W9-BGK-273

Pillsbury

HEALTHY·BAKING

FRESH APPROACHES TO MORE
THAN 200 FAVORITE RECIPES

Country Hearth Oatmeal Bread, p. 125; Hearty Pumpernickel Batter Bread, p. 140; Whole Wheat French Bread, p. 136

Pillsbury
HEALTHY·BAKING

FRESH APPROACHES TO MORE THAN 200 FAVORITE RECIPES

VIKING

PILLSBURY PUBLICATIONS
THE PILLSBURY COMPANY
Publisher: Sally Peters
Publication Managers: Diane B. Anderson, William Monn
Editors: Jackie Sheehan, Betsy Wray
Food Editor: Andrea Bidwell
Test Kitchen Coordinator: Pat Peterson
Production Coordinator: Michele Warren
Circulation Manager: Karen Goodsell
Circulation Coordinator: Rebecca Bogema
Recipe Typists: Bev Gustafson, Mary Thell
Publication Secretary: Jackie Ranney

HEALTHY BAKING
Publication Manager: Diane B. Anderson
Editors: Grace Wells, Nancy A. Lilleberg
Food Editor: Andrea Bidwell
Contributing Editor: Elizabeth Ward, M.S., R.D.
Nutrition Information: Guy Johnson, Ph.D., Indira Mehrotra, M.S., R.D.,
    Mary McFarland, R.D., Melissa Fraki, R.D., Karen Koke
Recipe Typists: Bev Gustafson, Mary Thell
Art Direction and Design: Tad Ware & Company, Inc.
Production Coordinator: Michele Warren
Food Stylist: Barb Standal
Text Photography: Studio 3, Glenn Peterson, Inc., Graham Brown
Cover Photography: Glenn Peterson, Inc.

VIKING
Published by the Penguin Group
Penguin Books USA Inc, 375 Hudson Street,
New York, New York 10014, U.S.A.
Penguin Books Ltd, 27 Wrights Lane,
London W8 5TZ, England
Penguin Books Australia Ltd, Ringwood,
Victoria, Australia
Penguin Books Canada Ltd, 10 Alcorn Avenue,
Toronto, Ontario, Canada M4V 3B2
Penguin Books (N.Z.) Ltd, 182-190 Wairau Road,
Auckland 10, New Zealand

Penguin Books Ltd, Registered Offices:
Harmondsworth, Middlesex, England

First published in 1994 by Viking Penguin,
a division of Penguin Books USA Inc.

10 9 8 7 6 5 4 3 2 1

Copyright © The Pillsbury Company, 1994
All rights reserved

ISBN 0-670-85723-8 CIP data available.

Printed in the United States of America

Without limiting the rights under copyright reserved above, no part of this
publication may be reproduced, stored in or introduced into a retrieval system,
or transmitted, in any form or by any means (electronic, mechanical, photo-
copying, recording or otherwise) without the prior written permission of both
the copyright owner and the above publisher of this book.

CONTENTS

Banana Blueberry Mini-Loaves, p. 104

INTRODUCTION

COMPONENTS OF A HEALTHY DIET

I f you're like most people, you want to eat a healthful and nutritious diet. But you don't want to be deprived of delicious foods.

There's no need to choose between good health and great taste, as long as you eat a wide variety of foods in moderation. Healthy eating even allows so-called "forbidden" favorites, such as apple pie or fudgy brownies. Adopting a more reasonable attitude toward eating does away with deprivation and promotes a long-lasting approach to good health.

Butter-rich cookies and gooey desserts often are perceived as sinful indulgences that wreak havoc on a healthy diet. But nutrition experts say there are no good or bad foods, only good or bad diets. A balanced, nutritious diet is made up of a wide array of foods, including occasional higher-fat choices.

The world of baked goods, too, is made up of a wide variety of choices. Some, like hearty breads, are naturally low in fat. Others, like cakes and pies, tip the scales. The beauty of this recipe collection is that we've taken many of those indulgent favorites and trimmed fat, without sacrificing flavor.

GOOD EATING GUIDELINES

Healthy eating gets easier when you know the basics of a wholesome diet. The government's Dietary Guidelines for Americans emphasize eating less fat and more complex carbohydrates:

- Eat a variety of foods.
- Maintain a healthy weight.
- Choose a diet low in fat, saturated fat and cholesterol.
- Choose a diet with plenty of vegetables, fruits and grain products.
- Use sugars only in moderation.
- Use salt and sodium only in moderation.
- If you drink alcoholic beverages, do so in moderation.

The beauty of this recipe collection is that we've taken many of those indulgent favorites and trimmed fat, without sacrificing flavor.

THE CARBOHYDRATE CONNECTION

Once shunned as fattening, carbohydrate-rich foods are now considered the cornerstone of a healthy diet, and should provide the bulk of your calories. Carbohydrates provide energy and come in two forms, simple and complex. Both types contain four calories per gram.

- Complex carbohydrates are found in breads, cereals, pasta, legumes, vegetables and grains, and are usually accompanied with vitamins and minerals.
- Simple carbohydrates, also known as sugars, come in many forms, including the natural sweeteners in table sugar, fruits and milk.

DIETARY FIBER

Fiber, found only in plant foods, fills you up, not out, which may decrease food intake and make weight control easier. It also keeps the digestive tract running smoothly and may help reduce the risk of some cancers and lower blood cholesterol.

Health professionals recommend consuming between 20 and 35 grams of dietary fiber daily. To give you an idea of the amount of fiber in foods, our bread recipes contain between 1 and 3 grams of dietary fiber per serving. Food labels list grams of dietary fiber.

THE POWER OF PROTEIN

Life revolves around protein, necessary for tissue growth and repair. But most Americans eat much more protein than they need and often choose protein-rich foods (meat, poultry, seafood, whole-milk dairy products and eggs) that may be higher in fat, calories and cholesterol. Lower-fat, non-cholesterol sources of protein include cereals, beans, vegetables, and grains. Protein has four calories per gram.

VITAMINS AND MINERALS

Your body makes only a few vitamins. But vitamins and minerals are dispersed widely throughout the foods we eat. Most of us can get all the vitamins and minerals we need from eating a wide range of grains, beans, legumes, meats, poultry, seafood, dairy foods, fruits and vegetables.

- Fat-soluble vitamins (A, D, E and K) are stored in body fat and need not be consumed every day. Megadoses can be toxic.

- B vitamins and vitamin C are considered water-soluble. Heat and water break down these vitamins both before and after they're eaten in foods. These need to be included in food choices every day.
- Minerals in varying amounts are essential to many body processes. To name a few, calcium and phosphorous provide structure and strength to such parts of the body as bones and teeth. Iron builds red blood cells, which carry oxygen to tissue, and sodium regulates fluid balance.

FAT FACTS

Food contains saturated and unsaturated fats. Saturated fats are found primarily in foods of animal origin and also in palm oil, palm kernel oil, coconut oil and cocoa butter, which are used to make processed foods such as cookies and crackers. Excessive saturated fat is considered the primary dietary villain in raising blood cholesterol levels, a major risk factor for heart disease.

Unsaturated fat is the predominant fat in most vegetable oils, nuts, peanut butter and margarine. In many cases you can substitute unsaturated fats, such as canola or sunflower oil, for saturated fats, such as butter and shortening without any noticeable change in the recipe.

Why Eat Fat?

Fat adds appeal to foods by providing flavor, aroma and texture. At nine calories per gram, fat provides energy—more than twice the energy of carbohydrate or protein. Fat lends satiety to meals, contains essential fatty acids not produced by the body, and is a carrier of vitamins A, D, E and K.

Cholesterol Confusion

Wax-like cholesterol isn't a fat and has no calories. It's actually part of the cell wall and aids in fat digestion. Indirectly, cholesterol orchestrates the workings of cells. Animals, including humans, make all the cholesterol they need, so it's not an essential nutrient. But if there's too much cholesterol and saturated fat in the diet, blood cholesterol levels may rise. Health experts recommend limiting cholesterol intake to 300 milligrams daily.

The 30-Percent Rule

Low-fat diets may decrease your risk for heart disease and certain types of cancer. That's the reasoning behind health experts' suggestion that fat should account for no more than 30 percent of your total calories.

To figure your fat allowance under the 30-percent rule, find your normal calorie level for a day in the chart below.

DAILY CALORIE INTAKE TO MAINTAIN OR LOSE WEIGHT	LIMIT DAILY FAT INTAKE TO:
1,200	40 grams or less
1,400	47 grams or less
1,600	53 grams or less
1,800	60 grams or less
2,000	67 grams or less
2,400	80 grams or less
2,800	93 grams or less

Here's another quick method to calculate your daily fat intake: Divide your target weight by two and the result will approximate your daily fat gram limit.

*FAT CONTENT
PER SERVING IN
HEALTHY BAKING*

Cookies: *3 grams or less*

Bars: *6 grams or less*

Yeast Breads and Quick Breads:
5 grams or less

Cakes, Pies, Tarts and Desserts:
10 grams or less

NUTRITION NOTES
EGGS

Egg yolks are cholesterol-rich. To decrease the cholesterol content of quick breads, muffins and scones, use either ¼ cup fat-free egg product or 2 egg whites for each egg. Fat-free egg products and egg whites are cholesterol-free.

But the 30-percent rule is not intended for every food that passes your lips. It applies to the diet as a whole and should be used as a guideline for balancing fat intake over a day or two. For example, foods such as meat and poultry are higher in fat, yet are a good source of many essential nutrients. A healthy diet can include moderate amounts of fatty foods in combination with low-fat foods during the course of the day.

THE FOUNDATION OF HEALTHY BAKING

Without a doubt, taste is top priority in baked goods. That's our logic behind using common ingredients such as flour, sugar, butter and eggs. Traditional ingredients lend baked products qualities that are difficult to duplicate.

How did we create healthier baked goods for this *Healthy Baking* book? By calling for less of the higher-fat ingredients. In doing so, we've cut calorie, fat and cholesterol content without sacrificing quality or taste. When necessary, lower-fat ingredients, such as skim milk or egg whites, were used to meet our fat guidelines. But flavor was never sacrificed.

INGREDIENTS
Each ingredient plays a specific role in a recipe. There is room for adjustment, however. That means you can alter some recipe ingredients to make them healthier without compromising quality.

Eggs
Eggs give baked goods structure, volume and tenderness. Eggs bind recipe ingredients together.

Fats
Butter, shortening, margarine and vegetable oil add richness, texture and tenderness and, in most cases, provide distinctive flavors. With the exception of reduced-fat and whipped varieties, fats contain between 100 and 135 calories per tablespoon. Reduced-fat and whipped varieties are not recommended for baking. Because air and/or water are whipped into them, the baked product may not turn out as expected.
- Oil is lower in saturated fat than margarine, butter and shortening, and it is cholesterol-free.
- Margarine, made from vegetable oils, has no cholesterol and

contains less saturated fat than butter. Tub margarine has the least saturated fat among all margarines but is not recommended for baking.

- Butter/margarine blends are typically 60 percent margarine, contain about 60 percent unsaturated fat and have significantly less cholesterol than butter.
- Butter is made from cream, so it contains cholesterol and saturated fat.
- Vegetable shortening is made from oil that has been partially solidified. Shortening has more saturated fat than oil and margarine. Cooks may consider its near tastelessness an advantage in baking.

Flour

Flour provides structure in baked goods.

- Flour is made by grinding grain, most commonly wheat.
- All-purpose flour is made from wheat and is used most often in baking. It contains moderate gluten, or protein, levels.
- Bleached flour undergoes an aging process that whitens it without affecting nutritional content. Bleached and unbleached flour perform equally well in baked goods and are interchangeable in recipes.
- Enriched flour contains added iron and B vitamins lost during the milling process. Most all-purpose flour is enriched.
- Whole wheat flour contains the entire wheat kernel. That gives it nearly five times the fiber of all-purpose flour, and more fat. Whole wheat flour produces denser baked goods.

Other Grains

Grains add texture, color and flavor to baked goods. For variety try different combinations.

- Cornmeal is ground dried corn kernels and may be white, yellow or blue. White and yellow are most commonly used for baking.
- Wheat germ is the section of the wheat kernel that sprouts and is a good source of some B vitamins, minerals, vitamin E, and fiber. It has a crunchy texture and nutty flavor. In baking, wheat germ flakes add texture.
- Old-fashioned and quick-cooking oats are suitable for baking and are interchangeable in most recipes. Instant oats are used primarily as breakfast cereal. Oat bran, the bran of the whole oat grain, is often used in muffins and quick breads as a partial or total substitute for flour.

NUTRITION NOTES
FATS

You may be able to successfully reduce the amount of oil in your favorite quick bread or muffin recipe by using ¼ to ⅓ less, but the same does not usually apply to cakes. A reduced-oil cake may be drier and less tender.

FLOUR

If you're looking to improve fiber, substitute some whole wheat flour for all-purpose. For best results, substitute whole wheat flour for up to half of the all-purpose flour in baking recipes. Too much whole wheat flour may make the batter or dough too heavy.

NUTRITION NOTES
MILK AND DAIRY PRODUCTS

A lower-fat milk may be substituted for whole milk in most recipes.

CULTURED DAIRY PRODUCTS

Reduced-fat sour cream may be substituted in some recipes, although the nonfat product may not be as successful in baked goods. Lowering the fat content of baked goods too much will result in dry products.

In some recipes, you may be able to substitute the same amount of plain low-fat yogurt for whole milk or sour cream to reduce calories, fat and cholesterol.

Milk and Dairy Products

Milk and milk products moisten ingredients and help activate yeast in bread recipes. Milk also gives bread a brown crust and sweet flavor.

- Whole milk contains the most calories, fat and cholesterol, but whole, 2%, 1% and skim milks have virtually the same vitamin and mineral content.
- Evaporated milk (whole, low-fat or skim) is cooked to decrease its water content. Reconstituted with an equal amount of water, it can be used in place of regular milk.
- Sweetened condensed milk is cooked milk with added sugar. It is very thick and is slightly higher in fat than whole evaporated milk.
- Whipping cream is between 32 and 40 percent fat by weight.
- Half-and-half is a mixture of milk and cream.

Cultured Dairy Products

- Buttermilk, whose name sounds fattening, is actually nonfat milk with added bacteria cultures. The cultures produce a thicker, tangier milk. Buttermilk is often used in quick breads and muffins, and is low-fat and butter-free.
- Sour cream is cultured cream with a tangy taste, thick texture and high fat content.
- Yogurt is cultured from milk (whole, reduced-fat or nonfat) to make it thick and tangy. Yogurt provides flavor and moistness.

Nuts

Nuts provide distinctive flavors, aromas and texture. On the nutrition front, nuts are most known for their fat content. But they are also good sources of protein and some minerals.

- To reduce fat content, substitute raisins or other chopped dried fruits for some of the nuts in quick breads, muffins and cookies.

Sweeteners

More than just a sweetener, sugar makes baked goods moist and tender. Sugar provides volume and contributes to a golden crust. In yeast bread recipes, sugar is vital to the yeast; cutting it out will stunt yeast growth.

- Sugar comes in many forms, including granulated, brown, powdered and superfine sugars, corn syrup, molasses, maple syrup and honey. Nutritionally, they're nearly the same.
- Brown sugar contains some molasses; dark brown sugar has more than light brown.

- Powdered sugar is finely granulated sugar with added cornstarch.
- Superfine sugar is finely granulated sugar well suited to meringues and cakes.
- Corn syrup is a liquid mixture of sugars.
- Honey has a distinctive flavor that sets it apart from other sweeteners.
- Maple syrup is made by boiling pure maple sap down to a thick syrup, while maple-flavored syrups are typically a blend of sugars, maple flavoring, coloring, thickening agents and preservatives.
- Molasses also has a distinctive flavor. It comes in light, dark and blackstrap, which is often too bitter for baking.
- Unless a recipe has been specially developed to use artificial sweeteners, we do not recommend them for baking. Artificial sweeteners cannot provide the necessary volume or structure and may not be heat tolerant.

Salt

Salt, made up of the minerals sodium and chloride, is a flavor enhancer. Purchased baked goods may be higher in sodium than homemade because some necessary preservatives contain sodium.

You can cut down on the salt in home-baked foods, but most recipes for baked goods need at least a small amount. Salt should never be eliminated from yeast bread recipes, where it is responsible for controlling the action of the yeast.

Baking Powder and Baking Soda

Baking powder and baking soda make baked goods rise.
- While they contain hefty amounts of sodium, you cannot eliminate baking powder and baking soda without suffering the consequences, typically a flat, leaden product.
- Baking powder loses its potency over time. Use this simple test to determine if it's still active: Add one teaspoon baking powder to ⅓ cup hot water. If the baking powder bubbles vigorously, then it's okay to use.

NUTRITION NOTES
NUTS

Instead of mixing nuts into a batter, sprinkle a smaller amount on top of baked goods. They'll toast during baking and add more flavor and have fewer calories because of the smaller amount used.

SWEETENERS

For regular muffin, quick bread, cookie, pie filling and fruit crisp recipes, try reducing sugar by one-fourth to one-third.

Cranberry and Vanilla Chip Cookies, p. 18; Wholesome Granola Bars, p. 43; Zucchini Bars with Penuche Frosting, p. 50

COOKIES & BARS

❧❦❧

*C*aught with your
hand in the cookie
jar? Don't worry. At no
more than three grams of
fat per cookie, and six or
fewer per bar, these melt-in-
your-mouth goodies have
about half the fat of regular
recipes.

Double Chocolate Chip Cookies, p. 17; Peanut Butter Cookies, p. 36

DOUBLE CHOCOLATE CHIP COOKIES

½ cup firmly packed brown sugar

¼ cup margarine or butter, softened

½ teaspoon vanilla

1 egg white

1 cup all purpose flour

3 tablespoons unsweetened cocoa

½ teaspoon baking soda

⅛ teaspoon salt

½ cup semi-sweet chocolate chips

Heat oven to 375°F. In large bowl, beat brown sugar and margarine until light and fluffy. Add vanilla and egg white; blend well. Add flour, cocoa, baking soda and salt; mix well. Stir in chocolate chips. Drop by teaspoonfuls 2 inches apart onto ungreased cookie sheets.

Bake at 375°F. for 8 to 9 minutes or until set. DO NOT OVERBAKE. Cool 1 minute; remove from cookie sheets.

2 dozen cookies.

TIP:

> If desired, cookies can be glazed. To make glaze, in small bowl combine ½ cup powdered sugar, 1½ teaspoons skim or 2% milk, 2 drops vanilla and 2 drops butter flavor, if desired. Stir to blend; drizzle glaze over cookies.

HIGH ALTITUDE – Above 3500 Feet: Increase flour to 1 cup plus 2 tablespoons. Bake as directed above.

The addition of cocoa boosts the chocolate flavor of these lower-fat chocolate chip cookies.

NUTRITION INFORMATION PER SERVING:

1 COOKIE		PERCENT U.S. RDA	
Calories	40	Protein	*
Protein	1 g	Vitamin A	*
Carbohydrate	6 g	Vitamin C	*
Dietary Fiber	0 g	Thiamine	*
Fat	2 g	Riboflavin	*
Polyunsaturated	0 g	Niacin	*
Saturated	1 g	Calcium	*
Cholesterol	0 mg	Iron	*
Sodium	35 mg	*Less than 2% U.S. RDA	
Potassium	25 mg		

DIETARY EXCHANGES: 1/2 Starch

CRANBERRY AND VANILLA CHIP COOKIES

*E*ach decadent bite of these cookies bursts with the flavor of white chocolate and cranberries. These treasures are low in fat, calories and sodium!

½ **cup margarine or butter, softened**

1⅓ **cups sugar**

½ **cup frozen fat-free egg product, thawed, or 2 eggs**

1 **teaspoon butter flavor**

1¾ **cups all purpose flour**

1 **cup rolled oats**

1½ **teaspoons baking soda**

½ **teaspoon salt**

1 **cup dried cranberries***

⅔ **cup vanilla milk chips**

Heat oven to 350°F. Spray cookie sheets with nonstick cooking spray. In large bowl, beat margarine and sugar until well blended. Add egg product and butter flavor; mix well. Add flour, oats, baking soda and salt; mix until well combined. Stir in cranberries and vanilla milk chips. Drop dough by tablespoonfuls 2 inches apart onto spray-coated cookie sheets.

Bake at 350°F. for 9 to 11 minutes or until edges are golden brown. Cool 1 minute; remove from cookie sheets. Cool completely on wire racks. Store in tightly covered container.
About 4 dozen cookies.

TIP:
 * Dried cranberries can be found in the serve-yourself bins in the produce section of large supermarkets.

HIGH ALTITUDE – Above 3500 Feet: Decrease sugar to 1¼ cups; increase flour to 2 cups. Bake at 350°F. for 10 to 12 minutes.

VARIATION:

GLAZED CRANBERRY AND VANILLA CHIP COOKIES: Prepare dough as directed above. Drop dough by heaping teaspoonfuls onto spray-coated cookie sheets. Bake at 350°F. for 9 to 11 minutes or until edges are golden brown. Cool 1 minute; remove from cookie sheets. Cool completely on wire racks. In small bowl, blend 1¼ cups powdered sugar and 5 to 6 teaspoons water until smooth and of desired drizzling consistency. Drizzle glaze over cooled cookies. Let glaze set before storing in tightly covered container.
About 6 dozen cookies.

NUTRITION INFORMATION PER SERVING:

1 COOKIE		PERCENT U.S. RDA	
Calories	90	Protein	*
Protein	1 g	Vitamin A	2%
Carbohydrate	13 g	Vitamin C	*
Dietary Fiber	1 g	Thiamine	2%
Fat	3 g	Riboflavin	2%
Polyunsaturated	1 g	Niacin	*
Saturated	1 g	Calcium	*
Cholesterol	1 mg	Iron	2%
Sodium	85 mg	*Less than 2% U.S. RDA	
Potassium	25 mg		

DIETARY EXCHANGES: 1 Starch, 1/2 Fat

CHOCOLATE CHIP YOGURT COOKIES

- ½ **cup sugar**
- ½ **cup firmly packed brown sugar**
- ¼ **cup margarine or butter, softened**
- ¼ **cup shortening**
- ½ **cup nonfat plain yogurt**
- 1½ **teaspoons vanilla**
- 1¾ **cups all purpose flour**
- ½ **teaspoon baking soda**
- ½ **teaspoon salt**
- ½ **cup miniature semi-sweet chocolate chips or carob chips**

Heat oven to 375°F. In large bowl, beat sugar, brown sugar, margarine and shortening until light and fluffy. Add yogurt and vanilla; blend well. Stir in flour, baking soda and salt; mix well. Stir in chocolate chips. Drop dough by rounded teaspoonfuls 2 inches apart onto ungreased cookie sheets.

Bake at 375°F. for 8 to 12 minutes or until light golden brown. Cool 1 minute; remove from cookie sheets.
3 dozen cookies.

HIGH ALTITUDE – Above 3500 Feet: Decrease granulated sugar to ⅓ cup; decrease brown sugar to ⅓ cup. Bake as directed above.

*H*ere's an all-time favorite you'll enjoy all the more because we've substituted yogurt for some of the fat.

NUTRITION INFORMATION PER SERVING:			
1 COOKIE		**PERCENT U.S. RDA**	
Calories	80	Protein	*
Protein	1 g	Vitamin A	*
Carbohydrate	12 g	Vitamin C	*
Dietary Fiber	0 g	Thiamine	2%
Fat	3 g	Riboflavin	2%
Polyunsaturated	1 g	Niacin	*
Saturated	1 g	Calcium	*
Cholesterol	0 mg	Iron	2%
Sodium	65 mg	*Less than 2% U.S. RDA	
Potassium	35 mg		

DIETARY EXCHANGES: 1/2 Starch, 1/2 Fat

Chocolate Chip Yogurt Cookies

OATMEAL RAISIN COOKIES

Every mouth-watering bite of these crispy-chewy oatmeal cookies is full of good tasting nuts and raisins.

NUTRITION INFORMATION PER SERVING:

1 COOKIE		PERCENT U.S. RDA	
Calories	70	Protein	*
Protein	1 g	Vitamin A	*
Carbohydrate	10 g	Vitamin C	*
Dietary Fiber	0 g	Thiamine	2%
Fat	3 g	Riboflavin	*
Polyunsaturated	1 g	Niacin	*
Saturated	1 g	Calcium	*
Cholesterol	5 mg	Iron	*
Sodium	55 mg	*Less than 2% U.S. RDA	
Potassium	35 mg		

DIETARY EXCHANGES: 1/2 Starch, 1/2 Fat

¾ cup sugar

¼ cup firmly packed brown sugar

½ cup margarine or butter, softened

½ teaspoon vanilla

1 egg

¾ cup all purpose flour

½ teaspoon baking soda

½ teaspoon cinnamon

¼ teaspoon salt

1½ cups quick-cooking rolled oats

½ cup raisins

½ cup chopped nuts

Heat oven to 375°F. Grease cookie sheets. In large bowl, combine sugar, brown sugar and margarine; beat until light and fluffy. Add vanilla and egg; blend well. Stir in flour, baking soda, cinnamon and salt; mix well. Stir in oats, raisins and nuts. Drop dough by rounded teaspoonfuls 2 inches apart onto greased cookie sheets.

Bake at 375°F. for 7 to 10 minutes or until edges are light golden brown. Cool 1 minute; remove from cookie sheets.
3½ dozen cookies.

HIGH ALTITUDE – Above 3500 Feet: Increase flour to 1 cup. Bake as directed above.

WHOLE WHEAT
APPLE-SPICE COOKIES

1 **cup all purpose flour**

1 **cup whole wheat flour**

1 **teaspoon cinnamon**

½ **teaspoon baking soda**

½ **teaspoon nutmeg**

¼ **teaspoon cloves**

⅛ **teaspoon salt**

1 **cup chopped unpeeled apples**

1 **(6-oz.) can frozen apple juice concentrate, thawed**

3 **egg whites**

¼ **cup firmly packed brown sugar**

Heat oven to 375°F. Spray cookie sheets with nonstick cooking spray. In large bowl, combine all purpose flour, whole wheat flour, cinnamon, baking soda, nutmeg, cloves and salt; blend well. Add apples and juice concentrate; stir just until dry ingredients are moistened. (Batter will be stiff.)

In small bowl, beat egg whites until frothy. Add brown sugar; beat until soft peaks form. Stir beaten egg whites into batter. Drop by teaspoonfuls 2 inches apart on spray-coated cookie sheets.

Bake at 375°F. for 9 to 11 minutes or until lightly browned. Immediately remove from cookie sheets; cool completely. Store in loosely covered container.

3 dozen cookies.

HIGH ALTITUDE – Above 3500 Feet: Increase all purpose flour to 1¼ cups. Bake as directed above.

*H*ere's great news for the cookie lover trying to watch fat intake. This fat-free cookie has a soft texture and a wonderfully spicy flavor.

NUTRITION INFORMATION PER SERVING:

1 COOKIE		PERCENT U.S. RDA	
Calories	45	Protein	*
Protein	1 g	Vitamin A	*
Carbohydrate	10 g	Vitamin C	*
Dietary Fiber	1 g	Thiamine	2%
Fat	0 g	Riboflavin	2%
Polyunsaturated	0 g	Niacin	2%
Saturated	0 g	Calcium	*
Cholesterol	0 mg	Iron	2%
Sodium	30 mg	*Less than 2% U.S. RDA	
Potassium	55 mg		

DIETARY EXCHANGES: 1/2 Starch

APRICOT OAT CRUNCHIES

These chewy cookies win on all counts—quick to make, nutritious and delicious! Team them with milk for a great wholesome after-school snack.

NUTRITION INFORMATION PER SERVING:

1 COOKIE		PERCENT U.S. RDA	
Calories	70	Protein	*
Protein	1 g	Vitamin A	4%
Carbohydrate	10 g	Vitamin C	*
Dietary Fiber	1 g	Thiamine	4%
Fat	3 g	Riboflavin	2%
Polyunsaturated	1 g	Niacin	2%
Saturated	1 g	Calcium	*
Cholesterol	6 mg	Iron	2%
Sodium	70 mg	*Less than 2% U.S. RDA	
Potassium	65 mg		

DIETARY EXCHANGES: 1/2 Starch, 1/2 Fat

¾   cup firmly packed brown sugar
½   cup margarine or butter, softened
1   teaspoon vanilla
1   egg
¾   cup all purpose flour
½   teaspoon baking soda
¼   teaspoon salt
¾   cup quick-cooking rolled oats
½   cup dried apricots, chopped
⅓   cup coconut
⅓   cup wheat germ
1   cup cornflakes cereal

Heat oven to 350°F. Grease cookie sheets. In large bowl, beat brown sugar and margarine until light and fluffy. Add vanilla and egg; blend well. Stir in flour, baking soda, salt, oats, apricots, coconut and wheat germ; mix well. Stir in cereal. Drop dough by rounded teaspoonfuls 2 inches apart onto greased cookie sheets.

Bake at 350°F. for 8 to 10 minutes or until light golden brown. Cool 1 minute; remove from cookie sheets.

3 dozen cookies.

HIGH ALTITUDE – Above 3500 Feet: Decrease brown sugar to ½ cup; increase flour to ¾ cup plus 2 tablespoons. Bake as directed above.

Apricot Oat Crunchies

CARROT RAISIN DROP COOKIES

Quick-cooking or old-fashioned oats can be used to make these frosted cookies. Old-fashioned oats will result in a cookie with a firmer texture. Both types of oats will yield the same nutritional value.

COOKIES

1 **cup rolled oats**
1 **cup firmly packed brown sugar**
½ **cup margarine or butter, softened**
1 **teaspoon vanilla**
1 **egg**
1 **cup all purpose flour**
2½ **teaspoons baking powder**
½ **teaspoon salt**
½ **teaspoon cinnamon**
⅛ **teaspoon cloves**
1 **cup (2 medium) finely shredded carrots**
½ **cup raisins or dried currants**

FROSTING

2 **cups powdered sugar**
2 **to 3 tablespoons orange juice**

Heat oven to 375°F. Spray cookie sheets with nonstick cooking spray. In food processor bowl with metal blade or blender container, process oats until of flour consistency; set aside.

In large bowl, combine brown sugar, margarine, vanilla and egg; beat until fluffy. Gradually beat in oats, flour, baking powder, salt, cinnamon and cloves. Stir in carrots and raisins. Drop by heaping teaspoonfuls onto spray-coated cookie sheets.

Bake at 375°F. for 8 to 10 minutes or until light golden brown. Remove from cookie sheets; cool completely.

In small bowl, beat powdered sugar and enough orange juice for desired spreading consistency. Frost cooled cookies.
3½ dozen cookies.

HIGH ALTITUDE – Above 3500 Feet: Decrease baking powder to 2 teaspoons; increase flour to 1¼ cups. Bake as directed above.

NUTRITION INFORMATION PER SERVING:

1 COOKIE		PERCENT U.S. RDA	
Calories	90	Protein	*
Protein	1 g	Vitamin A	15%
Carbohydrate	16 g	Vitamin C	*
Dietary Fiber	0 g	Thiamine	2%
Fat	2 g	Riboflavin	*
Polyunsaturated	1 g	Niacin	*
Saturated	1 g	Calcium	2%
Cholesterol	5 mg	Iron	2%
Sodium	75 mg	*Less than 2% U.S. RDA	
Potassium	55 mg		

DIETARY EXCHANGES: 1/2 Starch, 1/2 Fruit, 1/2 Fat

FROSTED CARROT DROPS

COOKIES

- ¾ cup sugar
- ½ cup margarine or butter, softened
- 1 teaspoon vanilla
- 1 egg
- 1¾ cups all purpose flour
- 1 teaspoon baking powder
- 1 cup (2 medium) finely shredded carrots
- ½ cup chopped walnuts or pecans
- ½ cup raisins

FROSTING

- 1 cup powdered sugar
- 1 teaspoon grated orange peel, if desired
- 3 to 5 teaspoons orange juice

These tender drop cookies are chock-full of carrots, walnuts and raisins. They're a softer cookie that's topped with an orange-flavored, quick and easy frosting.

Heat oven to 350°F. In large bowl, beat sugar and margarine until light and fluffy. Add vanilla and egg; blend well. Stir in flour and baking powder; mix well. Stir in carrots, walnuts and raisins. Drop dough by teaspoonfuls 2 inches apart onto ungreased cookie sheets.

Bake at 350°F. for 10 to 15 minutes or until edges are light golden brown. Remove from cookie sheets; cool completely.

In small bowl, combine all frosting ingredients, adding enough orange juice for desired spreading consistency; mix well. Frost cooled cookies.

3½ dozen cookies.

HIGH ALTITUDE – Above 3500 Feet: Increase flour to 1¾ cups plus 2 tablespoons. Bake as directed above.

NUTRITION INFORMATION PER SERVING:			
1 COOKIE		**PERCENT U.S. RDA**	
Calories	80	Protein	*
Protein	1 g	Vitamin A	15%
Carbohydrate	12 g	Vitamin C	*
Dietary Fiber	0 g	Thiamine	2%
Fat	3 g	Riboflavin	2%
Polyunsaturated	1 g	Niacin	*
Saturated	1 g	Calcium	*
Cholesterol	5 mg	Iron	*
Sodium	40 mg	*Less than 2% U.S. RDA	
Potassium	40 mg		

DIETARY EXCHANGES: 1/2 Starch, 1/2 Fat

Frosted Carrot Drops

LEMON GINGER CREAMS

A lemon frosting adds zest to this low-fat, soft, spicy drop cookie. After the frosting has set, store the cookies between layers of waxed paper in a container with a tight-fitting cover.

COOKIES

½ **cup sugar**

¼ **cup shortening**

½ **cup molasses**

½ **cup hot water**

1 **egg**

2 **cups all purpose flour**

1 **teaspoon baking soda**

½ **teaspoon salt**

½ **teaspoon ginger**

½ **teaspoon cinnamon**

¼ **teaspoon cloves**

FROSTING

2 **cups powdered sugar**

1 **teaspoon grated lemon peel**

2 **tablespoons margarine or butter, softened**

2 **tablespoons lemon juice**

1 **to 2 tablespoons 2% milk**

NUTRITION INFORMATION PER SERVING:

1 COOKIE		PERCENT U.S. RDA	
Calories	90	Protein	*
Protein	1 g	Vitamin A	*
Carbohydrate	18 g	Vitamin C	*
Dietary Fiber	0 g	Thiamine	4%
Fat	2 g	Riboflavin	2%
Polyunsaturated	1 g	Niacin	2%
Saturated	1 g	Calcium	*
Cholesterol	6 mg	Iron	2%
Sodium	75 mg	*Less than 2% U.S. RDA	
Potassium	80 mg		

DIETARY EXCHANGES: 1/2 Starch, 1/2 Fruit, 1/2 Fat

Heat oven to 375°F. Grease cookie sheets. In large bowl, combine sugar, shortening, molasses, water and egg; beat well. Add all remaining cookie ingredients; stir just until blended. Let stand 5 minutes. Drop by rounded teaspoonfuls 2 inches apart onto greased cookie sheets.

Bake at 375°F. for 8 to 12 minutes or until edges are light golden brown. Immediately remove from cookie sheets. Cool completely.

In small bowl, combine all frosting ingredients, adding enough milk for desired spreading consistency; blend until smooth. Spread frosting over cooled cookies.

3 dozen cookies.

HIGH ALTITUDE – Above 3500 Feet: No change.

Lemon Ginger Creams

CARROT RAISIN BRAN COOKIES

1 cup firmly packed brown sugar
1 cup margarine or butter, softened
1 cup (2 medium) shredded carrots
1 teaspoon vanilla
1 egg
1½ cups all purpose flour
1 teaspoon cinnamon
½ teaspoon baking soda
2½ cups bran flakes cereal with raisins

*E*veryone will enjoy these moist and chewy cereal cookies. When using young, tender carrots, just rinse and shred them. Older carrots should be peeled before they are shredded.

Heat oven to 375°F. In large bowl, beat brown sugar and margarine until light and fluffy. Add carrots, vanilla and egg; blend well. Stir in flour, cinnamon and baking soda; mix well. Stir in cereal. Drop dough by rounded teaspoonfuls 2 inches apart onto ungreased cookie sheets.

Bake at 375°F. for 9 to 14 minutes or until light golden brown. Cool 1 minute; remove from cookie sheets.

5½ dozen cookies.

HIGH ALTITUDE – Above 3500 Feet: No change.

NUTRITION INFORMATION PER SERVING:

1 COOKIE		PERCENT U.S. RDA	
Calories	60	Protein	*
Protein	1 g	Vitamin A	10%
Carbohydrate	7 g	Vitamin C	*
Dietary Fiber	0 g	Thiamine	2%
Fat	3 g	Riboflavin	2%
Polyunsaturated	1 g	Niacin	2%
Saturated	1 g	Calcium	*
Cholesterol	3 mg	Iron	6%
Sodium	55 mg	*Less than 2% U.S. RDA	
Potassium	30 mg		

DIETARY EXCHANGES: 1/2 Starch, 1/2 Fat

RASPBERRY MERINGUES

3 egg whites, room temperature
¼ teaspoon cream of tartar
Dash salt
¾ cup sugar
¼ cup raspberry preserves
5 to 6 drops red food color

*T*his low-calorie, fat-free cookie has a melt-in-your-mouth texture. It is a pretty addition to any cookie tray.

Heat oven to 225°F. Cover cookie sheets with parchment paper. In small bowl, beat egg whites, cream of tartar and salt until soft peaks form. Gradually add sugar, beating until *very* stiff peaks form, about 10 minutes. Add raspberry preserves and food color; beat 1 minute at highest speed. Drop teaspoonfuls of meringue mixture or pipe mixture into 1-inch mounds on paper-lined cookie sheets.

Bake at 225°F. for 2 hours. Cool completely. Remove from paper.

3 dozen cookies.

HIGH ALTITUDE – Above 3500 Feet: No change.

NUTRITION INFORMATION PER SERVING:

1 COOKIE		PERCENT U.S. RDA	
Calories	25	Protein	*
Protein	0 g	Vitamin A	*
Carbohydrate	6 g	Vitamin C	*
Dietary Fiber	0 g	Thiamine	*
Fat	0 g	Riboflavin	*
Polyunsaturated	0 g	Niacin	*
Saturated	0 g	Calcium	*
Cholesterol	0 mg	Iron	*
Sodium	10 mg	*Less than 2% U.S. RDA	
Potassium	10 mg		

DIETARY EXCHANGES: 1/2 Fruit

SPICED WHOLE WHEAT REFRIGERATOR COOKIES

½ cup sugar

½ cup firmly packed brown sugar

½ cup margarine or butter, softened

2 tablespoons water

2 teaspoons vanilla

1 egg

1¾ cups whole wheat flour

1 teaspoon baking powder

1 teaspoon cinnamon

½ teaspoon baking soda

¼ teaspoon salt

¼ teaspoon cloves

½ cup finely chopped pecans or walnuts

Because of its firm chewy texture, this traditional icebox cookie is ideal for mailing. Pack the cookies snugly in rows in a firm box or metal container. If necessary, cushion cookies with crumpled waxed paper.

In large bowl, beat sugar, brown sugar and margarine until light and fluffy. Add water, vanilla and egg; blend well. Add flour, baking powder, cinnamon, baking soda, salt and cloves; mix well. Stir in pecans. Shape dough into two 6-inch-long rolls. Wrap each roll in plastic wrap; refrigerate at least 2 hours or until firm.

Heat oven to 375°F. Using sharp knife, cut dough into ¼-inch slices. Place 2 inches apart on ungreased cookie sheets. Bake at 375°F. for 6 to 8 minutes or until set. Cool 1 minute; remove from cookie sheets.

3½ dozen cookies.

HIGH ALTITUDE – Above 3500 Feet: Decrease sugar to ⅓ cup; decrease brown sugar to ⅓ cup. Increase flour to 2 cups. Bake as directed above.

NUTRITION INFORMATION PER SERVING:			
1 COOKIE		**PERCENT U.S. RDA**	
Calories	70	Protein	*
Protein	1 g	Vitamin A	*
Carbohydrate	9 g	Vitamin C	*
Dietary Fiber	1 g	Thiamine	*
Fat	3 g	Riboflavin	*
Polyunsaturated	1 g	Niacin	*
Saturated	1 g	Calcium	*
Cholesterol	5 mg	Iron	*
Sodium	70 mg	*Less than 2% U.S. RDA	
Potassium	40 mg		

DIETARY EXCHANGES: 1/2 Starch, 1/2 Fat

DATE-FILLED WHOLE WHEAT COOKIES

*D*ates not only contain protein and iron but also are about 55% sugar so they add lots of natural sweetness to baked goods. In this updated version of an old favorite, we thicken the filling by processing it in the food processor instead of cooking it.

COOKIES

1 cup firmly packed brown sugar
¾ cup margarine or butter, softened
1 teaspoon vanilla
1 egg
1¼ cups all purpose flour
1 cup whole wheat flour
1½ teaspoons baking powder
1 teaspoon cinnamon
⅛ teaspoon salt

FILLING

¼ cup firmly packed brown sugar
¼ cup slivered almonds
⅓ cup orange juice
1 (8-oz.) pkg. chopped pitted dates

In large bowl, beat 1 cup brown sugar and margarine until light and fluffy. Add vanilla and egg; blend well. Add all purpose flour, whole wheat flour, baking powder, cinnamon and salt; mix well. Cover with plastic wrap; refrigerate 1 to 2 hours for easier handling.

Meanwhile, in food processor bowl with metal blade or blender container, combine all filling ingredients; process 1 to 2 minutes or until thickened.

Heat oven to 375°F. On lightly floured surface, roll out ⅓ of dough at a time to ⅛-inch thickness. Keep remaining dough refrigerated. Cut with floured 2½-inch round cookie cutter. Place rounds ½ inch apart on ungreased cookie sheets. Spoon scant 1 teaspoon filling onto center of each round; fold half of round over filling, creating half moon shape. Seal cut edges with tines of fork.

Bake at 375°F. for 5 to 10 minutes or until edges are golden brown. Immediately remove from cookie sheets.
4½ dozen cookies.

HIGH ALTITUDE – Above 3500 Feet: Increase all purpose flour to 1½ cups. Bake as directed above.

NUTRITION INFORMATION PER SERVING:

1 COOKIE		PERCENT U.S. RDA	
Calories	80	Protein	*
Protein	1 g	Vitamin A	2%
Carbohydrate	12 g	Vitamin C	*
Dietary Fiber	1 g	Thiamine	2%
Fat	3 g	Riboflavin	2%
Polyunsaturated	1 g	Niacin	2%
Saturated	1 g	Calcium	*
Cholesterol	4 mg	Iron	2%
Sodium	50 mg	*Less than 2% U.S. RDA	
Potassium	65 mg		

DIETARY EXCHANGES: 1/2 Starch, 1/2 Fruit, 1/2 Fat

GINGER SPICE COOKIES

1 cup sugar

⅓ cup margarine or butter, softened

¼ cup molasses

1 egg

1¾ cups all purpose flour

⅓ cup whole wheat flour

2 teaspoons baking soda

1 teaspoon cinnamon

1 teaspoon ginger

½ teaspoon cloves

3 tablespoons sugar

*E*njoy the aroma and old-fashioned flavor of freshly baked ginger cookies! This lower-calorie version is made with whole wheat flour and half the fat of regular ginger cookies.

Heat oven to 350°F. In large bowl, beat 1 cup sugar, margarine, molasses and egg until light and fluffy. Add all purpose flour, whole wheat flour, baking soda, cinnamon, ginger and cloves; mix well. Shape dough into 1-inch balls; dip half in 3 tablespoons sugar. Place sugar side up 2 inches apart on ungreased cookie sheets.

Bake at 350°F. for 6 to 8 minutes or until cookies are set and begin to crack. Cool 1 minute; remove from cookie sheets.
4 dozen cookies.

HIGH ALTITUDE – Above 3500 Feet: Decrease sugar in cookie dough to ¾ cup. Bake as directed above.

NUTRITION INFORMATION PER SERVING:

1 COOKIE		PERCENT U.S. RDA	
Calories	45	Protein	*
Protein	1 g	Vitamin A	*
Carbohydrate	8 g	Vitamin C	*
Dietary Fiber	0 g	Thiamine	2%
Fat	1 g	Riboflavin	*
Polyunsaturated	0 g	Niacin	*
Saturated	0 g	Calcium	*
Cholesterol	4 mg	Iron	*
Sodium	55 mg	*Less than 2% U.S. RDA	
Potassium	25 mg		

DIETARY EXCHANGES: 1/2 Starch

Anise Honey Bites

ANISE
HONEY BITES

½ cup sugar

½ cup honey

1 egg

1¾ to 2¼ cups all purpose flour

1½ teaspoons anise seed

1 teaspoon baking soda

⅛ teaspoon salt

2 tablespoons powdered sugar

*A*nise seeds give these bite-sized cookies a distinctive licorice flavor. The only fat in them comes from the egg yolk.

Heat oven to 350°F. Grease cookie sheets. In large bowl, combine sugar, honey and egg; blend well. Add remaining ingredients except powdered sugar, stirring in enough flour to form a soft dough; mix well. With floured hands, shape dough into 1-inch balls. Place 2 inches apart on greased cookie sheets.

Bake at 350°F. for 4 to 8 minutes or until bottoms of cookies are light golden brown. Immediately remove from cookie sheets. Cool completely. Sprinkle with powdered sugar.
3½ dozen cookies.

HIGH ALTITUDE – Above 3500 Feet: Increase flour to 2 to 2½ cups. Bake as directed above.

NUTRITION INFORMATION PER SERVING:

1 COOKIE		PERCENT U.S. RDA	
Calories	50	Protein	*
Protein	1 g	Vitamin A	*
Carbohydrate	11 g	Vitamin C	*
Dietary Fiber	0 g	Thiamine	2%
Fat	0 g	Riboflavin	2%
Polyunsaturated	0 g	Niacin	2%
Saturated	0 g	Calcium	*
Cholesterol	5 mg	Iron	2%
Sodium	40 mg	*Less than 2% U.S. RDA	
Potassium	10 mg		

DIETARY EXCHANGES: 1/2 Starch

HEALTH NOTES
SWEETENERS

Nutritionally, there's little difference among sweeteners. Granulated sugar (also known as table sugar), brown sugar, honey, corn syrup, maple syrup and fructose (the natural sweetener in fruit) all contain four calories per gram, and not much else. Molasses is the exception, however. The light and dark molasses varieties contain a bit more of the minerals calcium, potassium and iron. Blackstrap molasses has high levels of the same minerals, but it is too bitter for baking.

FAT-FREE MOLASSES COOKIES

*I*n this recipe all of the fat is replaced by prune puree—with delicious results. These cookies will soften when stored.

NUTRITION INFORMATION PER SERVING:

1 COOKIE		PERCENT U.S. RDA	
Calories	45	Protein	*
Protein	1 g	Vitamin A	*
Carbohydrate	10 g	Vitamin C	*
Dietary Fiber	0 g	Thiamine	2%
Fat	0 g	Riboflavin	*
Polyunsaturated	0 g	Niacin	*
Saturated	0 g	Calcium	*
Cholesterol	4 mg	Iron	2%
Sodium	50 mg	*Less than 2% U.S. RDA	
Potassium	40 mg		

DIETARY EXCHANGES: 1/2 Starch

- **5 oz. (¾ cup) pitted prunes**
- **⅓ cup hot water**
- **1 cup sugar**
- **¼ cup molasses**
- **1 egg**
- **2¼ cups all purpose flour**
- **2 teaspoons baking soda**
- **1 teaspoon cinnamon**
- **1 teaspoon ginger**
- **½ teaspoon cloves**
- **¼ teaspoon salt**
- **¼ cup sugar**

In blender container or food processor bowl with metal blade, combine prunes and hot water. Cover; process 2 to 3 minutes or until pureed. In large bowl, combine prune mixture, 1 cup sugar, molasses and egg; blend well. Stir in flour, baking soda, cinnamon, ginger, cloves and salt; mix well. Cover with plastic wrap; refrigerate 2 to 3 hours for easier handling.

Heat oven to 350°F. Shape dough into 1-inch balls; roll in ¼ cup sugar. Place 2 inches apart on ungreased cookie sheets. Bake at 350°F. for 8 to 12 minutes or until set. Cool 1 minute; remove from cookie sheets.

5 dozen cookies.

HIGH ALTITUDE – Above 3500 Feet: Decrease sugar in cookie dough to ¾ cup. Bake as directed above.

WHOLE WHEAT SUGAR COOKIES

- 1 **cup sugar**
- ½ **cup margarine or butter, softened**
- 2 **tablespoons 2% milk**
- 1 **teaspoon grated lemon peel**
- 1 **teaspoon vanilla**
- 1 **egg**
- 2 **cups whole wheat flour**
- 1 **teaspoon baking powder**
- ½ **teaspoon baking soda**
- ½ **teaspoon salt**
- ½ **teaspoon nutmeg**
- 2 **tablespoons sugar**
- ½ **teaspoon cinnamon**

In large bowl, beat 1 cup sugar and margarine until light and fluffy. Add milk, lemon peel, vanilla and egg; blend well. Add flour, baking powder, baking soda, salt and nutmeg; mix well. Cover with plastic wrap; refrigerate 1 hour for easier handling.

Heat oven to 375°F. In small bowl, combine 2 tablespoons sugar and cinnamon. Shape dough into 1-inch balls; roll in sugar-cinnamon mixture. Place 2 inches apart on ungreased cookie sheets. Bake at 375°F. for 8 to 10 minutes or until light golden brown. Cool 1 minute; remove from cookie sheets.

2 to 3 dozen cookies.

HIGH ALTITUDE – Above 3500 Feet: No change.

*W*hole wheat flour and nutmeg add new flavor to the all-time favorite sugar cookie. Just shape the dough into balls, roll them in the sugar-cinnamon mixture and bake. Their fabulous baking aroma will let everyone know that these home-baked goodies are ready to eat!

NUTRITION INFORMATION PER SERVING:

1 COOKIE		PERCENT U.S. RDA	
Calories	70	Protein	*
Protein	1 g	Vitamin A	2%
Carbohydrate	11 g	Vitamin C	*
Dietary Fiber	1 g	Thiamine	2%
Fat	3 g	Riboflavin	*
Polyunsaturated	1 g	Niacin	2%
Saturated	1 g	Calcium	*
Cholesterol	6 mg	Iron	*
Sodium	95 mg	*Less than 2% U.S. RDA	
Potassium	30 mg		

DIETARY EXCHANGES: 1/2 Starch, 1/2 Fat

PEANUT BUTTER COOKIES

*E*asily prepared and always a familiar favorite because of the traditional cross-hatched pattern, peanut butter cookies are great bake sale cookies. And the variations we've included add even more appeal.

½ **cup sugar**

½ **cup firmly packed brown sugar**

½ **cup margarine or butter, softened**

½ **cup peanut butter**

1 **teaspoon vanilla**

1 **egg**

1¼ **cups all purpose flour**

1 **teaspoon baking soda**

½ **teaspoon salt**

4 **teaspoons sugar**

Heat oven to 375°F. In large bowl, combine ½ cup sugar, brown sugar and margarine; beat until light and fluffy. Add peanut butter, vanilla and egg; blend well. Add flour, baking soda and salt; mix well. Shape into 1-inch balls. Place 2 inches apart on ungreased cookie sheets. With fork dipped in 4 teaspoons sugar, flatten balls in crisscross pattern.

Bake at 375°F. for 6 to 9 minutes or until golden brown and set. Immediately remove from cookie sheets.
4 dozen cookies.

HIGH ALTITUDE – Above 3500 Feet: Increase flour to 1½ cups. Bake as directed above.

VARIATIONS:

OATMEAL PEANUT BUTTER COOKIES: Prepare dough as directed above, decreasing flour to ¾ cup; stir in ¾ cup rolled oats. Cover dough with plastic wrap; refrigerate 2 hours for easier handling. With fork dipped in sugar, flatten balls in crisscross pattern. Bake at 375°F. for 6 to 10 minutes or until golden brown.
4 dozen cookies.

PEANUT BUTTER RAISIN COOKIE POPS: Prepare dough as directed above. Stir in 1 cup raisins. Shape into 2-inch balls. Place 4 cookies on each ungreased cookie sheet. With fork dipped in sugar, flatten balls in crisscross pattern. Insert wooden stick into each cookie. Bake at 350°F. for 7 to 11 minutes or until golden brown.
22 cookie pops.

NUTRITION INFORMATION PER SERVING:

1 COOKIE		PERCENT U.S. RDA	
Calories	60	Protein	*
Protein	1 g	Vitamin A	*
Carbohydrate	8 g	Vitamin C	*
Dietary Fiber	0 g	Thiamine	2%
Fat	3 g	Riboflavin	*
Polyunsaturated	1 g	Niacin	2%
Saturated	1 g	Calcium	*
Cholesterol	4 mg	Iron	*
Sodium	85 mg	*Less than 2% U.S. RDA	
Potassium	35 mg		

DIETARY EXCHANGES: 1/2 Starch, 1/2 Fat

MAPLE GINGER SNAPS

¾ cup sugar

¾ cup shortening

½ cup maple syrup or maple-flavored syrup

1 egg

2¼ cups all purpose flour

1¼ teaspoons baking soda

1 teaspoon ginger

½ teaspoon cinnamon

½ teaspoon cloves

¼ teaspoon salt

¼ cup sugar

1½ teaspoons cinnamon

In these cookies, maple syrup replaces the molasses used in traditional ginger snaps. The maple flavor is subtle and the cookies are delicious!

Grease cookie sheets. In large bowl, combine ¾ cup sugar, shortening, maple syrup and egg; blend well. Stir in flour, baking soda, ginger, ½ teaspoon cinnamon, cloves and salt; mix well. If necessary, cover with plastic wrap; refrigerate 1 to 2 hours for easier handling.

Heat oven to 350°F. In small bowl, combine ¼ cup sugar and 1½ teaspoons cinnamon; blend well. Shape dough into 1-inch balls; roll in sugar-cinnamon mixture. Place 2 inches apart on greased cookie sheets.

Bake at 350°F. for 7 to 10 minutes or until light golden brown. Cool 1 minute; remove from cookie sheets.

5 dozen cookies.

HIGH ALTITUDE – Above 3500 Feet: Increase flour to 2½ cups. Bake as directed above.

NUTRITION INFORMATION PER SERVING:

1 COOKIE		PERCENT U.S. RDA	
Calories	60	Protein	*
Protein	1 g	Vitamin A	*
Carbohydrate	9 g	Vitamin C	*
Dietary Fiber	0 g	Thiamine	2%
Fat	3 g	Riboflavin	*
Polyunsaturated	1 g	Niacin	*
Saturated	1 g	Calcium	*
Cholesterol	4 mg	Iron	*
Sodium	35 mg	*Less than 2% U.S. RDA	
Potassium	10 mg		

DIETARY EXCHANGES: 1/2 Starch, 1/2 Fat

WHOLE WHEAT SNICKERDOODLES

1½ **cups sugar**

½ **cup margarine or butter, softened**

1 **teaspoon vanilla**

2 **eggs**

1¾ **cups all purpose flour**

1 **cup whole wheat flour**

1 **teaspoon cream of tartar**

½ **teaspoon baking soda**

¼ **teaspoon salt**

2 **tablespoons sugar**

2 **teaspoons cinnamon**

Heat oven to 400°F. In large bowl, beat 1½ cups sugar and margarine until light and fluffy. Add vanilla and eggs; blend well. Add all purpose flour, whole wheat flour, cream of tartar, baking soda and salt; mix well. In small bowl, combine 2 tablespoons sugar and cinnamon. Shape dough into 1-inch balls; roll balls in sugar-cinnamon mixture. Place 2 inches apart on ungreased cookie sheets.

Bake at 400°F. for 8 to 10 minutes or until set. Immediately remove from cookie sheets.

4 dozen cookies.

HIGH ALTITUDE – Above 3500 Feet: No change.

VARIATION:

SNICKERDOODLES: Use 2¾ cups all purpose flour; omit whole wheat flour.

*S*nickerdoodle, the whimsical name for this popular cookie, originated in New England and is simply a nineteenth century nonsense word for a quickly made confection. You'll enjoy the whole wheat version.

NUTRITION INFORMATION PER SERVING:

1 COOKIE		PERCENT U.S. RDA	
Calories	70	Protein	*
Protein	1 g	Vitamin A	*
Carbohydrate	12 g	Vitamin C	*
Dietary Fiber	0 g	Thiamine	2%
Fat	2 g	Riboflavin	2%
Polyunsaturated	1 g	Niacin	2%
Saturated	0 g	Calcium	*
Cholesterol	9 mg	Iron	2%
Sodium	50 mg	*Less than 2% U.S. RDA	
Potassium	30 mg		

DIETARY EXCHANGES: 1/2 Starch, 1/2 Fat

KWIK-KRUMB RAISIN BARS

FILLING

2½ **cups raisins**
 1 **cup water**
 1 **cup applesauce**
 1 **teaspoon lemon juice**
 ¼ **teaspoon cinnamon**

BASE AND TOPPING

 2 **cups rolled oats**
 1 **cup all purpose flour**
 ½ **cup sugar**
 ½ **cup coconut**
 ¾ **cup margarine or butter**

In medium saucepan, bring raisins and water to a boil. Reduce heat; simmer 15 minutes. Drain; stir in applesauce, lemon juice and cinnamon. Set aside.

Heat oven to 350°F. In large bowl, combine oats, flour, sugar and coconut. Using pastry blender or fork, cut in margarine until mixture resembles coarse crumbs. Reserve 2½ cups crumb mixture for topping. Press remaining crumb mixture firmly in bottom of ungreased 13x9-inch pan. Spread evenly with filling. Sprinkle with reserved crumb mixture; press lightly.

Bake at 350°F. for 30 to 40 minutes or until light golden brown. Cool completely. Cut into bars.

36 bars.

HIGH ALTITUDE – Above 3500 Feet: No change.

Raisins have a high sugar content so are a great natural energy food. They also contain a variety of vitamins and minerals. These yummy bars, filled with the goodness of raisins and applesauce, are a favorite Pillsbury Bake-Off® recipe.

NUTRITION INFORMATION PER SERVING:

1 BAR		PERCENT U.S. RDA	
Calories	120	Protein	2%
Protein	2 g	Vitamin A	2%
Carbohydrate	18 g	Vitamin C	*
Dietary Fiber	1 g	Thiamine	4%
Fat	5 g	Riboflavin	2%
Polyunsaturated	1 g	Niacin	*
Saturated	1 g	Calcium	*
Cholesterol	0 mg	Iron	2%
Sodium	45 mg	*Less than 2% U.S. RDA	
Potassium	105 mg		

DIETARY EXCHANGES: 1/2 Starch, 1/2 Fruit, 1 Fat

PINEAPPLE CRANBERRY BARS

FILLING

*O*ats, cranberries and pineapple team up in this contemporary layered bar, which is reminiscent of an old-fashioned date bar.

- **1 cup fresh or frozen cranberries**
- **3 tablespoons brown sugar**
- **1½ teaspoons cornstarch**
- **1 (8-oz.) can crushed pineapple in its own juice, undrained**

CRUMB MIXTURE

- **1½ cups all purpose flour**
- **1 cup rolled oats**
- **1 cup firmly packed brown sugar**
- **½ cup chopped nuts**
- **¼ teaspoon salt**
- **¾ cup margarine or butter**

Heat oven to 350°F. Grease 13x9-inch pan. In medium saucepan, combine all filling ingredients. Bring to a boil over medium heat, stirring constantly. Reduce heat; cover and simmer 10 to 15 minutes or until cranberry skins pop and mixture thickens, stirring occasionally. Set aside.

Meanwhile, in large bowl combine all crumb mixture ingredients except margarine; mix well. Using pastry blender or fork, cut in margarine until mixture resembles coarse crumbs. Reserve 2 cups crumb mixture for topping; press remaining crumb mixture firmly in bottom of greased pan. Drop cranberry mixture by table-spoonfuls over crumb mixture in pan; spread evenly. Sprinkle with reserved crumb mixture; press lightly.

Bake at 350°F. for 20 to 30 minutes or until golden brown. Cool completely. Cut into bars.

36 bars.

HIGH ALTITUDE – Above 3500 Feet: No change.

NUTRITION INFORMATION PER SERVING:

1 BAR		PERCENT U.S. RDA	
Calories	110	Protein	*
Protein	1 g	Vitamin A	2%
Carbohydrate	14 g	Vitamin C	*
Dietary Fiber	1 g	Thiamine	4%
Fat	5 g	Riboflavin	2%
Polyunsaturated	2 g	Niacin	*
Saturated	1 g	Calcium	*
Cholesterol	0 mg	Iron	2%
Sodium	65 mg	*Less than 2% U.S. RDA	
Potassium	60 mg		

DIETARY EXCHANGES: 1/2 Starch, 1/2 Fruit, 1 Fat

Pineapple Cranberry Bars

OATMEAL PRUNE BARS

*T*hese delicious bars have a buttery fla-vored base and contain an excellent source of natural dietary fiber, prunes! The natural sweetness of prunes eliminates the need for additional sugar in the filling mixture.

NUTRITION INFORMATION PER SERVING:

1 BAR		PERCENT U.S. RDA	
Calories	130	Protein	2%
Protein	2 g	Vitamin A	8%
Carbohydrate	22 g	Vitamin C	*
Dietary Fiber	2 g	Thiamine	6%
Fat	5 g	Riboflavin	2%
Polyunsaturated	1 g	Niacin	2%
Saturated	1 g	Calcium	*
Cholesterol	0 mg	Iron	4%
Sodium	140 mg	*Less than 2% U.S. RDA	
Potassium	140 mg		

DIETARY EXCHANGES: 1 Starch, 1 Fat

FILLING

1¼ cups finely chopped dried pitted prunes

½ cup water

1 tablespoon lemon juice

BASE

1 cup quick-cooking rolled oats

⅔ cup all purpose flour

½ cup firmly packed brown sugar

¼ teaspoon baking soda

¼ teaspoon salt

¼ teaspoon cinnamon

6 tablespoons margarine or butter, melted

Grease 8-inch square pan. In medium saucepan, combine all filling ingredients; cook over medium heat until thick, stirring frequently. Cool slightly.

Heat oven to 350°F. In medium bowl, combine all base ingredients except margarine; blend well. Stir in margarine until mixture is crumbly. Reserve ¾ cup crumb mixture; press remaining mixture in bottom of greased pan. Spread filling over base. Sprinkle with reserved crumb mixture; press lightly.

Bake at 350°F. for 22 to 27 minutes or until light golden brown. Cool completely. Cut into bars.

16 bars.

HIGH ALTITUDE – Above 3500 Feet: No change.

WHOLESOME GRANOLA BARS

1¼ cups firmly packed brown sugar

¼ cup margarine or butter, softened

2 tablespoons honey

1 egg white

1 cup all purpose flour

1 teaspoon cinnamon

½ teaspoon baking powder

1 cup quick-cooking rolled oats

1 cup crisp rice cereal

1 cup raisins

½ cup shelled sunflower seeds

Heat oven to 350°F. Grease 13x9-inch pan or spray with nonstick cooking spray. In large bowl, combine brown sugar, margarine, honey and egg white; beat until well blended. Add flour, cinnamon and baking powder; mix well. Stir in oats, cereal, raisins and sunflower seeds. Press mixture firmly in bottom of greased pan.

Bake at 350°F. for 14 to 18 minutes or until edges are light golden brown and center appears set. Cool completely. Cut into bars. Store in tightly covered container.

36 bars.

HIGH ALTITUDE – Above 3500 Feet: No change.

VARIATION:

CHOCOLATE-TOPPED GRANOLA BARS: In small saucepan, combine ¼ cup semi-sweet chocolate chips and 1 teaspoon shortening. Cook and stir over low heat until melted and smooth. Drizzle over cooled, baked bars.

*I*n this recipe, we've combined traditional granola ingredients such as oats, sunflower seeds, raisins, honey and spices and created a wholesome, nutritious bar. When stored in an airtight container, they will stay soft and moist for several days.

NUTRITION INFORMATION PER SERVING:

1 BAR		PERCENT U.S. RDA	
Calories	90	Protein	2%
Protein	1 g	Vitamin A	*
Carbohydrate	16 g	Vitamin C	*
Dietary Fiber	1 g	Thiamine	4%
Fat	2 g	Riboflavin	2%
Polyunsaturated	1 g	Niacin	2%
Saturated	0 g	Calcium	*
Cholesterol	0 mg	Iron	4%
Sodium	35 mg	*Less than 2% U.S. RDA	
Potassium	85 mg		

DIETARY EXCHANGES: 1 Starch

APPLE GRANOLA BARS

*T*o reduce fat even more in these pack-able bars, try using one of the new lower-fat granolas that are available in the cold cereal section of the grocery store.

½ cup firmly packed brown sugar

¼ cup margarine or butter, softened

⅓ cup applesauce

1 egg

1 cup granola

½ cup whole wheat flour

¼ teaspoon baking soda

¼ to ½ teaspoon allspice

½ cup finely chopped dried apples

Heat oven to 350°F. Spray 8-inch square pan with nonstick cooking spray. In large bowl, combine brown sugar and margarine; beat well. Add applesauce and egg; blend well. Add granola, flour, baking soda and allspice; blend well. Stir in apples. Spread batter in spray-coated pan.

Bake at 350°F. for 20 to 25 minutes or until toothpick inserted in center comes out clean. Cool completely. Cut into bars.
16 bars.

HIGH ALTITUDE – Above 3500 Feet: No change.

NUTRITION INFORMATION PER SERVING:

1 BAR		PERCENT U.S. RDA	
Calories	120	Protein	2%
Protein	2 g	Vitamin A	2%
Carbohydrate	17 g	Vitamin C	*
Dietary Fiber	2 g	Thiamine	4%
Fat	5 g	Riboflavin	2%
Polyunsaturated	2 g	Niacin	2%
Saturated	1 g	Calcium	*
Cholesterol	13 mg	Iron	4%
Sodium	60 mg	*Less than 2% U.S. RDA	
Potassium	100 mg		

DIETARY EXCHANGES: 1 Starch, 1 Fat

PEANUTTY FIG BARS

*T*hese peanutty, high-energy bars contain an excellent source of natural dietary fiber—figs!

1 cup firmly packed brown sugar

2 eggs

¾ cup all purpose flour

¼ cup whole wheat flour

1 teaspoon baking powder

1 cup chopped figs

1 cup chopped peanuts

Heat oven to 350°F. Grease 9-inch square pan. In large bowl, beat brown sugar and eggs until light. Add all purpose flour, whole wheat flour and baking powder; mix well. Stir in figs and peanuts. Spread in greased pan.

Bake at 350°F. for 20 to 25 minutes or until crust is golden brown. Cool slightly. Cut into bars. Store in loosely covered container.
24 bars.

HIGH ALTITUDE – Above 3500 Feet: No change.

NUTRITION INFORMATION PER SERVING:

1 BAR		PERCENT U.S. RDA	
Calories	120	Protein	4%
Protein	3 g	Vitamin A	*
Carbohydrate	20 g	Vitamin C	*
Dietary Fiber	2 g	Thiamine	4%
Fat	4 g	Riboflavin	2%
Polyunsaturated	1 g	Niacin	6%
Saturated	1 g	Calcium	4%
Cholesterol	18 mg	Iron	4%
Sodium	80 mg	*Less than 2% U.S. RDA	
Potassium	150 mg		

DIETARY EXCHANGES: 1 Starch, 1 Fat

WHOLE WHEAT APPLE BARS

BARS

1 cup finely chopped dried apple slices

1 cup boiling water

1 cup all purpose flour

1 cup quick-cooking rolled oats

½ cup whole wheat flour

1 teaspoon baking soda

2 teaspoons cinnamon

½ teaspoon salt

¾ cup firmly packed brown sugar

½ cup margarine or butter, softened

1 egg

¾ cup unsweetened applesauce

GLAZE

¾ cup powdered sugar

3 to 4 teaspoons 2% milk

Heat oven to 350°F. Spray 13x9-inch pan with nonstick cooking spray. In small bowl, combine dried apples and boiling water; set aside.

In another small bowl, combine all purpose flour, oats, whole wheat flour, baking soda, cinnamon and salt; mix well. In large bowl, beat brown sugar and margarine until light and fluffy. Add egg; blend well. Alternately add flour mixture with applesauce and dried apple mixture, beginning and ending with flour mixture and beating well after each addition. Spread batter in spray-coated pan.

Bake at 350°F. for 20 to 30 minutes or until toothpick inserted in center comes out clean. Cool completely.

In small bowl, combine powdered sugar and enough milk for desired drizzling consistency; blend until smooth. Drizzle glaze over bars. Cut into bars.

36 bars.

HIGH ALTITUDE – Above 3500 Feet: No change.

*D*ried apples and apple-sauce combine to make this a healthful cake-like bar. If time is short, simply sprinkle the bars with powdered sugar instead of glazing them.

NUTRITION INFORMATION PER SERVING:

1 BAR		PERCENT U.S. RDA	
Calories	90	Protein	*
Protein	1 g	Vitamin A	2%
Carbohydrate	14 g	Vitamin C	*
Dietary Fiber	1 g	Thiamine	2%
Fat	3 g	Riboflavin	2%
Polyunsaturated	1 g	Niacin	*
Saturated	1 g	Calcium	*
Cholesterol	6 mg	Iron	2%
Sodium	95 mg	*Less than 2% U.S. RDA	
Potassium	55 mg		

DIETARY EXCHANGES: 1/2 Starch, 1/2 Fruit, 1/2 Fat

Apple Date Bars

APPLE
DATE BARS

¼   cup sugar

1   cup water

2   cups chopped peeled apples

1   (8-oz.) pkg. chopped dates

1¾ cups all purpose flour

½   teaspoon baking soda

¼   teaspoon salt

¾   cup margarine or butter

1½ cups rolled oats

1   cup firmly packed brown sugar

In medium saucepan, combine sugar, water, apples and dates. Bring to a boil. Reduce heat to low; cook until thickened, about 10 minutes, stirring occasionally. Cool slightly.

Heat oven to 375°F. Grease and flour 13x9-inch pan. In large bowl, combine flour, baking soda and salt. With pastry blender or fork, cut in margarine until mixture is crumbly. Add oats and brown sugar; mix well. Press 3 cups mixture evenly in greased and floured pan. Spread evenly with filling. Sprinkle with remaining crumb mixture; press lightly.

Bake at 375°F. for 18 to 28 minutes or until golden brown. Cool completely. Cut into bars.

36 bars.

HIGH ALTITUDE – Above 3500 Feet: No change.

*F*or a new version of the old-time "matrimonial bars," a moist and healthful apple date filling is enclosed between crisp crumb layers.

NUTRITION INFORMATION PER SERVING:

1 BAR		PERCENT U.S. RDA	
Calories	120	Protein	2%
Protein	1 g	Vitamin A	2%
Carbohydrate	20 g	Vitamin C	*
Dietary Fiber	1 g	Thiamine	4%
Fat	4 g	Riboflavin	2%
Polyunsaturated	1 g	Niacin	2%
Saturated	1 g	Calcium	*
Cholesterol	0 mg	Iron	4%
Sodium	75 mg	*Less than 2% U.S. RDA	
Potassium	90 mg		

DIETARY EXCHANGES: 1/2 Starch, 1/2 Fruit, 1 Fat

APPLESAUCE MOLASSES BARS

*W*hole wheat flour has a higher fiber, fat and nutritional content than all purpose flour. To prevent rancidity, always store whole wheat flour in the refrigerator or freezer.

NUTRITION INFORMATION PER SERVING:

1 BAR		PERCENT U.S. RDA	
Calories	80	Protein	*
Protein	1 g	Vitamin A	*
Carbohydrate	12 g	Vitamin C	*
Dietary Fiber	1 g	Thiamine	2%
Fat	3 g	Riboflavin	2%
Polyunsaturated	1 g	Niacin	2%
Saturated	1 g	Calcium	*
Cholesterol	9 mg	Iron	2%
Sodium	65 mg	*Less than 2% U.S. RDA	
Potassium	75 mg		

DIETARY EXCHANGES: 1/2 Starch, 1/2 Fat

1   cup firmly packed brown sugar
½   cup margarine or butter, softened
1   cup applesauce
⅓   cup light molasses
2   eggs
1½   cups all purpose flour
1   cup whole wheat flour
1   teaspoon baking soda
1   teaspoon cinnamon
¼   teaspoon salt
¼   teaspoon allspice
½   cup chopped nuts
1   tablespoon powdered sugar

Heat oven to 350°F. In large bowl, beat brown sugar and margarine until light and fluffy. Beat in applesauce, molasses and eggs until smooth. Add all purpose flour, whole wheat flour, baking soda, cinnamon, salt and allspice; blend well. Stir in nuts. Spread evenly in ungreased 15x10x1-inch baking pan.

Bake at 350°F. for 20 to 25 minutes or until toothpick inserted in center comes out clean. Cool completely. Sprinkle with powdered sugar. Cut into bars.
48 bars.

HIGH ALTITUDE – Above 3500 Feet: No change.

LIGHT AND SPICY PUMPKIN BARS

BARS

1	**cup all purpose flour**
1	**cup whole wheat flour**
1½	**cups firmly packed brown sugar**
2	**teaspoons baking powder**
1	**teaspoon baking soda**
1	**teaspoon cinnamon**
½	**teaspoon nutmeg**
½	**teaspoon cloves**
¼	**teaspoon salt**
½	**cup oil**
½	**cup apple juice**
1	**(16-oz.) can (2 cups) pumpkin**
2	**eggs**

FROSTING

1½	**cups powdered sugar**
2	**tablespoons margarine or butter, softened**
½	**teaspoon vanilla**
2	**to 3 tablespoons plain yogurt**

Heat oven to 350°F. Grease and flour 15x10x1-inch baking pan. In large bowl, combine all bar ingredients; beat at low speed until moistened. Beat 2 minutes at medium speed. Spread in greased and floured pan.

Bake at 350°F. for 20 to 30 minutes or until toothpick inserted in center comes out clean. Cool completely.

In medium bowl, combine all frosting ingredients, adding enough yogurt for desired spreading consistency; beat until smooth. Frost cooled bars; sprinkle with nutmeg, if desired. Refrigerate to set frosting. Cut into bars.

48 bars.

HIGH ALTITUDE – Above 3500 Feet: Increase all purpose flour to 1⅓ cups; decrease baking powder to 1 teaspoon. Bake as directed above.

*T*he combination of whole wheat flour, brown sugar and sweet spices gives these pumpkin bars a delicious rich flavor. And we've substituted yogurt in the frosting for the more traditional cream cheese to help lower the fat content. You'll like the creamy flavor and the high beta-carotene (vitamin A) content.

NUTRITION INFORMATION PER SERVING:

1 BAR		PERCENT U.S. RDA	
Calories	90	Protein	*
Protein	1 g	Vitamin A	40%
Carbohydrate	16 g	Vitamin C	*
Dietary Fiber	1 g	Thiamine	2%
Fat	3 g	Riboflavin	2%
Polyunsaturated	2 g	Niacin	*
Saturated	1 g	Calcium	*
Cholesterol	9 mg	Iron	2%
Sodium	65 mg	*Less than 2% U.S. RDA	
Potassium	40 mg		

DIETARY EXCHANGES: 1 Starch, 1/2 Fat

ZUCCHINI BARS WITH PENUCHE FROSTING

The cooked brown sugar frosting complements these light-colored cake-like zucchini bars.

NUTRITION INFORMATION PER SERVING:

1 BAR		PERCENT U.S. RDA	
Calories	130	Protein	*
Protein	1 g	Vitamin A	4%
Carbohydrate	21 g	Vitamin C	*
Dietary Fiber	0 g	Thiamine	4%
Fat	5 g	Riboflavin	2%
Polyunsaturated	1 g	Niacin	*
Saturated	1 g	Calcium	*
Cholesterol	10 mg	Iron	2%
Sodium	90 mg	*Less than 2% U.S. RDA	
Potassium	65 mg		

DIETARY EXCHANGES: 1/2 Starch, 1 Fruit, 1 Fat

BARS

- 1 **cup sugar**
- ¾ **cup margarine or butter, softened**
- 1 **teaspoon vanilla**
- 2 **eggs**
- 2 **cups all purpose flour**
- 1½ **teaspoons baking powder**
- ½ **teaspoon salt**
- 2 **cups shredded zucchini**
- ¾ **cup coconut**
- 1 **cup raisins**

FROSTING

- 3 **tablespoons margarine or butter**
- ½ **cup firmly packed brown sugar**
- ¼ **cup 2% milk**
- 2 **to 2½ cups powdered sugar**

Heat oven to 350°F. Grease 15x10x1-inch baking pan. In large bowl, beat sugar and ¾ cup margarine until light and fluffy. Add vanilla and eggs; blend well. Add flour, baking powder and salt; mix well. Stir in zucchini, coconut and raisins. Spread in greased pan.

Bake at 350°F. for 20 to 30 minutes or until light golden brown. Cool completely.

In medium saucepan, combine 3 tablespoons margarine and brown sugar. Bring to a boil. Cook over medium heat 1 minute or until slightly thickened, stirring constantly. Cool 10 minutes. Add milk; beat until smooth. Beat in enough powdered sugar for desired spreading consistency. Frost cooled bars. Cut into bars.
48 bars.

HIGH ALTITUDE – Above 3500 Feet: Decrease sugar in bars to ¾ cup. Bake as directed above.

LEMON ZUCCHINI YOGURT BARS

2 **cups all purpose flour**

1 **cup sugar**

1 **teaspoon baking soda**

¼ **teaspoon salt**

½ **cup nonfat lemon or plain yogurt**

¼ **cup margarine or butter, melted**

1 **tablespoon grated lemon peel**

1 **tablespoon lemon juice**

1 **cup shredded zucchini**

1 **tablespoon powdered sugar**

Heat oven to 350°F. Spray 9-inch square pan with nonstick cooking spray. In large bowl, combine flour, sugar, baking soda and salt; mix well. In small bowl, combine yogurt, margarine, lemon peel and lemon juice; blend well. Add to dry ingredients; stir just until moistened. Stir in zucchini. Spread batter in spray-coated pan.

Bake at 350°F. for 30 to 40 minutes or until toothpick inserted in center comes out clean. Cool completely. Sprinkle with powdered sugar. Cut into bars.

24 bars.

HIGH ALTITUDE – Above 3500 Feet: No change.

These moist cake-like bars could be served for breakfast as a coffee cake. Nonfat yogurt is used instead of egg in this recipe, helping to reduce the total amount of fat.

NUTRITION INFORMATION PER SERVING:

1 BAR		PERCENT U.S. RDA	
Calories	90	Protein	2%
Protein	1 g	Vitamin A	*
Carbohydrate	17 g	Vitamin C	*
Dietary Fiber	0 g	Thiamine	6%
Fat	2 g	Riboflavin	4%
Polyunsaturated	1 g	Niacin	2%
Saturated	0 g	Calcium	*
Cholesterol	0 mg	Iron	2%
Sodium	95 mg	*Less than 2% U.S. RDA	
Potassium	40 mg		

DIETARY EXCHANGES: 1 Starch

HEALTH NOTES
FAT-REDUCING COOKING TECHNIQUES

You know that using less fat in recipes reduces calories and cholesterol. But did you know that certain cooking techniques are particularly healthy? When baking, save calories by using nonstick aerosol cooking sprays instead of greasing pans with butter, margarine or shortening. These sprays now come in canola and butter-flavored varieties. Nonstick pans can substantially reduce the amount of fat used, too. And they make for easier and faster clean-up.

Frosted Chocolaty Brownies

FROSTED CHOCOLATY BROWNIES

BROWNIES

¾ cup all purpose flour

¾ cup sugar

¼ cup unsweetened cocoa

½ teaspoon baking powder

¼ teaspoon salt

¼ cup oil

2 teaspoons chocolate extract or flavor

2 eggs

FROSTING

¾ cup powdered sugar

1 tablespoon unsweetened cocoa

1 tablespoon skim or 2% milk

½ teaspoon chocolate extract or flavor

⅛ teaspoon butter flavor

Dash salt

*B*y using chocolate extract in the brownies and frosting, and a little butter flavor in the frosting, you can cut back on the fat and still have rich, fudgy brownies!

NUTRITION INFORMATION PER SERVING:

1 BAR		PERCENT U.S. RDA	
Calories	80	Protein	*
Protein	1 g	Vitamin A	*
Carbohydrate	13 g	Vitamin C	*
Dietary Fiber	0 g	Thiamine	2%
Fat	3 g	Riboflavin	2%
Polyunsaturated	1 g	Niacin	*
Saturated	1 g	Calcium	*
Cholesterol	18 mg	Iron	2%
Sodium	50 mg	*Less than 2% U.S. RDA	
Potassium	20 mg		

DIETARY EXCHANGES: 1/2 Starch, 1/2 Fat

Heat oven to 350°F. Grease bottom only of 8-inch square pan. In medium bowl, combine all brownie ingredients; mix well. Spread in greased pan.

Bake at 350°F. for 13 to 18 minutes or until top is dry and springs back when touched lightly in center. Cool 15 minutes.

In small bowl, combine all frosting ingredients; mix well. Spread over top of slightly cooled brownies. Cool completely. Cut into bars.

24 bars.

HIGH ALTITUDE – Above 3500 Feet: No change.

Honey Cornmeal Muffins, p. 78; Whole Wheat Banana Bread, p. 106

QUICK BREADS & MUFFINS

*G*reat tasting and good for you? You bet. At five fat grams or fewer for a serving, these healthful quick breads are sure to please, especially when you consider that traditional recipes contain up to three times the fat.

BUTTERMILK CORNMEAL BISCUITS

*F*or the most tender biscuits, mix gently and work quickly. Cut biscuits with a sharp-edged cutter. A dull edge will pinch the top and bottom together and the biscuits won't rise properly.

3½ cups all purpose flour
½ cup cornmeal
5 teaspoons baking powder
1 teaspoon baking soda
½ teaspoon salt
½ cup margarine or butter
1½ to 1¾ cups buttermilk

Heat oven to 400°F. Grease cookie sheet. In large bowl, combine flour, cornmeal, baking powder, baking soda and salt; mix well. With pastry blender or fork, cut in margarine until mixture resembles coarse crumbs. Stir in enough buttermilk to form a soft dough.

On lightly floured surface, shape dough into ball. Roll out to 1-inch thickness; cut with floured 2-inch round cutter. Place biscuits on greased cookie sheet.

Bake at 400°F. for 10 to 15 minutes or until light golden brown. Serve warm.

18 to 20 biscuits.

HIGH ALTITUDE – Above 3500 Feet: No change.

NUTRITION INFORMATION PER SERVING:

1 BISCUIT		PERCENT U.S. RDA	
Calories	140	Protein	4%
Protein	3 g	Vitamin A	4%
Carbohydrate	19 g	Vitamin C	*
Dietary Fiber	1 g	Thiamine	10%
Fat	5 g	Riboflavin	8%
Polyunsaturated	2 g	Niacin	6%
Saturated	1 g	Calcium	8%
Cholesterol	1 mg	Iron	6%
Sodium	260 mg	*Less than 2% U.S. RDA	
Potassium	70 mg		

DIETARY EXCHANGES: 1 Starch, 1 Fat

HEALTH NOTES
COMPARING FATS

Baked goods would surely be dull without fat and its different flavors. But eating too much fat can lead to a host of health problems. Dietary fat is a mixture of two fat types: saturated and unsaturated. Added fats, including margarine and vegetable oil, contain saturated fat, the kind that increases blood cholesterol levels. Butter and lard have high saturated fat levels, while vegetable oils and margarine have much lower levels. Cutting back on total fat intake is one way to decrease saturated fat consumption.

GORGONZOLA CHEESE BISCUITS

- **2 cups all purpose flour**
- **3 teaspoons baking powder**
- **½ teaspoon sugar**
- **¼ teaspoon salt**
- **¼ teaspoon baking soda**
- **¼ teaspoon nutmeg**
- **⅓ cup margarine or butter**
- **4 oz. crumbled gorgonzola cheese**
- **¾ to 1 cup buttermilk**

Heat oven to 425°F. Grease cookie sheet. In large bowl, combine flour, baking powder, sugar, salt, baking soda and nutmeg; mix well. Using fork or pastry blender, cut margarine and cheese into flour mixture until mixture resembles coarse crumbs. Add ¾ cup buttermilk; stir with fork until mixture leaves sides of bowl and forms a soft, moist dough, adding additional buttermilk if necessary.

On floured surface, toss dough lightly until no longer sticky. Roll out to ½-inch thickness; cut with floured 2-inch round cutter. Place on greased cookie sheet with sides touching.

Bake at 425°F. for 10 to 15 minutes or until light golden brown. Serve warm.

18 biscuits.

HIGH ALTITUDE – Above 3500 Feet: No change.

Because gorgonzola is similar to blue cheese and has a strong pungent flavor, only small amounts are used in most recipes. These cheesy biscuits are perfect to serve with an Italian meal— the gorgonzola cheese makes them just a bit different!

NUTRITION INFORMATION PER SERVING:

1 BISCUIT		PERCENT U.S. RDA	
Calories	110	Protein	4%
Protein	3 g	Vitamin A	4%
Carbohydrate	12 g	Vitamin C	*
Dietary Fiber	0 g	Thiamine	8%
Fat	5 g	Riboflavin	6%
Polyunsaturated	1 g	Niacin	4%
Saturated	2 g	Calcium	8%
Cholesterol	5 mg	Iron	4%
Sodium	240 mg	*Less than 2% U.S. RDA	
Potassium	55 mg		

DIETARY EXCHANGES: 1 Starch, 1 Fat

Parmesan Herb Biscuits

PARMESAN HERB BISCUITS

2 cups all purpose flour

¼ cup chopped fresh parsley

2 tablespoons grated Parmesan cheese

1 tablespoon sugar

3 teaspoons baking powder

½ teaspoon salt

½ teaspoon dried sage leaves

¾ to 1 cup half-and-half

1 tablespoon margarine or butter, melted

1 tablespoon grated Parmesan cheese

Heat oven to 425°F. In large bowl, combine flour, parsley, 2 tablespoons cheese, sugar, baking powder, salt and sage; mix well. Add ¾ cup half-and-half; stir with fork just until dry ingredients are moistened, adding additional half-and-half, 1 tablespoon at a time, if necessary to form a soft dough.

On floured surface, knead dough gently to form a smooth ball. Pat dough into ½-inch-thick square. Using knife, cut into 12 squares. Place on ungreased cookie sheet. Brush with melted margarine; sprinkle with 1 tablespoon cheese.

Bake at 425°F. for 8 to 14 minutes or until light golden brown. Serve warm.

12 biscuits.

HIGH ALTITUDE – Above 3500 Feet: Decrease baking powder to 2 teaspoons. Bake as directed above.

*H*ere's a new twist on rolled biscuits. Just pat the dough into a square and cut the biscuits with a knife. You don't need a biscuit cutter and there's no rerolling. We've used half-and-half in place of shortening to reduce the fat yet maintain high quality.

NUTRITION INFORMATION PER SERVING:

1 BISCUIT		PERCENT U.S. RDA	
Calories	120	Protein	4%
Protein	3 g	Vitamin A	4%
Carbohydrate	18 g	Vitamin C	2%
Dietary Fiber	1 g	Thiamine	10%
Fat	4 g	Riboflavin	8%
Polyunsaturated	1 g	Niacin	6%
Saturated	2 g	Calcium	10%
Cholesterol	9 mg	Iron	6%
Sodium	260 mg		
Potassium	60 mg		

DIETARY EXCHANGES: 1 Starch, 1 Fat

LIGHT SOUR CREAM DROP BISCUITS

*T*his recipe was developed with skim milk and light sour cream so that it would be lower in fat and calories, without sacrificing flavor or texture. Light and flaky, these biscuits are delicious warm from the oven.

2 **cups all purpose flour**
1 **tablespoon sugar**
3 **teaspoons baking powder**
½ **teaspoon salt**
3 **tablespoons shortening**
⅔ **cup skim or 2% milk**
⅔ **cup light sour cream**

Heat oven to 450°F. Grease cookie sheet. In medium bowl, combine flour, sugar, baking powder and salt; blend well. Using pastry blender or fork, cut in shortening until mixture is crumbly. In small bowl, combine milk and sour cream; blend well. Add to dry ingredients all at once, stirring just until moistened. (If dough is too dry, add additional milk 1 teaspoon at a time.) To form each biscuit, drop ¼ cup of dough onto greased cookie sheet.

Bake at 450°F. for 10 to 12 minutes or until peaks and bottoms are golden brown. Immediately remove from cookie sheet. Serve warm.

12 biscuits.

HIGH ALTITUDE – Above 3500 Feet: No change.

NUTRITION INFORMATION PER SERVING:

1 BISCUIT		PERCENT U.S. RDA	
Calories	130	Protein	4%
Protein	3 g	Vitamin A	*
Carbohydrate	18 g	Vitamin C	*
Dietary Fiber	1 g	Thiamine	10%
Fat	4 g	Riboflavin	6%
Polyunsaturated	1 g	Niacin	6%
Saturated	1 g	Calcium	6%
Cholesterol	2 mg	Iron	4%
Sodium	190 mg	*Less than 2% U.S. RDA	
Potassium	80 mg		

DIETARY EXCHANGES: 1 Starch, 1 Fat

Light Sour Cream Drop Biscuits

APPLE BREAKFAST POPOVER

This popover made with egg whites "pops" near the end of the baking time into an interesting shape that's delicious with the spicy apple topping. It's a pleasant low-fat change-of-pace breakfast idea.

POPOVER
- ½ **cup all purpose flour**
- ½ **cup skim or 2% milk**
- 1 **tablespoon margarine or butter, melted**
- ⅛ **teaspoon salt**
- 4 **egg whites**

TOPPING
- 1½ **cups chopped apples**
- ½ **cup apple jelly**
- 2 **tablespoons water**
- ⅛ **teaspoon cinnamon**

Heat oven to 400°F. Spray 8-inch square (1½-quart) baking dish with nonstick cooking spray. In medium bowl, beat flour and milk with wire whisk until well blended. Add margarine, salt and egg whites; beat well. Pour into spray-coated dish. Bake at 400°F. for 25 to 30 minutes or until puffed and golden brown.

Meanwhile, in small saucepan combine all topping ingredients; heat over low heat until jelly is melted and mixture is hot, stirring frequently. Immediately after removing popover from oven, cut into fourths and serve with hot topping.

4 servings.

NUTRITION INFORMATION PER SERVING:

1/4 OF RECIPE		PERCENT U.S. RDA	
Calories	240	Protein	10%
Protein	6 g	Vitamin A	4%
Carbohydrate	45 g	Vitamin C	4%
Dietary Fiber	2 g	Thiamine	10%
Fat	3 g	Riboflavin	15%
Polyunsaturated	1 g	Niacin	4%
Saturated	1 g	Calcium	6%
Cholesterol	1 mg	Iron	8%
Sodium	180 mg		
Potassium	200 mg		

DIETARY EXCHANGES: 2 Starch, 1 Fruit, 1/2 Fat

WHOLE WHEAT POPOVERS

When selecting bread to complement your menu, try to choose something with a minimum of fat, little or no sugar and a lot of whole grain flours. These light and airy popovers are a good example.

- 2 **eggs**
- ¾ **cup all purpose flour**
- ¼ **cup whole wheat flour**
- ½ **teaspoon salt**
- 1 **cup 2% milk**

Heat oven to 450°F. Generously grease 6 popover cups or deep custard cups.* In medium bowl, beat eggs slightly. Add all remaining ingredients; beat with rotary beater *just* until blended. *Do not overbeat.* Fill greased cups about ½ full.

Bake at 450°F. for 15 minutes. Reduce heat to 325°F.; bake an additional 25 to 30 minutes or until deep golden brown. Immediately remove from cups. Serve warm.

6 popovers.

TIP:
* A greased muffin pan can be substituted for the popover cups. Bake at 450°F. for 15 minutes. Reduce heat to 325°F.; bake an additional 20 to 25 minutes. 8 to 10 popovers.

HIGH ALTITUDE – Above 3500 Feet: No change.

NUTRITION INFORMATION PER SERVING:

1 POPOVER		PERCENT U.S. RDA	
Calories	120	Protein	8%
Protein	6 g	Vitamin A	4%
Carbohydrate	18 g	Vitamin C	*
Dietary Fiber	1 g	Thiamine	10%
Fat	3 g	Riboflavin	15%
Polyunsaturated	0 g	Niacin	6%
Saturated	1 g	Calcium	6%
Cholesterol	74 mg	Iron	6%
Sodium	220 mg	*Less than 2% U.S. RDA	
Potassium	120 mg		

DIETARY EXCHANGES: 1 Starch, 1/2 Fat

Apple Breakfast Popover

PUMPKIN SCONES

*P*umpkin is a great source of vitamin A and is naturally low in fat and calories. Serve these pumpkin-flavored biscuit wedges at breakfast, tea or your next brunch.

¼ cup sugar
1 teaspoon pumpkin pie spice
2½ cups all purpose flour
3 teaspoons baking powder
½ teaspoon baking soda
¼ teaspoon salt
3 tablespoons margarine or butter
1 cup canned pumpkin
¼ cup buttermilk

Heat oven to 400°F. Spray cookie sheet with nonstick cooking spray. In large bowl, combine sugar and pumpkin pie spice until well mixed; reserve 1½ teaspoons. Add flour, baking powder, baking soda and salt to remaining sugar-spice mixture; mix well. Using pastry blender or fork, cut in margarine until mixture resembles coarse crumbs. In small bowl with wire whisk, beat pumpkin and buttermilk until well combined. Add to flour mixture; toss with fork just until dry ingredients are moistened.

On floured surface, gently knead dough until smooth and no longer sticky. Shape into ball. Place on spray-coated cookie sheet; press into 9-inch circle. Sprinkle with reserved sugar-spice mixture. Cut into 8 wedges; separate slightly.

Bake at 400°F. for 18 to 24 minutes or until golden brown and toothpick inserted in center comes out clean. Serve warm.
8 scones.

TIP:
   If desired, ½ cup raisins or dried currants can be stirred into flour mixture.

HIGH ALTITUDE – Above 3500 Feet: No change.

NUTRITION INFORMATION PER SERVING:

1 SCONE		PERCENT U.S. RDA	
Calories	220	Protein	6%
Protein	5 g	Vitamin A	140%
Carbohydrate	37 g	Vitamin C	*
Dietary Fiber	2 g	Thiamine	20%
Fat	5 g	Riboflavin	10%
Polyunsaturated	2 g	Niacin	10%
Saturated	1 g	Calcium	10%
Cholesterol	0 mg	Iron	10%
Sodium	310 mg	*Less than 2% U.S. RDA	
Potassium	120 mg		

DIETARY EXCHANGES: 2 Starch, 1/2 Fruit, 1 Fat

WALNUT SCONE DROPS

2 **cups all purpose flour**

¼ **cup sugar**

2 **teaspoons baking powder**

½ **teaspoon salt**

¼ **teaspoon baking soda**

⅓ **cup margarine or butter**

⅔ **to ¾ cup buttermilk**

½ **cup chopped walnuts**

Heat oven to 375°F. Grease cookie sheets. In large bowl, combine flour, sugar, baking powder, salt and baking soda; blend well. Using fork or pastry blender, cut in margarine until mixture resembles coarse crumbs. Add buttermilk and walnuts; stir just until dry ingredients are moistened. Drop by heaping teaspoonfuls 2 inches apart onto greased cookie sheets.

Bake at 375°F. for 9 to 12 minutes or until light golden brown. Immediately remove from cookie sheets. Serve warm.
30 scones.

HIGH ALTITUDE – Above 3500 Feet: Decrease baking powder to 1½ teaspoons; increase buttermilk to ¾ cup plus 1 to 2 tablespoons. Bake as directed above.

*S*cones are Scottish in origin, and history says the name "scone" comes from the Stone of Destiny (or scone) where Scottish kings were once crowned. Serve this updated version of scones warm from the oven with fruit preserves.

NUTRITION INFORMATION PER SERVING:

1 SCONE		PERCENT U.S. RDA	
Calories	70	Protein	2%
Protein	1 g	Vitamin A	*
Carbohydrate	9 g	Vitamin C	*
Dietary Fiber	0 g	Thiamine	4%
Fat	3 g	Riboflavin	2%
Polyunsaturated	1 g	Niacin	2%
Saturated	1 g	Calcium	2%
Cholesterol	0 mg	Iron	2%
Sodium	110 mg	*Less than 2% U.S. RDA	
Potassium	30 mg		

DIETARY EXCHANGES: 1/2 Starch, 1/2 Fat

MOIST SPICED APPLE SCONES

Let the aroma of sweet spices and apples fill your kitchen when you make these nutritious coffee-cake style scones. They'll disappear quickly when you take them out of the oven.

SCONES

2 cups all purpose flour

½ cup firmly packed brown sugar

2 teaspoons baking powder

½ teaspoon cinnamon

¼ teaspoon nutmeg

¼ teaspoon ginger

⅛ teaspoon salt

2 tablespoons margarine or butter

1 cup chopped dried apples

½ cup unsweetened applesauce

¼ cup buttermilk

1 egg

TOPPING

1 teaspoon sugar

⅛ teaspoon cinnamon

Heat oven to 375°F. Spray large cookie sheet with nonstick cooking spray. In medium bowl, combine flour, brown sugar, baking powder, ½ teaspoon cinnamon, nutmeg, ginger and salt; mix well. Using pastry blender or fork, cut in margarine until mixture resembles coarse crumbs. Stir in apples. In small bowl, combine applesauce, buttermilk and egg; mix well. Add to dry ingredients; stir just until dry ingredients are moistened. (Dough will be sticky.)

Place dough on spray-coated cookie sheet. With wet fingers, shape into 8-inch circle, about ¾ inch thick. In small bowl, combine topping ingredients; sprinkle over top of dough. With sharp knife, score top surface into 8 wedges, cutting about ¼ inch deep.

Bake at 375°F. for 18 to 22 minutes or until golden brown and toothpick inserted in center comes out clean. Cut into wedges. Serve warm.

8 scones.

HIGH ALTITUDE – Above 3500 Feet: No change.

NUTRITION INFORMATION PER SERVING:

1 SCONE		PERCENT U.S. RDA	
Calories	240	Protein	6%
Protein	4 g	Vitamin A	2%
Carbohydrate	45 g	Vitamin C	*
Dietary Fiber	2 g	Thiamine	15%
Fat	4 g	Riboflavin	10%
Polyunsaturated	1 g	Niacin	10%
Saturated	1 g	Calcium	8%
Cholesterol	27 mg	Iron	10%
Sodium	170 mg	*Less than 2% U.S. RDA	
Potassium	160 mg		

DIETARY EXCHANGES: 2 Starch, 1 Fruit, 1/2 Fat

Moist Spiced Apple Scones

WHOLE WHEAT SCONES

*T*he original scones were made from oats and griddle-baked. Now, of course, scones are baked in an oven, but these whole grain scones are reminiscent of the original triangular-shaped version— they're tender and delicious.

1 cup all purpose flour
1 cup whole wheat flour
2 tablespoons sugar
1 tablespoon rolled oats
1½ teaspoons baking soda
¼ teaspoon salt
1 cup buttermilk
2 tablespoons buttermilk

Heat oven to 400°F. Grease cookie sheet. In large bowl, combine all ingredients except buttermilk; mix well. Add 1 cup buttermilk all at once; stir just until dry ingredients are moistened.

On lightly floured surface, gently knead until dough holds its shape. Place on greased cookie sheet; pat out to 7-inch circle. Cut into 8 wedges; separate slightly. Brush with 2 tablespoons buttermilk.

Bake at 400°F. for 12 to 14 minutes or until golden brown. Serve warm.
8 scones.

HIGH ALTITUDE – Above 3500 Feet: Increase all purpose flour to 1 cup plus 2 tablespoons. Bake as directed above.

NUTRITION INFORMATION PER SERVING:

1 SCONE		PERCENT U.S. RDA	
Calories	140	Protein	8%
Protein	5 g	Vitamin A	*
Carbohydrate	26 g	Vitamin C	*
Dietary Fiber	2 g	Thiamine	15%
Fat	1 g	Riboflavin	8%
Polyunsaturated	0 g	Niacin	8%
Saturated	0 g	Calcium	4%
Cholesterol	1 mg	Iron	8%
Sodium	310 mg	*Less than 2% U.S. RDA	
Potassium	130 mg		

DIETARY EXCHANGES: 2 Starch

MINIATURE CURRIED FENNEL SCONES

2 cups all purpose flour

3 teaspoons baking powder

¼ teaspoon curry powder

¼ teaspoon turmeric

¼ teaspoon fennel seed, crushed

¾ to 1 cup skim or 2% milk

2 tablespoons oil

SPREAD

½ cup light sour cream

4 teaspoons chopped fresh chives

Fresh fennel sprigs, if desired

Heat oven to 450°F. In medium bowl, combine flour, baking powder, curry powder, turmeric and fennel seed; blend well. Add ¾ cup milk and oil; stir just until dry ingredients are moistened, adding additional milk, 1 tablespoon at a time, if necessary to form a soft dough.

Turn dough out onto generously floured surface. With floured hands, knead dough 15 to 20 times. Pat into 1-inch-thick round; cut into 20 rounds with floured 1½-inch round cutter.* Place on ungreased cookie sheet.

Bake at 450°F. for 8 to 9 minutes or until light golden brown. Meanwhile, in small bowl combine sour cream and chives. Split hot scones; spread bottom half with about 1 teaspoon mixture. Place fennel sprigs over mixture. Place top halves over filling.

20 scones.

TIP:

* If desired, press dough into 1-inch-thick 5x4-inch rectangle; cut into 20 squares.

HIGH ALTITUDE – Above 3500 Feet: No change.

*T*he unusual combination of seasonings results in a delicious, savory scone with a subtle anise flavor. There's no added sugar and each scone boasts only 60 calories and 2 grams of fat! Delicious served as an appetizer or meal accompaniment.

NUTRITION INFORMATION PER SERVING:

1 SCONE		PERCENT U.S. RDA	
Calories	60	Protein	2%
Protein	2 g	Vitamin A	*
Carbohydrate	10 g	Vitamin C	*
Dietary Fiber	0 g	Thiamine	6%
Fat	2 g	Riboflavin	4%
Polyunsaturated	1 g	Niacin	4%
Saturated	0 g	Calcium	4%
Cholesterol	0 mg	Iron	2%
Sodium	50 mg	*Less than 2% U.S. RDA	
Potassium	35 mg		

DIETARY EXCHANGES: 1/2 Starch, 1/2 Fat

TOPPINGS FOR A DOZEN MUFFINS

TO ADD BEFORE BAKING:

*A*dd flavor and texture to a dozen muffins by sprinkling one of these simple topping mixtures over the batter just before baking.

CINNAMON SUGAR TOPPING

5½ teaspoons sugar

½ teaspoon cinnamon

In small bowl, combine sugar and cinnamon. Sprinkle ½ teaspoon mixture over batter in each muffin cup. Bake.

NUTRITION INFORMATION PER SERVING:

1/12 OF RECIPE		PERCENT U.S. RDA	
Calories	6	Protein	*
Protein	0 g	Vitamin A	*
Carbohydrate	2 g	Vitamin C	*
Dietary Fiber	0 g	Thiamine	*
Fat	0 g	Riboflavin	*
Polyunsaturated	0 g	Niacin	*
Saturated	0 g	Calcium	*
Cholesterol	0 mg	Iron	*
Sodium	0 mg	*Less than 2% U.S. RDA	
Potassium	0 mg		

DIETARY EXCHANGES: Free

OAT ALMOND TOPPING

5 tablespoons rolled oats

1 tablespoon chopped almonds

In small bowl, combine oats and almonds. Sprinkle 1½ teaspoons mixture over batter in each muffin cup; gently press into batter. Bake.

NUTRITION INFORMATION PER SERVING:

1/12 OF RECIPE		PERCENT U.S. RDA	
Calories	12	Protein	*
Protein	1 g	Vitamin A	*
Carbohydrate	2 g	Vitamin C	*
Dietary Fiber	0 g	Thiamine	*
Fat	1 g	Riboflavin	*
Polyunsaturated	0 g	Niacin	*
Saturated	0 g	Calcium	*
Cholesterol	0 mg	Iron	*
Sodium	0 mg	*Less than 2% U.S. RDA	
Potassium	10 mg		

DIETARY EXCHANGES: Free

CINNAMON HAZELNUT STREUSEL

2 tablespoons all purpose flour

2 tablespoons brown sugar

2 tablespoons finely chopped hazelnuts (filberts) or pecans

1 tablespoon oil

½ teaspoon cinnamon

In small bowl, combine all ingredients. Sprinkle 1½ teaspoons mixture over batter in each muffin cup; gently press into batter. Bake.

NUTRITION INFORMATION PER SERVING:

1/12 OF RECIPE		PERCENT U.S. RDA	
Calories	30	Protein	*
Protein	0 g	Vitamin A	*
Carbohydrate	3 g	Vitamin C	*
Dietary Fiber	0 g	Thiamine	*
Fat	2 g	Riboflavin	*
Polyunsaturated	1 g	Niacin	*
Saturated	0 g	Calcium	*
Cholesterol	0 mg	Iron	*
Sodium	0 mg	*Less than 2% U.S. RDA	
Potassium	15 mg		

DIETARY EXCHANGES: 1/2 Fat

CONTINUED

Muffin Toppings, pp. 70–73

RASPBERRY CRUMBLE TOPPING

¾ cup fresh raspberries or frozen unsweetened raspberries

2 tablespoons brown sugar

¼ teaspoon cinnamon

Press raspberries into batter in muffin cups. In small bowl, combine brown sugar and cinnamon. Sprinkle ½ teaspoon mixture over batter in each muffin cup. Bake.

NUTRITION INFORMATION PER SERVING:

1/12 OF RECIPE		PERCENT U.S. RDA	
Calories	12	Protein	*
Protein	0 g	Vitamin A	*
Carbohydrate	3 g	Vitamin C	2%
Dietary Fiber	0 g	Thiamine	*
Fat	0 g	Riboflavin	*
Polyunsaturated	0 g	Niacin	*
Saturated	0 g	Calcium	*
Cholesterol	0 mg	Iron	*
Sodium	0 mg	*Less than 2% U.S. RDA	
Potassium	20 mg		

DIETARY EXCHANGES: Free

SAVORY STREUSEL TOPPING

2 tablespoons all purpose flour

3 tablespoons wheat germ

1 teaspoon dried Italian seasoning

⅛ teaspoon salt

1 tablespoon oil

In small bowl, combine all ingredients; mix well. Sprinkle 1½ teaspoons mixture over batter in each muffin cup; gently press into batter. Bake.

NUTRITION INFORMATION PER SERVING:

1/12 OF RECIPE		PERCENT U.S. RDA	
Calories	20	Protein	*
Protein	1 g	Vitamin A	*
Carbohydrate	2 g	Vitamin C	*
Dietary Fiber	0 g	Thiamine	2%
Fat	1 g	Riboflavin	*
Polyunsaturated	1 g	Niacin	*
Saturated	0 g	Calcium	*
Cholesterol	0 mg	Iron	*
Sodium	20 mg	*Less than 2% U.S. RDA	
Potassium	20 mg		

DIETARY EXCHANGES: 1/2 Fat

TO ADD AFTER BAKING:

*D*ress up a dozen muffins warm from the oven with one of these simple topping combos.

HONEY SUNFLOWER NUT TOPPING

¼ cup honey, heated

2 tablespoons unsalted shelled sunflower seeds, toasted

Brush each warm muffin with 1 teaspoon honey; sprinkle each with ½ teaspoon sunflower seeds.

NUTRITION INFORMATION PER SERVING:

1/12 OF RECIPE		PERCENT U.S. RDA	
Calories	30	Protein	*
Protein	0 g	Vitamin A	*
Carbohydrate	6 g	Vitamin C	*
Dietary Fiber	0 g	Thiamine	*
Fat	1 g	Riboflavin	*
Polyunsaturated	0 g	Niacin	*
Saturated	0 g	Calcium	*
Cholesterol	0 mg	Iron	*
Sodium	0 mg	*Less than 2% U.S. RDA	
Potassium	15 mg		

DIETARY EXCHANGES: 1/2 Fruit

MAPLE WALNUT TOPPING

¾ **cup powdered sugar**

2 **to 3 tablespoons maple-flavored syrup, heated**

2 **tablespoons finely chopped walnuts**

In small bowl, combine powdered sugar and syrup; stir until smooth. Drizzle 1 teaspoon mixture over each warm muffin; sprinkle each with ½ teaspoon walnuts.

NUTRITION INFORMATION PER SERVING:

1/12 OF RECIPE		PERCENT U.S. RDA	
Calories	50	Protein	*
Protein	0 g	Vitamin A	*
Carbohydrate	11 g	Vitamin C	*
Dietary Fiber	0 g	Thiamine	*
Fat	1 g	Riboflavin	*
Polyunsaturated	1 g	Niacin	*
Saturated	0 g	Calcium	*
Cholesterol	0 mg	Iron	*
Sodium	0 mg	*Less than 2% U.S. RDA	
Potassium	10 mg		

DIETARY EXCHANGES: 1 Fruit

FRUIT AND PRESERVES TOPPING

¼ **cup light peach or apricot syrup**

¼ **cup dried mixed fruit bits, finely chopped**

Brush each warm muffin with 1 teaspoon peach syrup; sprinkle each with 1 teaspoon fruit bits.

NUTRITION INFORMATION PER SERVING:

1/12 OF RECIPE		PERCENT U.S. RDA	
Calories	18	Protein	*
Protein	0 g	Vitamin A	*
Carbohydrate	5 g	Vitamin C	*
Dietary Fiber	0 g	Thiamine	*
Fat	0 g	Riboflavin	*
Polyunsaturated	0 g	Niacin	*
Saturated	0 g	Calcium	*
Cholesterol	0 mg	Iron	*
Sodium	15 mg	*Less than 2% U.S. RDA	
Potassium	20 mg		

DIETARY EXCHANGES: 1/2 Fruit

LEMON DRIZZLE TOPPING

⅔ **cup powdered sugar**

2 **to 3 teaspoons lemon juice**

Grated lemon peel

In small bowl, combine powdered sugar and lemon juice; stir until smooth. Drizzle 1 teaspoon mixture over each warm muffin; sprinkle each with lemon peel.

NUTRITION INFORMATION PER SERVING:

1/12 OF RECIPE		PERCENT U.S. RDA	
Calories	25	Protein	*
Protein	0 g	Vitamin A	*
Carbohydrate	7 g	Vitamin C	*
Dietary Fiber	0 g	Thiamine	*
Fat	0 g	Riboflavin	*
Polyunsaturated	0 g	Niacin	*
Saturated	0 g	Calcium	*
Cholesterol	0 mg	Iron	*
Sodium	0 mg	*Less than 2% U.S. RDA	
Potassium	0 mg		

DIETARY EXCHANGES: 1/2 Fruit

LIGHT MUFFINS

*W*arm, fragrant and fresh from the oven, these muffins will satisfy many a craving for "homemade." Bake the basic muffins just as they are or try one of the many variations that we've included—they're all delicious!

2 cups all purpose flour

½ cup sugar

3 teaspoons baking powder

½ teaspoon salt

¾ cup 2% milk

3 tablespoons oil

1 egg, beaten

Heat oven to 400°F. Line 12 muffin cups with paper baking cups. In medium bowl, combine flour, sugar, baking powder and salt; mix well. In small bowl, combine milk, oil and egg; blend well. Add to dry ingredients; stir just until dry ingredients are moistened. Divide batter evenly among paper-lined muffin cups.

Bake at 400°F. for 18 to 23 minutes or until light golden brown. Cool 1 minute; remove from pan. Serve warm.

12 muffins.

▤ MICROWAVE DIRECTIONS: Prepare muffin batter as directed above. Using 6-cup microwave-safe muffin pan, line each cup with 2 paper baking cups to absorb moisture during baking. Fill cups ⅔ full. Microwave 6 muffins on HIGH for 2 to 3 minutes or until toothpick inserted in center comes out clean, rotating pan ½ turn halfway through cooking. Remove muffins from pan and immediately discard outer baking cups. Repeat with remaining batter.

HIGH ALTITUDE – Above 3500 Feet: Decrease sugar to ¼ cup. Bake as directed above.

VARIATIONS:

APPLE MUFFINS: Decrease sugar to ¼ cup. Add 1 teaspoon cinnamon and 1 cup finely chopped, peeled apple to dry ingredients. Substitute apple juice for milk.

BLUEBERRY MUFFINS: Stir 1 cup fresh or frozen blueberries (do not thaw) and 1 teaspoon grated lemon or orange peel into dry ingredients.

NUTRITION INFORMATION PER SERVING:

1 MUFFIN		PERCENT U.S. RDA	
Calories	150	Protein	4%
Protein	3 g	Vitamin A	*
Carbohydrate	25 g	Vitamin C	*
Dietary Fiber	1 g	Thiamine	10%
Fat	4 g	Riboflavin	8%
Polyunsaturated	2 g	Niacin	6%
Saturated	1 g	Calcium	8%
Cholesterol	19 mg	Iron	6%
Sodium	220 mg	*Less than 2% U.S. RDA	
Potassium	50 mg		

DIETARY EXCHANGES: 1-1/2 Starch, 1 Fat

CHOCOLATE CHIP MUFFINS: Add ¾ cup miniature chocolate chips to dry ingredients. Before baking, sprinkle tops of muffins with a combination of 3 tablespoons sugar and 2 tablespoons brown sugar.

JAM MUFFINS: Before baking, place ½ teaspoon any flavor jam on each muffin; press into batter. If desired, sprinkle with finely chopped nuts.

LEMON MUFFINS: Add 1 tablespoon grated lemon peel to dry ingredients.

ORANGE MUFFINS: Add 1 tablespoon grated orange peel to dry ingredients and substitute orange juice for milk.

STREUSEL-TOPPED MUFFINS: In small bowl, combine ¼ cup firmly packed brown sugar, 1 tablespoon margarine or butter, softened, ½ teaspoon cinnamon and ¼ cup chopped nuts or flaked coconut; with fork, mix until crumbly. Sprinkle over muffins before baking.

SUGAR-COATED MUFFINS: Brush tops of hot baked muffins with 2 tablespoons melted margarine or butter; dip in mixture of ¼ cup sugar and ½ teaspoon cinnamon.

WHOLE WHEAT MUFFINS: Use 1 cup all purpose flour and 1 cup whole wheat flour.

BROWN BREAD MUFFIN GEMS

*A*lthough there are no eggs or oil in these whole wheat muffins, you'll find them very moist and flavorful. The muffins are reminiscent of Boston brown bread and are perfect to serve with soup or stew.

1½	**cups whole wheat flour**
½	**cup cornmeal**
½	**cup chopped dates, if desired**
⅓	**cup sugar**
¼	**cup chopped nuts**
1	**teaspoon baking soda**
½	**teaspoon salt**
1	**cup buttermilk**
¼	**cup molasses**

Heat oven to 375°F. Grease bottoms only of 12 muffin cups. In medium bowl, combine flour, cornmeal, dates, sugar, nuts, baking soda and salt; mix well. Add buttermilk and molasses; stir just until dry ingredients are moistened. Fill greased muffin cups about ¾ full.

Bake at 375°F. for 16 to 25 minutes or until toothpick inserted in center comes out clean. Cool 1 minute; remove from pan. Serve warm.

12 muffins.

HIGH ALTITUDE – Above 3500 Feet: No change.

NUTRITION INFORMATION PER SERVING:

1 MUFFIN		PERCENT U.S. RDA	
Calories	150	Protein	6%
Protein	4 g	Vitamin A	*
Carbohydrate	32 g	Vitamin C	*
Dietary Fiber	3 g	Thiamine	8%
Fat	2 g	Riboflavin	4%
Polyunsaturated	1 g	Niacin	6%
Saturated	0 g	Calcium	4%
Cholesterol	1 mg	Iron	6%
Sodium	220 mg	*Less than 2% U.S. RDA	
Potassium	260 mg		

DIETARY EXCHANGES: 2 Starch

HEALTH NOTES

THE ROLE SALT PLAYS IN BAKED GOODS

If you or a family member is battling high blood pressure, you may wonder if recipes will "work" without salt, which is 40% sodium. In many cases, you may omit or cut back on salt in baked goods with little difference in the outcome. But this is not so with yeast breads. Salt regulates the action of yeast, and has a direct bearing on yeast bread quality. In cookie and quick bread recipes, use grated lemon or orange peel to mimic salt's flavor-enhancing qualities.

MOLASSES BRAN MUFFINS

2 cups shreds of whole bran cereal
1½ cups 2% milk
¼ cup molasses
¼ cup shortening
1 egg
1½ cups all purpose flour
½ cup sugar
1½ teaspoons baking soda
½ teaspoon salt
½ cup raisins

Heat oven to 400°F. Line with paper baking cups or grease 18 muffin cups. In medium bowl, combine cereal, milk and molasses; let stand 1 to 2 minutes until cereal is softened. Add shortening and egg; beat well. In large bowl, combine flour, sugar, baking soda and salt; mix well. Stir in raisins. Add cereal mixture all at once; stir just until dry ingredients are moistened. Divide batter evenly among paper-lined muffin cups.

Bake at 400°F. for 14 to 18 minutes or until toothpick inserted in center comes out clean. Immediately remove from pan. Serve warm.

18 muffins.

HIGH ALTITUDE – Above 3500 Feet: No change.

Molasses is available in many forms including light, dark and blackstrap. Light molasses is sweet and light in color. Dark molasses is darker, thicker and less sweet than light molasses; however, light and dark molasses are usually interchangeable in recipes. Blackstrap molasses is slightly bitter and very thick. We don't recommend it for baked goods.

NUTRITION INFORMATION PER SERVING:

1 MUFFIN		PERCENT U.S. RDA	
Calories	140	Protein	4%
Protein	3 g	Vitamin A	6%
Carbohydrate	25 g	Vitamin C	4%
Dietary Fiber	3 g	Thiamine	10%
Fat	4 g	Riboflavin	10%
Polyunsaturated	1 g	Niacin	8%
Saturated	1 g	Calcium	4%
Cholesterol	13 mg	Iron	10%
Sodium	240 mg		
Potassium	220 mg		

DIETARY EXCHANGES: 1 Starch, 1/2 Fruit, 1 Fat

HONEY CORNMEAL MUFFINS

A rule of thumb for filling muffin cups is to fill them ⅔ to ¾ full of batter. This recipe for honey-flavored dinner muffins doubles easily. Bake one batch to eat now and an extra batch to freeze for later.

1¼ **cups all purpose flour**
¾ **cup cornmeal**
3 **teaspoons baking powder**
½ **teaspoon salt**
1 **tablespoon grated lemon peel**
½ **cup skim or 2% milk**
½ **cup honey**
¼ **cup oil**
¼ **cup frozen fat-free egg product, thawed, or 1 egg, slightly beaten**

Heat oven to 375°F. Grease bottoms only of 12 muffin cups or line with paper baking cups. In large bowl, combine flour, cornmeal, baking powder, salt and lemon peel; mix well. Add milk, honey, oil and egg; stir just until dry ingredients are moistened. Fill greased muffin cups ⅔ full.

Bake at 375°F. for 13 to 18 minutes or until very light brown and toothpick inserted in center comes out clean. Immediately remove from pan. Serve warm.
12 muffins.

HIGH ALTITUDE – Above 3500 Feet: No change.

NUTRITION INFORMATION PER SERVING:			
1 MUFFIN		**PERCENT U.S. RDA**	
Calories	170	Protein	4%
Protein	3 g	Vitamin A	*
Carbohydrate	28 g	Vitamin C	*
Dietary Fiber	1 g	Thiamine	10%
Fat	5 g	Riboflavin	6%
Polyunsaturated	3 g	Niacin	4%
Saturated	1 g	Calcium	8%
Cholesterol	1 mg	Iron	6%
Sodium	230 mg	*Less than 2% U.S. RDA	
Potassium	65 mg		

DIETARY EXCHANGES: 1-1/2 Starch, 1 Fat

Honey Cornmeal Muffins

BOSTON BROWN BREAD MUFFINS

1½ cups all purpose flour

½   cup cornmeal

¼   cup firmly packed brown sugar

1   teaspoon baking soda

1   cup buttermilk

¼   cup molasses

¼   cup oil

½   cup golden raisins

¼   cup frozen fat-free egg product, thawed, or 1 egg,
    slightly beaten

Heat oven to 400°F. Line 12 muffin cups with paper baking cups or spray with nonstick cooking spray. In large bowl, combine flour, cornmeal, brown sugar and baking soda. In medium bowl, combine remaining ingredients; blend well. Add to dry ingredients all at once; stir just until dry ingredients are moistened. Fill paper-lined muffin cups ¾ full.

Bake at 400°F. for 13 to 18 minutes or until toothpick inserted in center comes out clean. Immediately remove from pan. Serve warm.

12 muffins.

HIGH ALTITUDE – Above 3500 Feet: Increase flour to 1½ cups plus 2 tablespoons. Bake as directed above.

Molasses, cornmeal, raisins and buttermilk are all ingredients used in making traditional New England brown bread. Molasses appears in many New England recipes, for good reason. Early colonists obtained both cane sugar and molasses from the West Indies but molasses was the cheaper of the two and so was more commonly used.

NUTRITION INFORMATION PER SERVING:

1 MUFFIN		PERCENT U.S. RDA	
Calories	180	Protein	4%
Protein	3 g	Vitamin A	*
Carbohydrate	31 g	Vitamin C	*
Dietary Fiber	1 g	Thiamine	10%
Fat	5 g	Riboflavin	8%
Polyunsaturated	3 g	Niacin	6%
Saturated	1 g	Calcium	4%
Cholesterol	1 mg	Iron	8%
Sodium	130 mg	*Less than 2% U.S. RDA	
Potassium	230 mg		

DIETARY EXCHANGES: 1 Starch, 1 Fruit, 1 Fat

ONION CHIVE MUFFINS

These savory muffins are at their best when served warm. To reduce the fat in each muffin to 3 grams, the recipe was developed with fat-free egg product.

NUTRITION INFORMATION PER SERVING:

1 MUFFIN		PERCENT U.S. RDA	
Calories	80	Protein	2%
Protein	2 g	Vitamin A	*
Carbohydrate	11 g	Vitamin C	*
Dietary Fiber	0 g	Thiamine	6%
Fat	3 g	Riboflavin	4%
Polyunsaturated	2 g	Niacin	2%
Saturated	1 g	Calcium	4%
Cholesterol	0 mg	Iron	2%
Sodium	150 mg	*Less than 2% U.S. RDA	
Potassium	50 mg		

DIETARY EXCHANGES: 1/2 Starch, 1/2 Fat

¾ cup chopped onions

1½ cups all purpose flour

¼ cup chopped fresh chives

2 tablespoons sugar

2 teaspoons baking powder

½ teaspoon salt

¼ teaspoon baking soda

1 cup buttermilk

¼ cup oil

¼ cup frozen fat-free egg product, thawed, or 1 egg, slightly beaten

Heat oven to 375°F. Grease bottoms only of 12 muffin cups or line with paper baking cups. Spray small skillet with nonstick cooking spray. Cook and stir onions over medium heat until crisp-tender; set aside.

In large bowl, combine flour, chives, sugar, baking powder, salt and baking soda. In small bowl, combine cooked onions, buttermilk, oil and egg product; mix well. Add to dry ingredients; stir just until dry ingredients are moistened. Fill greased muffin cups about ¾ full.

Bake at 375°F. for 12 to 14 minutes or until toothpick inserted in center comes out clean. (Muffins will be very light in color.) Immediately remove from pan. Serve warm.

12 muffins.

MICROWAVE DIRECTIONS: In small microwave-safe bowl, combine onions and *1 teaspoon oil.* Microwave on HIGH for 1½ to 2 minutes or until onions are crisp-tender. Prepare muffin batter as directed above. Using 6-cup microwave-safe muffin pan, line each cup with 2 paper baking cups to absorb moisture during baking. Fill cups about ½ full. Microwave 6 muffins on HIGH for 1¾ to 2 minutes or until toothpick inserted in center comes out clean, rotating pan ¼ turn once halfway through cooking. Immediately remove muffins from pan and discard outer baking cups. Cool 1 minute on wire rack before serving. Repeat with remaining batter.

18 muffins.

HIGH ALTITUDE – Above 3500 Feet: No change.

BLUEBERRY CORN MUFFINS

1¼ cups all purpose flour

¾ cup white cornmeal

½ cup sugar

3 teaspoons baking powder

½ teaspoon salt

¾ cup 2% milk

¼ cup margarine or butter, melted

1 egg, slightly beaten

1 cup fresh or frozen blueberries (do not thaw)

Heat oven to 400°F. Grease 12 muffin cups. In large bowl, combine flour, cornmeal, sugar, baking powder and salt; mix well. Add milk, margarine and egg; stir just until dry ingredients are moistened. Batter will be thin. Gently stir in blueberries. Fill greased muffin cups ⅔ full.

Bake at 400°F. for 20 to 25 minutes or until light golden brown. Cool 1 minute; remove from pan. Serve warm.

12 muffins.

HIGH ALTITUDE – Above 3500 Feet: Increase flour to 1⅓ cups. Bake as directed above.

*W*hite cornmeal has a sweeter, milder flavor than yellow cornmeal and provides a crunchy texture to these muffins. However, yellow cornmeal can be substituted for white in the recipe.

NUTRITION INFORMATION PER SERVING:

1 MUFFIN		PERCENT U.S. RDA	
Calories	160	Protein	4%
Protein	3 g	Vitamin A	4%
Carbohydrate	27 g	Vitamin C	*
Dietary Fiber	1 g	Thiamine	10%
Fat	5 g	Riboflavin	8%
Polyunsaturated	1 g	Niacin	6%
Saturated	1 g	Calcium	8%
Cholesterol	19 mg	Iron	6%
Sodium	270 mg	*Less than 2% U.S. RDA	
Potassium	75 mg		

DIETARY EXCHANGES: 1 Starch, 1/2 Fruit, 1 Fat

WHOLE WHEAT APPLE MUFFINS

A *streusel topping adds sweetness and crunch to these warm-from-the-oven muffins. They're great with milk as an after-school snack.*

NUTRITION INFORMATION PER SERVING:

1 MUFFIN		PERCENT U.S. RDA	
Calories	180	Protein	4%
Protein	3 g	Vitamin A	4%
Carbohydrate	32 g	Vitamin C	*
Dietary Fiber	1 g	Thiamine	10%
Fat	5 g	Riboflavin	6%
Polyunsaturated	2 g	Niacin	6%
Saturated	1 g	Calcium	8%
Cholesterol	0 mg	Iron	8%
Sodium	190 mg	*Less than 2% U.S. RDA	
Potassium	130 mg		

DIETARY EXCHANGES: 1 Starch, 1 Fruit, 1 Fat

MUFFINS

1½ cups all purpose flour

1½ cups chopped peeled apples

½ cup whole wheat flour

½ cup firmly packed brown sugar

2 teaspoons baking powder

¼ teaspoon salt

¼ teaspoon cinnamon

½ cup skim or 2% milk

¼ cup margarine or butter, melted

¼ cup frozen fat-free egg product, thawed, or 1 egg, slightly beaten

TOPPING

¼ cup firmly packed brown sugar

1 tablespoon finely chopped nuts

¼ teaspoon cinnamon

Heat oven to 400°F. Grease bottoms only of 12 muffin cups or line with paper baking cups. In small bowl, combine ½ cup of the all purpose flour and apples; stir until apples are well coated.

In large bowl, combine remaining all purpose flour, whole wheat flour, ½ cup brown sugar, baking powder, salt and ¼ teaspoon cinnamon; mix well. Add apples and remaining muffin ingredients; stir just until dry ingredients are moistened. In small bowl, combine all topping ingredients; mix well. Divide batter evenly among greased muffin cups; sprinkle each with about 2 teaspoons topping.

Bake at 400°F. for 20 to 25 minutes or until toothpick inserted in center comes out clean. Immediately remove from pan. Serve warm.

12 muffins.

▤ MICROWAVE DIRECTIONS: Prepare muffin batter and topping as directed above. Using 6-cup microwave-safe muffin pan, line each cup with 2 paper baking cups to absorb moisture during baking. Fill cups ½ full; sprinkle each with scant 2 teaspoons topping. Microwave 6 muffins on HIGH for 2½ to 3 minutes or until toothpick inserted in center comes out clean, rotating pan ½ turn halfway through cooking. Immediately remove muffins from pan and discard outer baking cups. Repeat, making 6 additional muffins. With remaining batter, make 3 muffins; microwave 3 muffins on HIGH for 1½ to 2 minutes, rotating pan ½ turn halfway through cooking.

15 muffins.

HIGH ALTITUDE – Above 3500 Feet: No change.

WHOLE WHEAT MAPLE MUFFINS

MUFFINS

1½ **cups whole wheat flour**

½ **cup firmly packed brown sugar**

2 **teaspoons baking powder**

½ **teaspoon salt**

1 **egg**

½ **cup skim or 2% milk**

½ **cup unsweetened applesauce**

¼ **cup oil**

2 **tablespoons maple flavor**

½ **cup chopped dates**

GLAZE

¼ **cup powdered sugar**

1 **teaspoon maple flavor**

¼ **to ½ teaspoon skim or 2% milk**

*T*uck these moist, whole grain muffins in lunch boxes or serve a basketful at a morning coffee break.

NUTRITION INFORMATION PER SERVING:

1 MUFFIN		PERCENT U.S. RDA	
Calories	170	Protein	4%
Protein	3 g	Vitamin A	*
Carbohydrate	30 g	Vitamin C	*
Dietary Fiber	3 g	Thiamine	4%
Fat	5 g	Riboflavin	4%
Polyunsaturated	3 g	Niacin	6%
Saturated	1 g	Calcium	8%
Cholesterol	18 mg	Iron	6%
Sodium	190 mg	*Less than 2% U.S. RDA	
Potassium	170 mg		

DIETARY EXCHANGES: 1 Starch, 1 Fruit, 1 Fat

Heat oven to 375°F. Line 12 muffin cups with paper baking cups or spray with nonstick cooking spray. In large bowl, combine whole wheat flour, brown sugar, baking powder and salt; mix well. In small bowl, beat egg until foamy. Add ½ cup milk, applesauce, oil and 2 tablespoons maple flavor; mix well. Add to dry ingredients; stir just until dry ingredients are moistened. Stir in dates. Fill paper-lined muffin cups ¾ full.

Bake at 375°F. for 19 to 22 minutes or until toothpick inserted in center comes out clean. Immediately remove from pan. In small bowl, combine all glaze ingredients, adding enough milk for desired drizzling consistency; mix well. Drizzle over warm muffins. Serve warm.

12 muffins.

HIGH ALTITUDE – Above 3500 Feet: No change.

WHOLE WHEAT PUMPKIN MUFFINS

*S*erve these whole grain, vitamin A-rich muffins as an early morning or mid-afternoon treat, or make a batch for a special friend.

NUTRITION INFORMATION PER SERVING:

1 MUFFIN		PERCENT U.S. RDA	
Calories	170	Protein	4%
Protein	3 g	Vitamin A	45%
Carbohydrate	29 g	Vitamin C	*
Dietary Fiber	3 g	Thiamine	6%
Fat	5 g	Riboflavin	4%
Polyunsaturated	3 g	Niacin	6%
Saturated	1 g	Calcium	8%
Cholesterol	18 mg	Iron	6%
Sodium	190 mg	*Less than 2% U.S. RDA	
Potassium	190 mg		

DIETARY EXCHANGES: 1 Starch, 1 Fruit, 1 Fat

MUFFINS

1½ cups whole wheat flour
½ cup firmly packed brown sugar
2 teaspoons baking powder
1 teaspoon pumpkin pie spice
½ teaspoon salt
1 egg
½ cup skim or 2% milk
½ cup canned pumpkin
¼ cup oil
½ teaspoon grated orange peel
½ cup dried currants

GLAZE

¼ cup powdered sugar
1 to 1½ teaspoons orange juice

Heat oven to 375°F. Line 12 muffin cups with paper baking cups or spray with nonstick cooking spray. In large bowl, combine whole wheat flour, brown sugar, baking powder, pumpkin pie spice and salt; mix well. In small bowl, beat egg until foamy. Add milk, pumpkin, oil and orange peel; mix well. Add to dry ingredients; stir just until dry ingredients are moistened. Stir in currants. Fill paper-lined muffin cups ¾ full.

Bake at 375°F. for 15 to 18 minutes or until toothpick inserted in center comes out clean. Immediately remove from pan. In small bowl, combine powdered sugar and enough orange juice for desired drizzling consistency; mix well. Drizzle over warm muffins. Serve warm.

12 muffins.

HIGH ALTITUDE – Above 3500 Feet: No change.

Whole Wheat Pumpkin Muffins

WHOLE WHEAT BANANA MUFFINS

⅓ cup margarine or butter, softened

½ cup firmly packed brown sugar

1½ cups (3 medium) mashed ripe bananas

½ cup frozen fat-free egg product, thawed, or 2 eggs

¼ cup skim or 2% milk

1 teaspoon vanilla

¾ cup all purpose flour

¾ cup whole wheat flour

½ cup wheat germ

1 teaspoon baking powder

1 teaspoon baking soda

3 tablespoons chopped walnuts

Heat oven to 375°F. Grease 18 muffin cups. In large bowl, beat margarine and brown sugar until fluffy. Add bananas, egg product, milk and vanilla; blend well. Stir in all purpose flour, whole wheat flour, wheat germ, baking powder and baking soda just until dry ingredients are moistened. Fill muffin cups ⅔ full. Sprinkle with walnuts.

Bake at 375°F. for 20 to 25 minutes or until toothpick inserted in center comes out clean. Cool 5 minutes; remove from pan. Serve warm.

18 muffins.

HIGH ALTITUDE – Above 3500 Feet: Increase all purpose flour to 1 cup. Bake as directed above.

Mmm-mmm! Make the sun shine on the dreariest day with these fragrant, warm, whole grain muffins. For optimum flavor, use well-ripened bananas and mash completely before adding them to the batter.

NUTRITION INFORMATION PER SERVING:

1 MUFFIN		PERCENT U.S. RDA	
Calories	130	Protein	4%
Protein	3 g	Vitamin A	4%
Carbohydrate	20 g	Vitamin C	2%
Dietary Fiber	2 g	Thiamine	10%
Fat	5 g	Riboflavin	6%
Polyunsaturated	2 g	Niacin	4%
Saturated	1 g	Calcium	2%
Cholesterol	0 mg	Iron	6%
Sodium	150 mg		
Potassium	170 mg		

DIETARY EXCHANGES: 1/2 Starch, 1 Fruit, 1 Fat

DRIED BLUEBERRY WHOLE WHEAT MUFFINS

*D*ried blueberries, cherries and cranberries are usually available in the produce section of large grocery stores. It's convenient to have these ingredients on hand so you can make these lower-fat whole grain muffins.

NUTRITION INFORMATION PER SERVING:

1 MUFFIN		PERCENT U.S. RDA	
Calories	170	Protein	4%
Protein	4 g	Vitamin A	4%
Carbohydrate	28 g	Vitamin C	*
Dietary Fiber	1 g	Thiamine	8%
Fat	5 g	Riboflavin	8%
Polyunsaturated	3 g	Niacin	6%
Saturated	1 g	Calcium	6%
Cholesterol	1 mg	Iron	6%
Sodium	220 mg	*Less than 2% U.S. RDA	
Potassium	150 mg		

DIETARY EXCHANGES: 1-1/2 Starch, 1 Fat

1	cup all purpose flour
¾	cup whole wheat flour
½	cup firmly packed brown sugar
2	teaspoons baking powder
½	teaspoon baking soda
½	teaspoon salt
1	cup buttermilk
¼	cup oil
2	egg whites
½	cup dried blueberries, dried tart cherries, dried cranberries or raisins

Heat oven to 400°F. Spray 12 muffin cups with nonstick cooking spray, or line muffin cups with paper baking cups and spray paper cups with nonstick cooking spray.

In large bowl, combine all purpose flour, whole wheat flour, brown sugar, baking powder, baking soda and salt; mix well. In small bowl, combine buttermilk, oil and egg whites; blend well. Add to dry ingredients all at once; stir just until dry ingredients are moistened. Gently stir in dried blueberries. Spoon batter evenly into spray-coated muffin cups.

Bake at 400°F. for 14 to 19 minutes or until light golden brown and toothpick inserted in center comes out clean. Immediately remove from pan. Serve warm.

12 muffins.

HIGH ALTITUDE – Above 3500 Feet: Increase all purpose flour to 1¼ cups. Bake at 400°F. for 17 to 21 minutes.

NECTARINE YOGURT MUFFINS

2 cups all purpose flour

½ cup firmly packed brown sugar

2 teaspoons baking powder

½ teaspoon baking soda

½ teaspoon salt

1 (8-oz.) carton vanilla yogurt

¼ cup margarine or butter, melted

1 egg

1 nectarine or peeled peach, pitted, chopped

¼ cup sliced almonds

*W*e tested these luscious muffins with both nectarines and peaches with equally delicious results. Nectarines are used unpeeled and peaches are best when peeled.

Heat oven to 400°F. Grease bottoms only of 15 muffin cups or line with paper baking cups. In large bowl, combine flour, brown sugar, baking powder, baking soda and salt. In small bowl, combine yogurt, margarine and egg; blend well. Add to dry ingredients; stir just until dry ingredients are moistened. (Batter will be very thick.) Stir in nectarine. Fill greased muffin cups ¾ full. Sprinkle almonds over batter.

Bake at 400°F. for 15 to 22 minutes or until golden brown and toothpick inserted in center comes out clean. Cool 1 minute; remove from pan. Serve warm.

15 muffins.

MICROWAVE DIRECTIONS: Prepare muffin batter as directed above. Using 6-cup microwave-safe muffin pan, line each cup with 2 paper baking cups to absorb moisture during cooking. Fill cups ⅔ full. Microwave 6 muffins on HIGH for 3 to 3½ minutes or until toothpick inserted in center comes out clean, rotating pan ½ turn halfway through cooking. Remove muffins from pan and immediately discard outer baking cups. Cool 1 minute on wire rack before serving. Repeat, making 6 additional muffins. With remaining batter, make 3 muffins; microwave 3 muffins on HIGH for 1¾ to 2 minutes, rotating pan ½ turn halfway through cooking.

HIGH ALTITUDE – Above 3500 Feet: No change.

NUTRITION INFORMATION PER SERVING:			
1 MUFFIN		**PERCENT U.S. RDA**	
Calories	150	Protein	4%
Protein	3 g	Vitamin A	4%
Carbohydrate	24 g	Vitamin C	*
Dietary Fiber	1 g	Thiamine	10%
Fat	5 g	Riboflavin	8%
Polyunsaturated	1 g	Niacin	6%
Saturated	1 g	Calcium	8%
Cholesterol	15 mg	Iron	6%
Sodium	230 mg	*Less than 2% U.S. RDA	
Potassium	115 mg		

DIETARY EXCHANGES: 1 Starch, 1/2 Fruit, 1 Fat

PLUMP CARROT MUFFINS

*T*hese muffins contain far less fat than typical carrot muffins and a lot more beta-carotene (vitamin A). Bake and freeze a batch to warm in the toaster oven or microwave on busy days.

1¾ cups all purpose flour	¾ cup orange juice
⅓ cup firmly packed brown sugar	2 tablespoons oil
1 teaspoon baking powder	1½ teaspoons grated orange peel
1 teaspoon baking soda	1 teaspoon vanilla
1 teaspoon cinnamon	1 egg
¼ teaspoon salt	⅓ cup golden raisins
½ cup shredded carrot	

Heat oven to 375°F. Spray bottoms only of 12 muffin cups with nonstick cooking spray or line with paper baking cups. In large bowl, combine flour, brown sugar, baking powder, baking soda, cinnamon and salt; mix well. In small bowl, combine carrot, orange juice, oil, orange peel, vanilla and egg; blend well. Add to dry ingredients; stir just until dry ingredients are moistened. Stir in raisins. Fill spray-coated muffin cups ¾ full.

Bake at 375°F. for 15 to 18 minutes or until toothpick inserted in center comes out clean. Cool in pan 1 minute; remove from pan. Serve warm.

12 muffins.

HIGH ALTITUDE – Above 3500 Feet: Increase flour to 2 cups. Divide batter evenly among 14 muffin cups. Bake as directed above.

NUTRITION INFORMATION PER SERVING:

1 MUFFIN		PERCENT U.S. RDA	
Calories	140	Protein	4%
Protein	3 g	Vitamin A	25%
Carbohydrate	26 g	Vitamin C	8%
Dietary Fiber	1 g	Thiamine	10%
Fat	3 g	Riboflavin	6%
Polyunsaturated	1 g	Niacin	6%
Saturated	1 g	Calcium	4%
Cholesterol	18 mg	Iron	6%
Sodium	200 mg		
Potassium	120 mg		

DIETARY EXCHANGES: 1 Starch, 1/2 Fruit, 1/2 Fat

Plump Carrot Muffins

CARROT ZUCCHINI MUFFINS

- 2 cups all purpose flour
- 1 cup rolled oats
- ¾ cup firmly packed brown sugar
- 3 teaspoons baking powder
- ½ teaspoon cinnamon
- ¼ teaspoon salt
- ⅔ cup skim or 2% milk
- 3 tablespoons oil
- 2 egg whites
- 1 cup finely shredded carrots
- ½ cup (1 small) shredded unpeeled zucchini

Heat oven to 400°F. Spray 12 muffin cups with nonstick cooking spray, or line muffin cups with paper baking cups and spray paper cups with nonstick cooking spray.

In large bowl, combine flour, oats, brown sugar, baking powder, cinnamon and salt; mix well. In small bowl, combine milk, oil and egg whites; blend well. Add to dry ingredients all at once; stir just until dry ingredients are moistened. Stir in carrot and zucchini just until blended. Spoon batter evenly into spray-coated muffin cups.

Bake at 400°F. for 16 to 21 minutes or until golden brown and toothpick inserted in center comes out clean. Immediately remove from pan. Serve warm.

12 muffins.

HIGH ALTITUDE – Above 3500 Feet: Decrease brown sugar to ⅔ cup. Bake at 400°F. for 18 to 22 minutes.

*A*mong the best sources of dietary fiber are fruits, vegetables, whole grain cereals, nuts, seeds and legumes. Sources of dietary fiber in this recipe for tasty muffins include oats, carrots and zucchini. The carrots add good amounts of beta-carotene (vitamin A) to these muffins, too.

NUTRITION INFORMATION PER SERVING:

1 MUFFIN		PERCENT U.S. RDA	
Calories	200	Protein	6%
Protein	4 g	Vitamin A	50%
Carbohydrate	36 g	Vitamin C	*
Dietary Fiber	2 g	Thiamine	15%
Fat	4 g	Riboflavin	10%
Polyunsaturated	2 g	Niacin	6%
Saturated	1 g	Calcium	8%
Cholesterol	0 mg	Iron	10%
Sodium	140 mg	*Less than 2% U.S. RDA	
Potassium	170 mg		

DIETARY EXCHANGES: 2 Starch, 1 Fat

REFRIGERATOR BRAN MUFFINS

A batch of these fragrant, flavorful muffins is great to have on hand for hurried mornings. Pop as many as you need in the oven to bake. They are ready to eat in minutes.

2½ cups buttermilk
⅓ cup oil
2 eggs
3 cups bran flakes cereal with or without raisins
2½ cups all purpose flour
1 cup sugar
1¼ teaspoons baking soda
1 teaspoon baking powder
½ teaspoon salt

In large bowl, combine buttermilk, oil and eggs; beat well. Add remaining ingredients; stir just until moistened. Batter can be baked immediately or stored in tightly covered container in refrigerator for up to 2 weeks.

When ready to bake, heat oven to 400°F. Line desired number of muffin cups with paper baking cups. Stir batter; fill paper-lined muffin cups ⅔ full.

Bake at 400°F. for 20 to 25 minutes or until toothpick inserted in center comes out clean. Immediately remove from pan. Serve warm.

30 muffins.

HIGH ALTITUDE – Above 3500 Feet: Increase flour to 3 cups. Bake as directed above.

NUTRITION INFORMATION PER SERVING:			
1 MUFFIN		**PERCENT U.S. RDA**	
Calories	110	Protein	4%
Protein	3 g	Vitamin A	4%
Carbohydrate	19 g	Vitamin C	*
Dietary Fiber	1 g	Thiamine	8%
Fat	3 g	Riboflavin	8%
Polyunsaturated	2 g	Niacin	6%
Saturated	1 g	Calcium	4%
Cholesterol	15 mg	Iron	15%
Sodium	160 mg	*Less than 2% U.S. RDA	
Potassium	70 mg		

DIETARY EXCHANGES: 1 Starch, 1/2 Fat

Refrigerator Bran Muffins

REFRIGERATOR APPLE BRAN MUFFINS

*T*he batter for these whole grain muffins is stored in the refrigerator, so the muffins can be baked any time you want them. They're deliciously sweetened with applesauce and raisins.

2	cups shreds of whole bran cereal
1½	cups buttermilk
1	cup unsweetened applesauce
½	cup oil
4	egg whites
2	cups all purpose flour
½	cup whole wheat flour

1	cup sugar
1	teaspoon baking powder
1	teaspoon baking soda
1	teaspoon cinnamon
1	teaspoon ginger
¼	teaspoon salt
½	cup raisins

NUTRITION INFORMATION PER SERVING:

1/30 OF RECIPE		PERCENT U.S. RDA	
Calories	120	Protein	4%
Protein	3 g	Vitamin A	2%
Carbohydrate	21 g	Vitamin C	2%
Dietary Fiber	2 g	Thiamine	8%
Fat	4 g	Riboflavin	8%
Polyunsaturated	2 g	Niacin	6%
Saturated	1 g	Calcium	2%
Cholesterol	0 mg	Iron	6%
Sodium	130 mg		
Potassium	115 mg		

DIETARY EXCHANGES: 1 Starch, 1 Fat

In large bowl, combine cereal and buttermilk; let stand 5 minutes or until cereal is softened. Add applesauce, oil and egg whites; blend well. Stir in remaining ingredients; mix well. Batter can be baked immediately or stored in tightly covered container in refrigerator for up to 2 weeks.

When ready to bake, heat oven to 400°F. Grease desired number of muffin cups or line with paper baking cups. Stir batter; fill greased muffin cups ¾ full. Sprinkle with sugar, if desired.

Bake at 400°F. for 15 to 20 minutes or until toothpick inserted in center comes out clean. Immediately remove from pan. Serve warm.

30 muffins.

▦ MICROWAVE DIRECTIONS: Prepare muffin batter as directed above. Using 6-cup microwave-safe muffin pan, line each cup with 2 paper baking cups to absorb moisture during cooking. Fill cups ½ full. Sprinkle with sugar, if desired. Microwave on HIGH as directed below or until toothpick inserted in center comes out clean, rotating pan ½ turn halfway through cooking. Remove muffins from pan and immediately discard outer baking cups.

45 muffins.

6 muffins – 3 to 3½ minutes.
4 muffins – 2½ to 2¾ minutes.
2 muffins – 2 to 2¼ minutes.

HIGH ALTITUDE – Above 3500 Feet: Increase all purpose flour to 2¼ cups. Bake as directed above.

PINEAPPLE OAT BRAN MUFFINS

- 1½ **cups oat bran**
- ½ **cup all purpose flour**
- 2 **teaspoons baking powder**
- ¼ **teaspoon nutmeg**
- ⅓ **cup honey**
- ¼ **cup oil**
- 2 **egg whites**
- 1 **(8-oz.) can crushed pineapple in its own juice, undrained**

Heat oven to 425°F. Line 12 muffin cups with paper baking cups. In large bowl, combine oat bran, flour, baking powder and nutmeg; blend well. In small bowl, combine honey, oil, egg whites and pineapple; mix well. Add to dry ingredients; stir just until dry ingredients are moistened. Divide evenly among paper-lined muffin cups.

Bake at 425°F. for 18 to 20 minutes or until toothpick inserted in center comes out clean. Immediately remove from pan. Serve warm.

12 muffins.

HIGH ALTITUDE – Above 3500 Feet: Increase flour to ¾ cup. Bake as directed above.

*O*at bran is rich in soluble fiber, which is believed to help lower blood cholesterol. It also gives these pineapple-flavored muffins texture and flavor that is irresistible.

NUTRITION INFORMATION PER SERVING:

1 MUFFIN		PERCENT U.S. RDA	
Calories	130	Protein	4%
Protein	3 g	Vitamin A	*
Carbohydrate	23 g	Vitamin C	2%
Dietary Fiber	2 g	Thiamine	10%
Fat	5 g	Riboflavin	4%
Polyunsaturated	3 g	Niacin	2%
Saturated	1 g	Calcium	6%
Cholesterol	0 mg	Iron	6%
Sodium	90 mg	*Less than 2% U.S. RDA	
Potassium	110 mg		

DIETARY EXCHANGES: 1 Starch, 1 Fat

HEALTH NOTES

BRAN AND HEALTH

What do wheat bran and oat bran have in common? They both play a role in a healthy diet. Wheat bran contains insoluble fiber, prized for keeping your digestive tract running smoothly and for warding off colon cancer. On the other hand, oat bran is rich in soluble fiber, the type thought to lower blood cholesterol levels. Neither bran is better, since both are needed for good health. Focus on eating more of these whole grains to increase bran intake.

FRUITY ORANGE REFRIGERATOR MUFFINS

*C*hock-full of healthful ingredients, this muffin batter is great to have on hand for hurried mornings. We've even included easy microwave directions for breakfast-on-the-run kinds of days!

1½ cups all purpose flour
1 cup whole wheat flour
2 cups shreds of whole bran cereal
1½ cups sugar
1¼ teaspoons baking soda
1 teaspoon baking powder
½ teaspoon salt
¼ teaspoon allspice
1 tablespoon grated orange peel
2½ cups buttermilk
½ cup oil
2 eggs, slightly beaten
1 (6-oz.) pkg. dried fruit bits

In large bowl, combine all purpose flour, whole wheat flour, cereal, sugar, baking soda, baking powder, salt, allspice and orange peel. Add buttermilk, oil and eggs; mix well. Stir in fruit bits. Cover tightly; refrigerate at least 3 hours or up to 2 weeks.

When ready to bake, heat oven to 400°F. Grease desired number of muffin cups or line with paper baking cups. Stir batter; fill greased muffin cups ¾ full.

Bake at 400°F. for 18 to 20 minutes or until toothpick inserted in center comes out clean. Immediately remove from pan. Serve warm.

24 to 30 muffins.

▤ MICROWAVE DIRECTIONS: Prepare and refrigerate muffin batter as directed above. Using 6-cup microwave-safe muffin pan, line each cup with 2 paper baking cups to absorb moisture during baking. Fill cups ½ full. Microwave on HIGH as indicated below or until toothpick inserted in center comes out clean, rotating pan ½ turn halfway through cooking. Remove muffins from pan and immediately discard outer baking cups. Cool 1 minute on wire rack before serving.

36 to 45 muffins.

   6 muffins −3 to 4 minutes.
   4 muffins −2 to 2½ minutes.
   2 muffins −1¼ minutes to 1¾ minutes.

HIGH ALTITUDE – Above 3500 Feet: No change.

NUTRITION INFORMATION PER SERVING:

1 MUFFIN		PERCENT U.S. RDA	
Calories	140	Protein	4%
Protein	3 g	Vitamin A	6%
Carbohydrate	25 g	Vitamin C	2%
Dietary Fiber	3 g	Thiamine	8%
Fat	4 g	Riboflavin	8%
Polyunsaturated	2 g	Niacin	6%
Saturated	1 g	Calcium	4%
Cholesterol	15 mg	Iron	6%
Sodium	170 mg		
Potassium	140 mg		

DIETARY EXCHANGES: 1 Starch, 1/2 Fruit, 1 Fat

APRICOT SUNSHINE MUFFINS

1 **cup all purpose flour**	½ **cup chopped dried apricots**
1 **cup whole wheat flour**	⅓ **cup orange juice**
1½ **teaspoons baking soda**	¼ **cup honey**
1 **teaspoon grated orange peel**	¼ **cup oil**
¼ **teaspoon salt**	1 **egg, slightly beaten**
1 **(8-oz.) container low-fat apricot or orange yogurt**	

Heat oven to 375°F. Line 12 muffin cups with paper baking cups or grease bottoms only. In large bowl, combine all purpose flour, whole wheat flour, baking soda, orange peel and salt; mix well. In medium bowl, combine all remaining ingredients; mix well. Add to dry ingredients; stir just until dry ingredients are moistened. Divide batter evenly among paper-lined muffin cups.

Bake at 375°F. for 14 to 18 minutes or until toothpick inserted in center comes out clean. Immediately remove from pan. Serve warm.

12 muffins.

HIGH ALTITUDE – Above 3500 Feet: No change.

*T*he secret to making moist, tender muffins is to mix the batter just until the dry ingredients are moistened. Serve these wonderful honey and orange-sweetened apricot muffins for breakfast or brunch.

NUTRITION INFORMATION PER SERVING:

1 MUFFIN		PERCENT U.S. RDA	
Calories	180	Protein	6%
Protein	4 g	Vitamin A	8%
Carbohydrate	29 g	Vitamin C	4%
Dietary Fiber	2 g	Thiamine	8%
Fat	5 g	Riboflavin	8%
Polyunsaturated	3 g	Niacin	6%
Saturated	1 g	Calcium	4%
Cholesterol	19 mg	Iron	6%
Sodium	220 mg		
Potassium	190 mg		

DIETARY EXCHANGES: 1 Starch, 1 Fruit, 1 Fat

Apricot Sunshine Muffins

BANANA NUTMEG MINI-MUFFINS

*O*riginally, buttermilk was the liquid left after butter was churned. Today it is made commercially by adding special bacteria to nonfat or low-fat milk. Either nonfat or low-fat buttermilk works well for these tasty muffins.

1	cup all purpose flour
1	cup whole wheat flour
½	cup sugar
2	teaspoons baking powder
½	teaspoon baking soda
½	teaspoon nutmeg
⅛	teaspoon salt
⅛	teaspoon allspice
1	egg
½	cup buttermilk
½	cup (1 medium) mashed ripe banana
⅓	cup oil

Heat oven to 400°F. Spray 36 miniature muffin cups with nonstick cooking spray or line with paper baking cups. In large bowl, combine all purpose flour, whole wheat flour, sugar, baking powder, baking soda, nutmeg, salt and allspice; mix well. Beat egg in small bowl. Add buttermilk, banana and oil; mix well. Add to dry ingredients; stir just until dry ingredients are moistened. Divide batter evenly among spray-coated muffin cups, filling each ⅔ full.

Bake at 400°F. for 10 to 15 minutes or until light golden brown and toothpick inserted in center comes out clean. Immediately remove from pan. Serve warm.

36 mini-muffins.

TIP:

Batter can be baked in batches. Any batter not baked immediately should be refrigerated and baked as soon as possible.

HIGH ALTITUDE – Above 3500 Feet: Decrease sugar to ¼ cup. Bake as directed above.

NUTRITION INFORMATION PER SERVING:

1 MINI-MUFFIN		PERCENT U.S. RDA	
Calories	60	Protein	*
Protein	1 g	Vitamin A	*
Carbohydrate	9 g	Vitamin C	*
Dietary Fiber	1 g	Thiamine	2%
Fat	2 g	Riboflavin	2%
Polyunsaturated	1 g	Niacin	2%
Saturated	0 g	Calcium	2%
Cholesterol	6 mg	Iron	*
Sodium	60 mg	*Less than 2% U.S. RDA	
Potassium	35 mg		

DIETARY EXCHANGES: 1/2 Starch, 1/2 Fat

Banana Nutmeg Mini–Muffins, p. 96; Strawberry Mini–Muffins, p. 98

STRAWBERRY MINI-MUFFINS

Make these special muffins in the spring when juicy, ripe strawberries are at their peak. You'll enjoy the sugar coating on top.

NUTRITION INFORMATION PER SERVING:

1 MINI-MUFFIN		PERCENT U.S. RDA	
Calories	60	Protein	*
Protein	1 g	Vitamin A	*
Carbohydrate	10 g	Vitamin C	4%
Dietary Fiber	0 g	Thiamine	4%
Fat	2 g	Riboflavin	2%
Polyunsaturated	1 g	Niacin	2%
Saturated	0 g	Calcium	2%
Cholesterol	6 mg	Iron	2%
Sodium	75 mg	*Less than 2% U.S. RDA	
Potassium	25 mg		

DIETARY EXCHANGES: 1/2 Starch, 1/2 Fat

2 **cups all purpose flour**

½ **cup sugar**

1 **tablespoon baking powder**

½ **teaspoon salt**

¾ **cup 2% milk**

⅓ **cup oil**

1 **egg**

1 **cup chopped fresh strawberries**

2 **tablespoons sugar**

Heat oven to 375°F. Spray 36 miniature muffin cups with non-stick cooking spray. In large bowl, combine flour, ½ cup sugar, baking powder and salt; mix well. In small bowl, combine milk, oil and egg; blend well. Add to dry ingredients; stir just until dry ingredients are moistened. Gently stir in strawberries. Spoon rounded tablespoonful batter into each spray-coated muffin cup; sprinkle 2 tablespoons sugar evenly over batter in muffin cups.

Bake at 375°F. for 12 to 16 minutes or until edges are very light brown and toothpick inserted in center comes out clean. Cool 3 minutes; remove from pan. Serve warm.
36 mini-muffins.

TIP:

Batter can be baked in batches. Any batter not baked immediately should be refrigerated and baked as soon as possible.

HIGH ALTITUDE – Above 3500 Feet: No change.

ORANGE POPPY SEED MINI-MUFFINS

½ cup margarine or butter, softened

⅓ cup sugar

1½ cups all purpose flour

1 tablespoon poppy seed

¾ teaspoon baking powder

½ teaspoon salt

1 (6-oz.) container orange yogurt

3 tablespoons orange juice

1 tablespoon grated orange peel

1 egg

Powdered sugar

These bite-sized puffs are bursting with orange flavor. Poppy seed makes the texture interesting. Because the recipe makes a big batch, you may want to freeze some for later use.

Heat oven to 375°F. Grease bottoms only of 36 miniature muffin cups or line with paper baking cups.* In large bowl, beat margarine and sugar until light and fluffy. Add remaining ingredients except powdered sugar; stir just until ingredients are moistened. Fill greased muffin cups ¾ full.

Bake at 375°F. for 15 to 20 minutes or until edges are light golden brown. Run knife around edges to loosen; immediately remove muffins from pan. Sprinkle with powdered sugar. Serve warm.

36 mini-muffins.

TIPS:

* Recipe can be baked in regular muffin cups. Grease bottoms only of 12 muffin cups or line with paper baking cups. Bake at 375°F. for 20 to 25 minutes or until edges are light golden brown.

Batter can be baked in batches. Any batter not baked immediately should be refrigerated and baked as soon as possible.

HIGH ALTITUDE – Above 3500 Feet: Increase flour to 1¾ cups. Bake as directed above.

NUTRITION INFORMATION PER SERVING:

1 MINI-MUFFIN		PERCENT U.S. RDA	
Calories	60	Protein	*
Protein	1 g	Vitamin A	2%
Carbohydrate	7 g	Vitamin C	*
Dietary Fiber	0 g	Thiamine	2%
Fat	3 g	Riboflavin	2%
Polyunsaturated	1 g	Niacin	*
Saturated	1 g	Calcium	*
Cholesterol	6 mg	Iron	*
Sodium	75 mg	*Less than 2% U.S. RDA	
Potassium	20 mg		

DIETARY EXCHANGES: 1/2 Starch, 1/2 Fat

BLUEBERRY MINI-MUFFINS

When using frozen blueberries for breads, always stir them in while still frozen. If thawed, they will discolor the batter.

NUTRITION INFORMATION PER SERVING:

1 MINI-MUFFIN		PERCENT U.S. RDA	
Calories	60	Protein	*
Protein	1 g	Vitamin A	*
Carbohydrate	9 g	Vitamin C	*
Dietary Fiber	0 g	Thiamine	4%
Fat	2 g	Riboflavin	2%
Polyunsaturated	1 g	Niacin	2%
Saturated	0 g	Calcium	2%
Cholesterol	6 mg	Iron	2%
Sodium	35 mg	*Less than 2% U.S. RDA	
Potassium	20 mg		

DIETARY EXCHANGES: 1/2 Starch, 1/2 Fat

2 **cups all purpose flour**

½ **cup sugar**

3 **teaspoons baking powder**

½ **teaspoon cinnamon**

⅛ **teaspoon salt**

1 **egg**

¾ **cup 2% milk**

⅓ **cup oil**

1 **teaspoon vanilla**

1 **cup fresh or frozen blueberries (do not thaw)**

Heat oven to 400°F. Spray 36 miniature muffin cups with nonstick cooking spray or line with paper baking cups. In large bowl, combine flour, sugar, baking powder, cinnamon and salt; mix well. Beat egg in small bowl. Add milk, oil and vanilla; mix well. Add to dry ingredients; stir just until dry ingredients are moistened. Carefully stir in blueberries. Fill spray-coated muffin cups ⅔ full.

Bake at 400°F. for 10 to 15 minutes or until light golden brown and toothpick inserted in center comes out clean. Immediately remove muffins from pan. Serve warm.

36 mini-muffins.

TIP:

Batter can be baked in batches. Any batter not baked immediately should be refrigerated and baked as soon as possible.

HIGH ALTITUDE – Above 3500 Feet: No change.

SWEET POTATO MINI-MUFFINS

- **1 cup all purpose flour**
- **½ cup sugar**
- **¾ teaspoon baking powder**
- **½ teaspoon cinnamon**
- **¼ teaspoon salt**
- **⅛ teaspoon allspice**
- **⅛ teaspoon cloves**
- **¼ cup golden raisins**
- **½ cup mashed cooked sweet potatoes**
- **½ cup buttermilk**
- **2 tablespoons oil**
- **1 egg**

Heat oven to 375°F. Spray 24 miniature muffin cups with nonstick cooking spray. In large bowl, combine flour, sugar, baking powder, cinnamon, salt, allspice and cloves. Stir in raisins. In medium bowl, combine sweet potatoes, buttermilk, oil and egg; mix well. Add to dry ingredients; stir just until dry ingredients are moistened. Fill muffin cups ¾ full.

Bake at 375°F. for 14 to 19 minutes or just until edges begin to brown and tops are no longer wet. Immediately remove from pans. Serve warm or place on wire racks to cool.

24 mini-muffins.

HIGH ALTITUDE – Above 3500 Feet: No change.

Lightly spiced, flavored with sweet potatoes and dotted with raisins, these unique muffins are perfect with breakfast or for a delicious snack.

NUTRITION INFORMATION PER SERVING:

1 MINI-MUFFIN		PERCENT U.S. RDA	
Calories	60	Protein	*
Protein	1 g	Vitamin A	15%
Carbohydrate	11 g	Vitamin C	*
Dietary Fiber	0 g	Thiamine	2%
Fat	1 g	Riboflavin	2%
Polyunsaturated	1 g	Niacin	*
Saturated	0 g	Calcium	*
Cholesterol	9 mg	Iron	2%
Sodium	50 mg	*Less than 2% U.S. RDA	
Potassium	40 mg		

DIETARY EXCHANGES: 1/2 Starch, 1/2 Fat

CORIANDER CORN MUFFINS

*C*oriander and corn—
what an unusual com-
bination, but what delicious
results!

NUTRITION INFORMATION PER SERVING:

1 MUFFIN		PERCENT U.S. RDA	
Calories	170	Protein	4%
Protein	3 g	Vitamin A	*
Carbohydrate	28 g	Vitamin C	*
Dietary Fiber	1 g	Thiamine	10%
Fat	5 g	Riboflavin	8%
Polyunsaturated	3 g	Niacin	6%
Saturated	1 g	Calcium	6%
Cholesterol	0 mg	Iron	6%
Sodium	135 mg	*Less than 2% U.S. RDA	
Potassium	95 mg		

DIETARY EXCHANGES: 1-1/2 Starch, 1 Fat

1½ **cups all purpose flour**

½ **cup yellow cornmeal**

¼ **cup sugar**

¼ **cup firmly packed brown sugar**

3 **teaspoons baking powder**

½ **teaspoon coriander**

¼ **teaspoon salt**

½ **cup skim or 2% milk**

¼ **cup oil**

2 **egg whites**

1 **cup frozen whole kernel corn, thawed, well drained***

Heat oven to 400°F. Spray 12 muffin cups with nonstick cooking spray, or line muffin cups with paper baking cups and spray paper cups with nonstick cooking spray.

In large bowl, combine flour, cornmeal, sugar, brown sugar, baking powder, coriander and salt; mix well. In small bowl, combine milk, oil and egg whites; blend well. Add to dry ingredients all at once; stir just until dry ingredients are moistened. Gently stir in corn. Spoon batter evenly into spray-coated muffin cups.

Bake at 400°F. for 14 to 19 minutes or until toothpick inserted in center comes out clean and muffins are light golden brown. Immediately remove from pan. Serve warm.
12 muffins.

TIP:

* To thaw corn, place frozen corn in strainer or colander; rinse with warm water until corn is thawed. Drain thoroughly.

HIGH ALTITUDE – Above 3500 Feet: Decrease baking powder to 2 teaspoons. Bake as directed above.

BANANA-WHEAT QUICK BREAD

1¼ cups all purpose flour

½ cup whole wheat flour

1 cup sugar

1 teaspoon baking soda

1 teaspoon salt

1½ cups (3 medium) mashed ripe bananas

¼ cup margarine or butter, softened

2 tablespoons orange juice

¼ teaspoon lemon juice, if desired

1 egg

¼ to ½ cup raisins

Heat oven to 350°F. Grease and flour bottom only of 9x5 or 8x4-inch loaf pan. In large bowl, combine all ingredients except raisins; beat 3 minutes at medium speed. Fold in raisins. Pour batter into greased and floured pan.

Bake at 350°F. for 55 to 65 minutes or until toothpick inserted in center comes out clean. Cool 10 minutes; remove from pan. Cool on wire rack. Wrap tightly and store in refrigerator.

1 (16-slice) loaf.

HIGH ALTITUDE – Above 3500 Feet: Increase all purpose flour to 1½ cups. Bake as directed above.

Quick bread is simply bread that is quick to make because it doesn't require kneading or rising time. The leavening in quick bread is usually baking powder and /or baking soda. You'll like the down-home goodness of this wholesome banana bread.

NUTRITION INFORMATION PER SERVING:

1 SLICE		PERCENT U.S. RDA	
Calories	160	Protein	2%
Protein	2 g	Vitamin A	2%
Carbohydrate	31 g	Vitamin C	2%
Dietary Fiber	1 g	Thiamine	8%
Fat	3 g	Riboflavin	6%
Polyunsaturated	1 g	Niacin	4%
Saturated	1 g	Calcium	*
Cholesterol	13 mg	Iron	4%
Sodium	250 mg	*Less than 2% U.S. RDA	
Potassium	150 mg		

DIETARY EXCHANGES: 1-1/2 Starch, 1/2 Fruit, 1/2 Fat

HEALTH NOTES
BREAD TOPPINGS

You've just baked delicious muffins or a quick bread. What should you top them with? Use the chart below to make healthier choices.

TOPPING (ONE TABLESPOON)	CALORIES	FAT (MG.)	CHOLESTEROL (MG.)
Butter	108	12	33
Margarine	100	11	0
Reduced-calorie margarine	50	6	0
Cream cheese	50	5	16
Reduced-fat cream cheese	31	2	8
Jam or jelly	52	0	0

BANANA BLUEBERRY MINI-LOAVES

1   **cup sugar**

½   **cup oil**

1   **cup (2 medium) mashed ripe bananas**

½   **cup low fat plain yogurt**

1   **teaspoon vanilla**

2   **eggs**

2   **cups all purpose flour**

1   **teaspoon baking soda**

½   **teaspoon salt**

1   **cup fresh or frozen blueberries (do not thaw)**

*B*ananas and blueberries are featured in this moist, flavorful quick bread. The mini-loaves are an ideal size for singles or small families. For convenience, use the disposable foil mini-loaf pans available in supermarkets. Plan to freeze one or two of the loaves for later use.

Heat oven to 350°F. Grease and flour bottoms only of three 6x3½-inch loaf pans.* In large bowl, combine sugar and oil; beat well. Add bananas, yogurt, vanilla and eggs; blend well. Add flour, baking soda and salt; stir just until dry ingredients are moistened. Gently stir in blueberries. Pour into greased and floured pans.

Bake at 350°F. for 40 to 50 minutes or until toothpick inserted in center comes out clean. Cool 5 minutes; remove from pans. Cool completely. Wrap tightly and store in refrigerator.
3 (12-slice) loaves.

TIP:
   *Recipe can be baked in one 9x5-inch loaf pan. Grease and flour bottom only of pan. Bake at 350°F. for 60 to 70 minutes.

HIGH ALTITUDE – Above 3500 Feet: Increase flour to 2¼ cups. Bake 6x3½-inch pans at 375°F. for 30 to 40 minutes. Bake 9x5-inch pan at 375°F. for 50 to 60 minutes.

NUTRITION INFORMATION PER SERVING:

1 SLICE		PERCENT U.S. RDA	
Calories	90	Protein	2%
Protein	1 g	Vitamin A	*
Carbohydrate	13 g	Vitamin C	*
Dietary Fiber	0 g	Thiamine	4%
Fat	3 g	Riboflavin	4%
Polyunsaturated	2 g	Niacin	2%
Saturated	1 g	Calcium	*
Cholesterol	12 mg	Iron	2%
Sodium	70 mg	*Less than 2% U.S. RDA	
Potassium	45 mg		

DIETARY EXCHANGES: 1 Starch, 1/2 Fat

Banana Blueberry Mini-Loaves

WHOLE WHEAT BANANA BREAD

*F*oods such as this quick bread that contain complex carbohydrates are a good source of energy.

NUTRITION INFORMATION PER SERVING:			
1 SLICE		**PERCENT U.S. RDA**	
Calories	150	Protein	4%
Protein	3 g	Vitamin A	4%
Carbohydrate	27 g	Vitamin C	*
Dietary Fiber	1 g	Thiamine	8%
Fat	4 g	Riboflavin	6%
Polyunsaturated	1 g	Niacin	4%
Saturated	1 g	Calcium	*
Cholesterol	0 mg	Iron	4%
Sodium	200 mg	*Less than 2% U.S. RDA	
Potassium	105 mg		

DIETARY EXCHANGES: 1 Starch, 1/2 Fruit, 1 Fat

1   cup sugar

⅓   cup margarine or butter, melted

1   cup (2 medium) mashed ripe bananas

⅓   cup water

½   cup frozen fat-free egg product, thawed, or 2 eggs, slightly beaten

1   cup all purpose flour

1   cup whole wheat flour

1   teaspoon baking soda

½   teaspoon salt

Heat oven to 350°F. Grease bottom only of 9x5 or 8x4-inch loaf pan. In large bowl, combine sugar and margarine; beat well. Add bananas, water and egg product; mix well. In medium bowl, combine all purpose flour, whole wheat flour, baking soda and salt; mix well. Add dry ingredients gradually to banana mixture, mixing until well combined. Pour batter into greased pan.

Bake at 350°F. for 55 to 65 minutes or until toothpick inserted in center comes out clean. Cool 10 minutes; remove from pan. Cool completely before slicing. Wrap tightly and store in refrigerator.

1 (16-slice) loaf.

HIGH ALTITUDE – Above 3500 Feet: No change.

Whole Wheat Banana Bread

WHOLE WHEAT PEAR QUICK BREAD

1¼ **cups all purpose flour**

½ **cup whole wheat flour**

¾ **cup sugar**

1 **teaspoon baking soda**

½ **teaspoon salt**

½ **teaspoon cinnamon**

¼ **teaspoon ginger**

¼ **cup oil**

2 **egg whites**

1 **(8.5-oz.) can light pear halves, drained, chopped, reserving ¼ cup liquid**

¼ **cup coarsely chopped pecans, if desired**

Heat oven to 325°F. Grease and flour bottom only of 8x4-inch loaf pan. In large bowl, combine all purpose flour, whole wheat flour, sugar, baking soda, salt, cinnamon, ginger, oil, egg whites, pears and reserved ¼ cup pear liquid. Blend at low speed until moistened; beat 3 minutes at medium speed. Stir in pecans. Pour batter into greased and floured pan.

Bake at 325°F. for 65 to 75 minutes or until toothpick inserted in center comes out clean. Cool 5 minutes; remove from pan. Cool on wire rack. Wrap tightly and store in refrigerator.

1 (16-slice) loaf.

HIGH ALTITUDE – Above 3500 Feet: Bake at 350°F. for 53 to 58 minutes.

*C*innamon and ginger add delightful flavor to this healthful quick bread. To reduce fat even further, omit the pecans.

NUTRITION INFORMATION PER SERVING:

1 SLICE		PERCENT U.S. RDA	
Calories	140	Protein	2%
Protein	2 g	Vitamin A	*%
Carbohydrate	22 g	Vitamin C	*%
Dietary Fiber	1 g	Thiamine	6%
Fat	5 g	Riboflavin	4%
Polyunsaturated	2 g	Niacin	4%
Saturated	1 g	Calcium	*%
Cholesterol	0 mg	Iron	4%
Sodium	150 mg	*Less than 2% U.S. RDA	
Potassium	45 mg		

DIETARY EXCHANGES: 1 Starch, 1/2 Fruit, 1 Fat

BLUEBERRY OATMEAL BREAD

*W*ho can resist home-made blueberry quick bread? This large moist loaf uses skim milk and is lower in fat and sugar than most quick breads.

NUTRITION INFORMATION PER SERVING:

1 SLICE		PERCENT U.S. RDA	
Calories	170	Protein	6%
Protein	4 g	Vitamin A	*
Carbohydrate	27 g	Vitamin C	*
Dietary Fiber	1 g	Thiamine	10%
Fat	5 g	Riboflavin	8%
Polyunsaturated	3 g	Niacin	4%
Saturated	1 g	Calcium	6%
Cholesterol	0 mg	Iron	6%
Sodium	190 mg	*Less than 2% U.S. RDA	
Potassium	85 mg		

DIETARY EXCHANGES: 1-1/2 Starch, 1 Fat

2 **cups all purpose flour**

1 **cup quick-cooking rolled oats**

¾ **cup sugar**

2 **teaspoons baking powder**

½ **teaspoon baking soda**

½ **teaspoon salt**

1¼ **cups skim or 2% milk**

⅓ **cup oil**

2 **teaspoons vanilla**

1 **teaspoon grated lemon peel**

½ **cup frozen fat-free egg product, thawed, or 2 eggs, slightly beaten**

1 **cup fresh or frozen blueberries (do not thaw)**

Heat oven to 350°F. Grease bottom only of 9x5-inch loaf pan. In large bowl, combine flour, oats, sugar, baking powder, baking soda and salt; mix well. In small bowl, combine milk, oil, vanilla, lemon peel and egg product; blend well. Add to dry ingredients all at once; stir just until dry ingredients are moistened. Gently fold in blueberries. Pour into greased pan.

Bake at 350°F. for 50 to 60 minutes or until toothpick inserted in center comes out clean. Cool 10 minutes; remove from pan. Cool completely. Wrap tightly and store in refrigerator.

1 (16-slice) loaf.

HIGH ALTITUDE – Above 3500 Feet: Increase flour to 2 cups plus 2 tablespoons. Bake as directed above.

ZUCCHINI CHEESE BREAD

1 cup all purpose flour

1 teaspoon baking powder

½ teaspoon onion salt

¼ teaspoon garlic powder

1 cup coarsely shredded unpeeled zucchini

¼ cup low-fat plain yogurt

1 (2-oz.) jar chopped pimiento, drained

2 tablespoons grated Parmesan cheese

¼ teaspoon hot pepper sauce

1 egg

1 oz. (¼ cup) shredded reduced-fat Swiss cheese

This colorful wholesome bread is chock-full of good things. Using low-fat yogurt instead of oil reduces the fat considerably. The Swiss and Parmesan cheeses add calcium, riboflavin (vitamin B2) and protein.

Heat oven to 350°F. Spray 8 or 9-inch round cake pan with nonstick cooking spray. In large bowl, combine flour, baking powder, onion salt and garlic powder; mix well. In medium bowl, combine zucchini, yogurt, pimiento, Parmesan cheese, hot pepper sauce and egg; blend well. Add to dry ingredients; stir just until dry ingredients are moistened. Spread batter evenly in spray-coated pan.

Bake at 350°F. for 30 to 35 minutes or until toothpick inserted in center comes out clean. Sprinkle Swiss cheese over top; bake an additional 2 to 3 minutes or until cheese is melted.

8 servings.

HIGH ALTITUDE – Above 3500 Feet: No change.

NUTRITION INFORMATION PER SERVING:

1/8 OF RECIPE		PERCENT U.S. RDA	
Calories	90	Protein	8%
Protein	5 g	Vitamin A	4%
Carbohydrate	13 g	Vitamin C	6%
Dietary Fiber	1 g	Thiamine	8%
Fat	2 g	Riboflavin	8%
Polyunsaturated	0 g	Niacin	4%
Saturated	1 g	Calcium	10%
Cholesterol	30 mg	Iron	4%
Sodium	200 mg		
Potassium	95 mg		

DIETARY EXCHANGES: 1 Starch, 1/2 Fat

Hearty Grain Quick Loaf

HEARTY GRAIN QUICK LOAF

2 cups all purpose flour

1 cup whole wheat flour

½ cup quick-cooking rolled oats

¼ cup sugar

3 teaspoons baking powder

¾ teaspoon salt

1½ cups 2% milk

3 tablespoons oil

1 egg

1 to 2 tablespoons quick-cooking rolled oats

*T*his recipe makes a lovely round loaf of wholesome bread. It's delicious to serve with a meal or just as a snack with milk.

Heat oven to 350°F. Grease bottom only of 8-inch round cake pan. In large bowl, combine all purpose flour, whole wheat flour, ½ cup oats, sugar, baking powder and salt; mix well. In small bowl, combine milk, oil and egg; beat well. Add to dry ingredients all at once; stir just until dry ingredients are moistened. Spread dough in greased pan. Sprinkle with 1 to 2 tablespoons oats.

Bake at 350°F. for 42 to 47 minutes or until golden brown and toothpick inserted in center comes out clean. Cool 5 minutes; remove from pan. Serve warm.

1 (16-slice) loaf.

HIGH ALTITUDE – Above 3500 Feet: Spread dough in greased 9-inch round cake pan. Bake as directed above.

NUTRITION INFORMATION PER SERVING:

1 SLICE		PERCENT U.S. RDA	
Calories	150	Protein	6%
Protein	4 g	Vitamin A	*
Carbohydrate	24 g	Vitamin C	*
Dietary Fiber	2 g	Thiamine	10%
Fat	4 g	Riboflavin	8%
Polyunsaturated	2 g	Niacin	6%
Saturated	1 g	Calcium	8%
Cholesterol	15 mg	Iron	6%
Sodium	210 mg	*Less than 2% U.S. RDA	
Potassium	100 mg		

DIETARY EXCHANGES: 1-1/2 Starch, 1 Fat

CHEDDAR AND DILL CORN BREAD

1 **cup all purpose flour**

2 **tablespoons sugar**

4 **teaspoons baking powder**

½ **teaspoon salt**

1 **cup yellow cornmeal**

4 **oz. (1 cup) shredded Cheddar cheese**

2 **teaspoons dried dill weed**

3 **egg whites**

1 **cup skim or 2% milk**

¼ **cup nonfat plain yogurt**

Heat oven to 425°F. Spray 9-inch square pan with nonstick cooking spray. In large bowl, combine flour, sugar, baking powder, salt, cornmeal, cheese and dill; mix well. In small bowl, combine egg whites, milk and yogurt; mix well. Add to dry ingredients all at once; stir just until dry ingredients are moistened. (Batter will be lumpy.) Pour into spray-coated pan.

Bake at 425°F. for 14 to 17 minutes or until top is light golden brown. Cut into squares; serve warm.

12 servings.

HIGH ALTITUDE – Above 3500 Feet: No change.

*C*ornmeal is simply finely ground white or yellow corn. It's the yellow cornmeal that gives cornbread its characteristic golden color. From a nutritional standpoint, the two types of corn are much the same except yellow cornmeal has slightly more vitamin A.

NUTRITION INFORMATION PER SERVING:

1/12 OF RECIPE		PERCENT U.S. RDA	
Calories	140	Protein	8%
Protein	6 g	Vitamin A	4%
Carbohydrate	20 g	Vitamin C	*
Dietary Fiber	1 g	Thiamine	8%
Fat	4 g	Riboflavin	10%
Polyunsaturated	0 g	Niacin	4%
Saturated	2 g	Calcium	15%
Cholesterol	10 mg	Iron	6%
Sodium	280 mg	*Less than 2% U.S. RDA	
Potassium	115 mg		

DIETARY EXCHANGES: 1-1/2 Starch, 1/2 Fat

Cheddar and Dill Corn Bread

SPOON BREAD WITH CORN

Spoon bread, a popular Southern mealtime accompaniment, is a soft custard-like corn bread that is baked in a casserole. Its moist souffle-like texture is at its best served immediately from the oven. It is usually served as a side dish, often in small bowls, and is eaten with a spoon or fork.

1½ cups water
1 cup white or yellow cornmeal
½ teaspoon salt
2 tablespoons margarine or butter
2 teaspoons baking powder
1 (8-oz.) container nonfat plain yogurt
2 eggs, separated
1 (7-oz.) can whole kernel corn, undrained

Heat oven to 375°F. Grease 1-quart souffle dish or 8-inch square pan. Bring water to a boil in medium saucepan. Slowly stir in cornmeal and salt. Cook 1 to 2 minutes or until mixture becomes very thick, stirring constantly. Remove from heat; stir in margarine. Gradually beat in baking powder, yogurt and 2 egg yolks. Stir in undrained corn.

In small bowl, beat 2 egg whites until stiff. Fold into cornmeal mixture. Pour batter into greased dish. If desired, sprinkle top with additional cornmeal.

Bake at 375°F. for 40 to 50 minutes or until knife inserted near center comes out clean.

8 (½-cup) servings.

TIP:
Two teaspoons finely chopped fresh sage or ½ teaspoon dried sage leaves can be added with the corn.

HIGH ALTITUDE – Above 3500 Feet: No change.

NUTRITION INFORMATION PER SERVING:

1/2 CUP		PERCENT U.S. RDA	
Calories	140	Protein	6%
Protein	5 g	Vitamin A	6%
Carbohydrate	20 g	Vitamin C	*
Dietary Fiber	2 g	Thiamine	10%
Fat	4 g	Riboflavin	25%
Polyunsaturated	1 g	Niacin	6%
Saturated	1 g	Calcium	10%
Cholesterol	54 mg	Iron	6%
Sodium	390 mg	*Less than 2% U.S. RDA	
Potassium	140 mg		

DIETARY EXCHANGES: 1 Starch, 1 Fat

MAPLE AND SPICE CORN BREAD

1   cup all purpose flour

1   cup cornmeal

½   cup raisins

2   teaspoons baking powder

1   teaspoon cinnamon

½   teaspoon salt

½   teaspoon nutmeg

½   teaspoon grated orange peel

⅔   cup 2% milk

½   cup maple-flavored syrup

¼   cup margarine or butter, melted

½   cup frozen fat-free egg product, thawed, or 2 eggs, slightly beaten

Heat oven to 400°F. Grease 8 or 9-inch square pan. In large bowl, combine flour, cornmeal, raisins, baking powder, cinnamon, salt, nutmeg and orange peel; mix well. Add milk, syrup, margarine and egg product; stir just until dry ingredients are moistened. Pour into greased pan.

Bake at 400°F. for 17 to 22 minutes or until toothpick inserted in center comes out clean. Serve warm.

12 servings.

HIGH ALTITUDE – Above 3500 Feet: No change.

*L*ightly spiced, sweetened with maple syrup and dotted with raisins, this unique corn bread is a perfect accompaniment to a hearty chili meal. And because it's a quick bread, it's extra easy to make!

NUTRITION INFORMATION PER SERVING:

1/12 OF RECIPE		PERCENT U.S. RDA	
Calories	170	Protein	4%
Protein	3 g	Vitamin A	6%
Carbohydrate	31 g	Vitamin C	*
Dietary Fiber	1 g	Thiamine	10%
Fat	5 g	Riboflavin	8%
Polyunsaturated	1 g	Niacin	4%
Saturated	1 g	Calcium	8%
Cholesterol	1 mg	Iron	8%
Sodium	240 mg	*Less than 2% U.S. RDA	
Potassium	150 mg		

DIETARY EXCHANGES: 1 Starch, 1 Fruit, 1 Fat

HEALTH NOTES
THE INCREDIBLE EGG

Dietary wisdom dictates consuming a wide variety of foods in moderation. Happily, that includes eggs. Once hailed as the perfect food, eggs have fallen from grace with many people put off by eggs' high cholesterol content. In fact, eggs have less cholesterol than previously thought. Eggs alone are typically not to blame for high blood cholesterol levels, either. Some side dishes, such as bacon and sausage, may be at fault, because of their saturated fat and cholesterol content. To cut dietary cholesterol without nixing eggs, limit egg yolk consumption to four per week. You can reduce the cholesterol level of baked goods by opting for two egg whites or ¼ cup fat-free egg product instead of a whole egg. Egg whites and fat-free egg products contain no cholesterol.

GRAHAM CRACKER BROWN BREAD

The secret ingredient in this unusual bread is graham crackers—they add color, texture and flavor appeal. The recipe makes two loaves. Have one now and freeze one to serve later.

NUTRITION INFORMATION PER SERVING:

1 SLICE		PERCENT U.S. RDA	
Calories	110	Protein	2%
Protein	2 g	Vitamin A	*
Carbohydrate	17 g	Vitamin C	*
Dietary Fiber	0 g	Thiamine	4%
Fat	4 g	Riboflavin	4%
Polyunsaturated	1 g	Niacin	2%
Saturated	1 g	Calcium	2%
Cholesterol	14 mg	Iron	4%
Sodium	180 mg	*Less than 2% U.S. RDA	
Potassium	180 mg		

DIETARY EXCHANGES: 1 Starch, 1 Fat

2 cups graham cracker crumbs or finely crushed graham crackers (30 squares)

½ cup shortening

1¾ cups buttermilk

¾ cup molasses

2 eggs, slightly beaten

1¾ cups all purpose flour

2 teaspoons baking soda

1 teaspoon salt

¼ to ½ teaspoon nutmeg

1 cup raisins

Heat oven to 375°F. Grease and flour bottoms only of two 8x4-inch loaf pans. In large bowl, combine graham cracker crumbs and shortening; beat until well blended. Add buttermilk, molasses and eggs; blend well. In small bowl, combine flour, baking soda, salt and nutmeg; mix well. Add to graham cracker mixture; mix at low speed until well blended. Fold in raisins. Pour batter into greased and floured pans.

Bake at 375°F. for 35 to 40 minutes or until toothpick inserted in center comes out clean. Cool 5 minutes; remove from pans. Cool on wire racks. Wrap tightly and store in refrigerator.
2 (16-slice) loaves.

HIGH ALTITUDE – Above 3500 Feet: Increase flour to 2¼ cups. Bake as directed above.

FRUITED IRISH SODA BREAD

2 cups all purpose flour

½ cup whole wheat flour

3 tablespoons brown sugar

1 teaspoon baking powder

1 teaspoon baking soda

¼ teaspoon salt

¼ teaspoon cinnamon

¼ cup margarine or butter

1¼ cups buttermilk

1 cup dried fruit bits

¼ cup candied orange peel, finely chopped

Heat oven to 375°F. Lightly grease cookie sheet. In large bowl, combine all purpose flour, whole wheat flour, brown sugar, baking powder, baking soda, salt and cinnamon; mix well. Using fork or pastry blender, cut in margarine until crumbly. Add buttermilk, fruit bits and orange peel; blend well.

On well-floured surface, knead dough gently until no longer sticky, 1 to 2 minutes. Form dough into ball and place on greased cookie sheet. With sharp knife, cut an "X" ¼ inch deep on top of loaf.

Bake at 375°F. for 40 to 45 minutes or until golden brown and toothpick inserted in center comes out clean. Immediately remove from pan; serve warm or cool.

1 (16-slice) loaf.

HIGH ALTITUDE – Above 3500 Feet: No change.

This traditional coarse-textured bread can be served as a coffee cake or snack with tea or coffee. It's called soda bread because it's leavened with baking soda.

NUTRITION INFORMATION PER SERVING:

1 SLICE		PERCENT U.S. RDA	
Calories	140	Protein	4%
Protein	3 g	Vitamin A	6%
Carbohydrate	26 g	Vitamin C	*
Dietary Fiber	2 g	Thiamine	10%
Fat	3 g	Riboflavin	6%
Polyunsaturated	1 g	Niacin	6%
Saturated	1 g	Calcium	4%
Cholesterol	1 mg	Iron	6%
Sodium	200 mg	*Less than 2% U.S. RDA	
Potassium	135 mg		

DIETARY EXCHANGES: 1-1/2 Starch, 1/2 Fat

Country Hearth Oatmeal Bread, p. 125; Hearty Pumpernickel Batter Bread, p. 140; Whole Wheat French Bread, p. 136

YEAST BREADS

*N*othing compares to bread fresh from the oven, the ultimate comfort food. Few foods are as appealing or as naturally low in fat. Ours are no different, at a maximum of five fat grams per serving.

Golden Party Loaves

GOLDEN PARTY LOAVES

4½ to 5½ cups all purpose flour
1½ cups finely shredded carrots
1 teaspoon salt
1 pkg. active dry yeast
¾ cup apricot nectar
½ cup plain low fat yogurt
¼ cup honey
¼ cup margarine or butter
1 egg
Margarine or butter, softened

Carrots add color, texture and flavor to these party perfect mini-loaves.

NUTRITION INFORMATION PER SERVING:

1 SLICE		PERCENT U.S. RDA	
Calories	90	Protein	2%
Protein	2 g	Vitamin A	25%
Carbohydrate	15 g	Vitamin C	*
Dietary Fiber	1 g	Thiamine	8%
Fat	2 g	Riboflavin	6%
Polyunsaturated	1 g	Niacin	4%
Saturated	0 g	Calcium	*
Cholesterol	5 mg	Iron	4%
Sodium	70 mg	*Less than 2% U.S. RDA	
Potassium	50 mg		

DIETARY EXCHANGES: 1 Starch, 1/2 Fat

In large bowl, combine 2 cups flour, carrots, salt and yeast; blend well. In small saucepan, heat apricot nectar, yogurt, honey and ¼ cup margarine until very warm (120 to 130°F.). Add warm liquid and egg to flour mixture. Blend at low speed until moistened; beat 3 minutes at medium speed. By hand, stir in an additional 2 to 2½ cups flour to form a stiff dough.

On floured surface, knead in remaining ½ to 1 cup flour until dough is smooth and elastic, about 5 minutes. Place dough in greased bowl; cover loosely with plastic wrap and cloth towel. Let rise in warm place (80 to 85°F.) until light and doubled in size, about 1 hour.

Grease and flour two 9x5 or 8x4-inch loaf pans. Punch down dough several times to remove all air bubbles. Divide dough in half. Work dough with hands to remove large air bubbles. Divide each half into thirds. Shape each third into a small loaf. Spread sides of loaves with softened margarine. Place 3 loaves crosswise in each greased and floured pan. Cover; let rise in warm place until light and doubled in size, about 45 minutes.

Heat oven to 375°F. Uncover dough. Bake 30 to 35 minutes or until loaves are deep golden brown and sound hollow when lightly tapped. Immediately remove from pans; cool on wire racks. Brush warm loaves with softened margarine.

6 (7-slice) loaves.

HIGH ALTITUDE – Above 3500 Feet: No change.

CRACKED WHEAT
RAISIN BREAD

*T*he cracked wheat adds a pleasant nutty texture to these wholesome loaves. Try the bread toasted—it's sensational!

NUTRITION INFORMATION PER SERVING:

1 SLICE		PERCENT U.S. RDA	
Calories	120	Protein	4%
Protein	3 g	Vitamin A	*
Carbohydrate	24 g	Vitamin C	*
Dietary Fiber	2 g	Thiamine	10%
Fat	1 g	Riboflavin	8%
Polyunsaturated	0 g	Niacin	8%
Saturated	0 g	Calcium	*
Cholesterol	5 mg	Iron	6%
Sodium	120 mg	*Less than 2% U.S. RDA	
Potassium	85 mg		

DIETARY EXCHANGES: 1-1/2 Starch

1½ **cups cracked wheat**
1 **cup raisins**
½ **cup firmly packed brown sugar**
2 **teaspoons salt**
3 **tablespoons margarine or butter**
2 **cups boiling water**
2 **pkg. active dry yeast**
⅔ **cup warm water**
5 **to 6 cups all purpose flour**
   Beaten egg

In large bowl, combine cracked wheat, raisins, brown sugar, salt, margarine and 2 cups boiling water. Mix well and allow to cool to 105 to 115°F. In small bowl, dissolve yeast in warm water (105 to 115°F.). Add to cooled cracked wheat mixture. Add 2 cups flour to cracked wheat mixture. Blend at low speed until moistened; beat 2 minutes at medium speed. By hand, stir in an additional 2½ to 3 cups flour until dough pulls cleanly away from sides of bowl.

On floured surface, knead in remaining ½ to 1 cup flour until dough is smooth and elastic, about 10 minutes. Place dough in greased bowl; cover loosely with plastic wrap and cloth towel. Let rise in warm place (80 to 85°F.) until light and doubled in size, 45 to 60 minutes.

Grease large cookie sheet. Punch down dough several times to remove all air bubbles. Divide dough in half; shape into balls. Place on greased cookie sheet. Cover; let rise in warm place until light and doubled in size, 45 to 60 minutes.

Heat oven to 350°F. Uncover dough. With sharp knife, slash a ½-inch deep lattice design on top of each loaf. Brush with beaten egg. Bake at 350°F. for 35 to 45 minutes or until loaves sound hollow when lightly tapped. Immediately remove from cookie sheet; cool on wire racks.

2 (20-slice) loaves.

HIGH ALTITUDE – Above 3500 Feet: No change.

Cracked Wheat Raisin Bread

Speedy Mustard Rye Bread

SPEEDY MUSTARD RYE BREAD

    3 to 4 cups all purpose flour
    2 teaspoons salt
    3 pkg. active dry yeast
    2 cups water
   ¼ cup Dijon mustard
    3 tablespoons brown sugar
    3 tablespoons margarine or butter
 2½ cups medium rye flour
    1 egg, beaten
    1 to 2 teaspoons caraway seed, if desired

In large bowl, combine 2 cups all purpose flour, salt and yeast; blend well. In small saucepan, heat water, mustard, brown sugar and margarine until very warm (120 to 130°F.). Add warm liquid to flour mixture. Blend at low speed until moistened; beat 3 minutes at medium speed. Stir in rye flour and an additional ¾ to 1½ cups all purpose flour until dough pulls away from sides of bowl.

On floured surface, knead in remaining ¼ to ½ cup all purpose flour until dough is smooth and elastic, about 5 minutes. Place dough in greased bowl; cover loosely with plastic wrap and cloth towel. Place bowl in pan of warm water (about 95°F.); let rise 15 minutes.

Grease large cookie sheet. Punch down dough several times to remove all air bubbles. Divide dough in half; shape into balls. Place on greased cookie sheet. Press down slightly. Cover; let rise in warm place until light and doubled in size, about 15 minutes.

Heat oven to 375°F. Uncover dough. With sharp knife, slash a ¼-inch deep lattice design in top of each loaf. Brush with beaten egg; sprinkle with caraway seed. Bake at 375°F. for 25 to 35 minutes or until loaves sound hollow when lightly tapped. Immediately remove from cookie sheet; cool on wire rack.
2 (20-slice) loaves.

HIGH ALTITUDE – Above 3500 Feet: No change.

*H*ere's a hearty bread that's perfect for holiday gift-giving. It makes two loaves so you can give one to a friend in an attractive bread basket, and keep the other for yourself.

NUTRITION INFORMATION PER SERVING:

1 SLICE		PERCENT U.S. RDA	
Calories	90	Protein	2%
Protein	2 g	Vitamin A	*
Carbohydrate	16 g	Vitamin C	*
Dietary Fiber	1 g	Thiamine	8%
Fat	1 g	Riboflavin	6%
Polyunsaturated	0 g	Niacin	4%
Saturated	0 g	Calcium	*
Cholesterol	5 mg	Iron	4%
Sodium	160 mg	*Less than 2% U.S. RDA	
Potassium	55 mg		

DIETARY EXCHANGES: 1 Starch

GARDEN PEPPER BREAD

This bountiful bread has tasty bits of color-ful peppers dotting every slice. The recipe makes two hearty loaves. Plan to freeze one for later. Serve the bread warm or cool.

NUTRITION INFORMATION PER SERVING:

1 SLICE		PERCENT U.S. RDA	
Calories	170	Protein	6%
Protein	5 g	Vitamin A	4%
Carbohydrate	30 g	Vitamin C	6%
Dietary Fiber	1 g	Thiamine	20%
Fat	3 g	Riboflavin	15%
Polyunsaturated	1 g	Niacin	10%
Saturated	1 g	Calcium	*
Cholesterol	1 mg	Iron	8%
Sodium	120 mg	*Less than 2% U.S. RDA	
Potassium	75 mg		

DIETARY EXCHANGES: 2 Starch, 1/2 Fat

2 **tablespoons margarine or butter**
½ **cup chopped onion**
⅓ **cup chopped red bell pepper**
⅓ **cup chopped green bell pepper**
7 **to 8 cups all purpose flour**
½ **cup sugar**
½ **to 1 teaspoon salt**
⅛ **teaspoon pepper**
2 **pkg. active dry yeast**
1 **cup 2% milk**
¾ **cup water**
⅓ **cup margarine or butter**
6 **egg whites or 3 whole eggs**

Melt 2 tablespoons margarine in small skillet over medium heat. Add onion and bell peppers; cook 4 to 5 minutes or until vegetables are tender, stirring occasionally. Set aside.

In large bowl, combine 2 cups flour, sugar, salt, pepper and yeast; blend well. In small saucepan, heat milk, water and ⅓ cup margarine until very warm (120 to 130°F.). Add warm liquid to flour mixture. Blend at low speed until moistened; beat 3 minutes at medium speed. Add egg whites, cooked vegetable mixture and 1 cup flour; beat at medium speed 3 minutes. By hand, stir in an additional 3 to 3½ cups flour to make a stiff dough.

On floured surface, knead in remaining 1 to 1½ cups flour until dough is smooth and elastic, about 10 minutes. (Dough will be slightly sticky.) Place dough in greased bowl; cover loosely with plastic wrap and cloth towel. Let rise in warm place (80 to 85°F.) until light and doubled in size, about 40 minutes.

Grease two 9x5 or three 8x4-inch loaf pans. Punch down dough several times to remove all air bubbles. Divide dough in half; shape into loaves. Place in greased pans. Cover with greased plastic wrap and cloth towel; let rise in warm place until light and doubled in size, about 40 minutes.

Heat oven to 375°F. Uncover dough. Bake 30 to 40 minutes or until loaves are deep golden brown and sound hollow when lightly tapped. Cover with foil during last 10 minutes of baking if neces-sary to avoid excessive browning. Immediately remove from pans; cool on wire racks.

2 (15-slice) loaves.

HIGH ALTITUDE – Above 3500 Feet: No change.

ORANGE RYE BREAD

2	pkg. active dry yeast
1	cup warm water
½	cup orange juice
¼	cup molasses
¼	cup margarine or butter
2¼ to 3¼	cups all purpose flour
¼	cup sugar
1	teaspoon salt
1	teaspoon cardamom
4	teaspoons grated orange peel
1½	cups medium rye flour

In small bowl, dissolve yeast in warm water (105 to 115°F.). In medium saucepan, heat orange juice, molasses and margarine until warm (105 to 115°F.). In large bowl, combine 1½ cups all purpose flour, sugar, salt, cardamom and orange peel. Add dissolved yeast and warm liquids. Blend at low speed until moistened; beat 2 minutes at medium speed. By hand, stir in rye flour and an additional ½ to 1 cup all purpose flour until dough pulls cleanly away from sides of bowl.

On floured surface, knead in remaining ¼ to ¾ cup all purpose flour until dough is smooth and elastic, about 10 minutes. Place dough in greased bowl; cover loosely with plastic wrap and cloth towel. Let rise in warm place (80 to 85°F.) until light and doubled in size, 1 to 1½ hours.

Grease two 8x4-inch loaf pans. Punch down dough several times to remove all air bubbles. Divide dough in half; shape into balls. Shape into loaves by rolling dough into two 14x7-inch rectangles. Starting with shorter side, roll up tightly; pinch edges and ends firmly to seal. Place seam side down in greased pans. Cover; let rise in warm place until dough fills pans and tops of loaves are about 1 inch above pan edges, 1 to 1½ hours.

Heat oven to 375°F. Uncover dough. Bake 35 to 45 minutes or until loaves sound hollow when lightly tapped. Immediately remove from pans; cool on wire racks.

2 (18-slice) loaves.

HIGH ALTITUDE – Above 3500 Feet: No change.

Because rye flour is milled from hardy cereal grass, it contains less gluten than all purpose or whole wheat flour. For rye bread to rise properly, the rye flour must be combined with a larger amount of all purpose or whole wheat flour. Although there are several types available, medium rye flour is the most common.

NUTRITION INFORMATION PER SERVING:

1 SLICE		PERCENT U.S. RDA	
Calories	80	Protein	2%
Protein	2 g	Vitamin A	*
Carbohydrate	15 g	Vitamin C	*
Dietary Fiber	1 g	Thiamine	8%
Fat	1 g	Riboflavin	4%
Polyunsaturated	1 g	Niacin	4%
Saturated	0 g	Calcium	*
Cholesterol	0 mg	Iron	4%
Sodium	75 mg	*Less than 2% U.S. RDA	
Potassium	75 mg		

DIETARY EXCHANGES: 1 Starch

GOLDEN SESAME LOAVES

5 **to 6 cups all purpose flour**
½ **cup instant nonfat dry milk**
½ **cup oat bran**
½ **cup sesame seed, toasted**
1½ **teaspoons salt**
1 **teaspoon sugar**
2 **pkg. active dry yeast**
1¾ **cups water**
¼ **cup oil**
¼ **cup honey**
1 **egg**
1 **egg white, beaten**
1 **tablespoon sesame seed**

*A*ccording to history books, sesame seed is the first recorded seasoning, dating back to 3000 B.C. It is now grown widely in India and throughout the Orient. Toasting the seeds enhances their flavor and, in this recipe, adds a slightly sweet, nutty flavor to the bread.

In large bowl, combine 2 cups flour, dry milk, oat bran, ½ cup toasted sesame seed, salt, sugar and yeast; blend well. In small saucepan, heat water, oil and honey until very warm (120 to 130°F.). Add warm liquid and 1 egg to flour mixture. Blend at low speed until moistened; beat 3 minutes at medium speed. Stir in an additional 2¾ to 3½ cups flour until dough pulls cleanly away from sides of bowl.

On floured surface, knead in remaining ¼ to ½ cup flour until dough is smooth and elastic, about 10 minutes. Place dough in greased bowl; cover loosely with plastic wrap and cloth towel. Let rise in warm place (80 to 85°F.) until light and doubled in size, about 45 to 55 minutes.

Grease two 9x5 or three 7x3-inch loaf pans. Punch down dough several times to remove all air bubbles. Divide dough in half; shape into balls. Shape into loaves by rolling each half into 12x8-inch rectangle. Starting with shortest side, roll up; pinch edges firmly to seal. Place seam side down in greased pans. Cover; let rise in warm place until dough fills pans and tops of loaves are about 1 inch above pan edges, 30 to 35 minutes.

Heat oven to 350°F. Uncover dough. Carefully brush loaves with egg white; sprinkle with 1 tablespoon sesame seed. Bake at 350°F. for 30 to 40 minutes or until loaves sound hollow when lightly tapped. Immediately remove from pans; cool on wire racks. **2 (16-slice) loaves.**

HIGH ALTITUDE – Above 3500 Feet: Decrease each rise time by about 15 minutes. Bake at 350°F. for 25 to 35 minutes.

NUTRITION INFORMATION PER SERVING:

1 SLICE		PERCENT U.S. RDA	
Calories	130	Protein	6%
Protein	4 g	Vitamin A	*
Carbohydrate	22 g	Vitamin C	*
Dietary Fiber	1 g	Thiamine	15%
Fat	3 g	Riboflavin	10%
Polyunsaturated	2 g	Niacin	8%
Saturated	1 g	Calcium	2%
Cholesterol	7 mg	Iron	8%
Sodium	110 mg	*Less than 2% U.S. RDA	
Potassium	75 mg		

DIETARY EXCHANGES: 1-1/2 Starch, 1/2 Fat

Golden Sesame Loaves

HONEY GRANOLA BREAD

*W*hole wheat flour, honey and granola make this a wholesome tasty sandwich bread for the school lunch box. Lower fat granola cereal is now available and can be used to make the bread.

NUTRITION INFORMATION PER SERVING:

1 SLICE		PERCENT U.S. RDA	
Calories	150	Protein	6%
Protein	4 g	Vitamin A	*
Carbohydrate	27 g	Vitamin C	*
Dietary Fiber	2 g	Thiamine	15%
Fat	3 g	Riboflavin	10%
Polyunsaturated	2 g	Niacin	8%
Saturated	1 g	Calcium	2%
Cholesterol	13 mg	Iron	8%
Sodium	135 mg	*Less than 2% U.S. RDA	
Potassium	100 mg		

DIETARY EXCHANGES: 1-1/2 Starch, 1/2 Fat

5 **to 5½ cups all purpose flour**
1 **cup granola cereal**
2 **teaspoons salt**
2 **pkg. active dry yeast**
1½ **cups water**
1 **cup plain low fat yogurt**
½ **cup honey**
¼ **cup oil or shortening**
2 **eggs**
2 **cups whole wheat flour**

In large bowl, combine 3 cups all purpose flour, granola cereal, salt and yeast; blend well. In medium saucepan, heat water, yogurt, honey and oil until very warm (120 to 130°F.). Add warm liquid and eggs to flour mixture. Blend at low speed until moistened; beat 3 minutes at medium speed. By hand, stir in whole wheat flour and an additional 1 cup all purpose flour to form a stiff dough.

On floured surface, knead in remaining 1 to 1½ cups all purpose flour until dough is smooth and elastic, about 10 minutes. Place dough in greased bowl; cover loosely with plastic wrap and cloth towel. Let rise in warm place (80 to 85°F.) until light and doubled in size, about 1 hour.

Generously grease two 9x5 or 8x4-inch loaf pans. Punch down dough several times to remove all air bubbles. Divide dough in half; shape into loaves. Place in greased pans. Cover; let rise in warm place until light and doubled in size, 30 to 45 minutes.

Heat oven to 350°F. Uncover dough. Bake 30 to 40 minutes or until loaves sound hollow when lightly tapped. Immediately remove from pans; cool on wire racks. If desired, brush loaves with melted margarine.

2 (17-slice) loaves.

HIGH ALTITUDE – Above 3500 Feet: Bake at 350°F. for 40 to 50 minutes.

HEARTY OATS 'N WHEAT LOAVES

2 to 2½ cups all purpose flour
1 cup rolled oats
2 teaspoons salt
3 pkg. active dry yeast
1¾ cups water
½ cup corn syrup
½ cup margarine or butter
1 egg
1 egg, separated
2 cups whole wheat flour
1 cup medium rye flour
1 tablespoon water
4 teaspoons sesame seed

In large bowl, combine 1½ cups all purpose flour, oats, salt and yeast; blend well. In medium saucepan, heat 1¾ cups water, corn syrup and margarine until very warm (120 to 130°F.). Add warm liquid, 1 egg and 1 egg yolk (reserve egg white) to flour mixture. Blend at low speed until moistened; beat 3 minutes at medium speed. By hand, stir in whole wheat flour and rye flour to form a soft dough.

On floured surface, knead in remaining ½ to 1 cup all purpose flour until dough is smooth and elastic, about 10 minutes. Place dough in greased bowl; cover loosely with plastic wrap and cloth towel. Let rise in warm place (80 to 85°F.) until light and doubled in size, about 1 hour.

Generously grease two 8x4 or 9x5-inch loaf pans. Punch down dough several times to remove all air bubbles. Divide dough in half; shape into loaves. Place in greased pans. Cover; let rise in warm place until light and doubled in size, about 1 hour.

Heat oven to 375°F. Uncover dough. In small bowl, combine reserved egg white and 1 tablespoon water; brush over loaves. Sprinkle with sesame seed. Bake at 375°F. for 30 to 40 minutes or until loaves are golden brown and sound hollow when lightly tapped. Immediately remove from pans; cool on wire racks.
2 (12-slice) loaves.

HIGH ALTITUDE – Above 3500 Feet: Decrease yeast to 2 packages. Bake as directed above.

The best thing about making your own bread is that you can serve it warm from the oven. This hearty whole grain bread is the perfect accompaniment to a steaming bowl of soup.

NUTRITION INFORMATION PER SERVING:

1 SLICE		PERCENT U.S. RDA	
Calories	170	Protein	6%
Protein	5 g	Vitamin A	4%
Carbohydrate	28 g	Vitamin C	*
Dietary Fiber	3 g	Thiamine	15%
Fat	5 g	Riboflavin	10%
Polyunsaturated	1 g	Niacin	8%
Saturated	1 g	Calcium	*
Cholesterol	18 mg	Iron	8%
Sodium	240 mg	*Less than 2% U.S. RDA	
Potassium	105 mg		

DIETARY EXCHANGES: 1-1/2 Starch, 1 Fat

Nutty Wheat Bread

NUTTY WHEAT BREAD

3½ to 4 cups all purpose flour

1 teaspoon salt

2 pkg. active dry yeast

1½ cups 2% milk

½ cup water

⅓ cup honey

¼ cup margarine or butter

1½ cups whole wheat flour

¾ cup chopped walnuts

¼ cup wheat germ

In large bowl, combine 2 cups all purpose flour, salt and yeast; mix well. In small saucepan, heat milk, water, honey and margarine until very warm (120 to 130°F.). Add warm liquid to flour mixture. Blend at low speed until moistened; beat 2 minutes at medium speed. By hand, stir in whole wheat flour, an additional 1 cup all purpose flour, walnuts and wheat germ.

On floured surface, knead in remaining ½ to 1 cup all purpose flour until dough is smooth and elastic, about 5 minutes. Place dough in greased bowl; cover loosely with plastic wrap and cloth towel. Let rise in warm place (80 to 85°F.) until light and doubled in size, about 1 hour.

Grease two 8x4-inch loaf pans. Punch down dough several times to remove all air bubbles. Divide dough in half. On lightly floured surface, roll out half of dough to 10x8-inch rectangle. Starting with shorter side, roll up tightly; pinch edges and ends firmly to seal. Place seam side down in greased pan. Repeat with other half of dough. Cover; let rise in warm place until dough fills pans and tops of loaves are about 1 inch above pan edges, 30 to 45 minutes.

Heat oven to 350°F. Uncover dough. Bake 30 to 40 minutes or until loaves sound hollow when lightly tapped. Immediately remove from pans; cool on wire racks.

2 (16-slice) loaves.

HIGH ALTITUDE – Above 3500 Feet: No change.

Whole wheat flour is milled from the entire wheat kernel—endosperm, bran and germ. It has a higher fiber, nutritional and fat content than all purpose flour. Breads made with whole wheat flour have a heavier, more compact texture.

NUTRITION INFORMATION PER SERVING:

1 SLICE		PERCENT U.S. RDA	
Calories	130	Protein	6%
Protein	4 g	Vitamin A	*
Carbohydrate	21 g	Vitamin C	*
Dietary Fiber	1 g	Thiamine	10%
Fat	4 g	Riboflavin	8%
Polyunsaturated	2 g	Niacin	8%
Saturated	1 g	Calcium	2%
Cholesterol	1 mg	Iron	6%
Sodium	90 mg	*Less than 2% U.S. RDA	
Potassium	90 mg		

DIETARY EXCHANGES: 1-1/2 Starch, 1/2 Fat

WHOLE WHEAT FRENCH BREAD

*T*his delicious bread boasts only 1 gram of fat and no cholesterol per serving. Enjoy it warm or cool.

2¾ to 3¾ cups all purpose flour
1 tablespoon sugar
2 teaspoons salt
2 pkg. active dry yeast
2 cups water
2 tablespoons shortening
2 cups whole wheat flour
1 tablespoon water
1 egg white, slightly beaten

In large bowl, combine 2 cups all purpose flour, sugar, salt and yeast; blend well. In small saucepan, heat 2 cups water and shortening until very warm (120 to 130°F.). Add warm liquid to flour mixture. Blend at low speed until moistened; beat 3 minutes at medium speed. By hand, stir in whole wheat flour and an additional ½ to 1 cup all purpose flour until dough pulls cleanly away from sides of bowl.

On floured surface, knead in remaining ¼ to ¾ cup all purpose flour until dough is smooth and elastic, about 5 minutes. Place dough in greased bowl; cover loosely with plastic wrap and cloth towel. Let rise in warm place (80 to 85°F.) until light and doubled in size, about 45 minutes.

Grease 2 large cookie sheets. Punch down dough several times to remove all air bubbles. Divide dough in half; shape into balls. Shape balls into two 18-inch oblong loaves; round ends. Place on greased cookie sheets. Combine 1 tablespoon water and egg white; brush some of mixture over loaves. Cover; let rise in warm place until light and doubled in size, 10 to 15 minutes.

Heat oven to 375°F. Uncover dough; brush loaves with remaining egg white mixture. With sharp knife, make four ½-inch deep diagonal slashes in top of each loaf. Bake at 375°F. for 30 to 40 minutes or until loaves are golden brown and sound hollow when lightly tapped. Immediately remove from cookie sheets; cool on wire racks.

2 (18-slice) loaves.

HIGH ALTITUDE – Above 3500 Feet: Decrease first rise time by 15 minutes. Bake as directed above.

NUTRITION INFORMATION PER SERVING:

1 SLICE		PERCENT U.S. RDA	
Calories	80	Protein	4%
Protein	3 g	Vitamin A	*
Carbohydrate	15 g	Vitamin C	*
Dietary Fiber	1 g	Thiamine	8%
Fat	1 g	Riboflavin	6%
Polyunsaturated	0 g	Niacin	6%
Saturated	0 g	Calcium	*
Cholesterol	0 mg	Iron	4%
Sodium	120 mg	*Less than 2% U.S. RDA	
Potassium	50 mg		

DIETARY EXCHANGES: 1 Starch

OAT BRAN FRENCH BREAD

2¼	to 2¾ cups all purpose flour	1	cup water
⅓	cup oat bran	1	tablespoon honey
1	pkg. active dry yeast	1	tablespoon cornmeal
1	teaspoon salt	½	teaspoon cornstarch
		¼	cup water

In large bowl, combine 1 cup flour, oat bran, yeast and salt; blend well. In small saucepan, heat 1 cup water and honey until very warm (120 to 130°F.). Add warm liquid to flour mixture. Blend at low speed until moistened; beat 3 minutes at medium speed. By hand, stir in an additional 1 to 1¼ cups flour to form a stiff dough.

On floured surface, knead in remaining ¼ to ½ cup flour until dough is smooth and elastic, about 5 minutes. Place dough in greased bowl; cover loosely with plastic wrap and cloth towel. Let rise in warm place (80 to 85°F.) until almost doubled in size, about 30 minutes.

Grease cookie sheet; sprinkle with cornmeal.* Punch down dough several times to remove all air bubbles. Shape dough by rolling back and forth on counter into a 15-inch long loaf. Place on greased cookie sheet. Cover; let rise in warm place until almost doubled in size, about 15 minutes.

Heat oven to 400°F. In small saucepan, combine cornstarch and ¼ cup water; mix well. Bring to a boil; cook until mixture is thickened and clear. Remove from heat; cool, stirring occasionally. Uncover dough. With very sharp knife, cut four ½-inch deep diagonal slashes on top of loaf. Brush loaf with thin layer of cornstarch mixture. Bake at 400°F. for 10 minutes. Brush with cornstarch mixture again. Bake an additional 15 to 20 minutes or until loaf is golden brown and loaf sounds hollow when lightly tapped. Immediately remove from cookie sheet; cool on wire rack.
1 (15-slice) loaf.

TIP:
* French bread stick pans can be substituted for cookie sheet. Grease pans; sprinkle with cornmeal. To shape bread, divide dough in half. Gently elongate each half by rolling it back and forth to 1 inch shorter than length of pan. Place in greased pans. Continue as directed above.

HIGH ALTITUDE – Above 3500 Feet: No change.

News of oat bran as a tool to help lower cholesterol has encouraged many cooks to add it to their recipes. In this recipe, we've incorporated this ingredient into a crusty loaf of one of America's favorite breads. Serve it anytime that you would regular French bread.

NUTRITION INFORMATION PER SERVING:

1 SLICE		PERCENT U.S. RDA	
Calories	100	Protein	4%
Protein	3 g	Vitamin A	*
Carbohydrate	21 g	Vitamin C	*
Dietary Fiber	1 g	Thiamine	15%
Fat	0 g	Riboflavin	8%
Polyunsaturated	0 g	Niacin	8%
Saturated	0 g	Calcium	*
Cholesterol	0 mg	Iron	6%
Sodium	140 mg	*Less than 2% U.S. RDA	
Potassium	50 mg		

DIETARY EXCHANGES: 1-1/2 Starch

Garden Batter Bread

GARDEN BATTER BREAD

> 3 **cups all purpose flour**
>
> 1 **pkg. fast-acting dry yeast**
>
> 1 **teaspoon salt**
>
> 1¼ **cups very warm water**
>
> ¼ **cup light molasses**
>
> 2 **tablespoons margarine or butter, melted**
>
> 1 **egg**
>
> 1 **cup wheat germ**
>
> 1 **cup coarsely grated carrots**
>
> ¼ **cup chopped fresh parsley or 2 tablespoons dried parsley flakes**
>
> **Margarine or butter, melted**

Generously grease 2-quart casserole. In large bowl, combine 2 cups flour, yeast and salt; blend well. Add very warm water (120 to 130°F.), molasses, 2 tablespoons melted margarine and egg; beat at low speed until moistened, occasionally scraping down sides of bowl. Beat 3 minutes at medium speed. By hand, stir in remaining 1 cup flour, wheat germ, carrots and parsley to make a stiff batter. Turn into greased casserole. Cover loosely with greased plastic wrap and cloth towel. Let rise in warm place (80 to 85°F.) until almost doubled in size, 30 to 40 minutes.

Heat oven to 350°F. Uncover dough. Bake 50 to 60 minutes or until deep golden brown. Immediately remove from casserole; place on wire rack. Brush with melted margarine.
1 (16-slice) loaf.

HIGH ALTITUDE – Above 3500 Feet: Decrease wheat germ to ¾ cup. Let dough rise in bowl in warm place (80 to 85°F.) until doubled in size. Stir down batter, beating well. Turn into greased casserole. Bake at 375°F. for 40 to 50 minutes.

This easy no-knead casserole loaf combines a tasty blend of wheat germ, carrots, parsley and molasses. For even rising, you must beat the batter well to distribute the yeast. It is typical for batter breads to have a coarser texture than kneaded yeast breads.

NUTRITION INFORMATION PER SERVING:

1 SLICE		PERCENT U.S. RDA	
Calories	150	Protein	6%
Protein	5 g	Vitamin A	40%
Carbohydrate	26 g	Vitamin C	2%
Dietary Fiber	2 g	Thiamine	25%
Fat	3 g	Riboflavin	10%
Polyunsaturated	1 g	Niacin	10%
Saturated	1 g	Calcium	2%
Cholesterol	13 mg	Iron	10%
Sodium	160 mg		
Potassium	210 mg		

DIETARY EXCHANGES: 1-1/2 Starch, 1/2 Fat

HEARTY PUMPERNICKEL BATTER BREAD

*P*umpernickel is tradi-tionally a coarse dark bread made with both rye and wheat flours. This no-knead version has authentic, robust pumpernickel flavor. It's a great bread to slice and eat as is or to use for hearty sandwiches.

1	pkg. active dry yeast
1¼	cups warm water
1	tablespoon sugar
1	teaspoon salt
¾	teaspoon onion powder
½	teaspoon instant coffee granules or crystals
2	tablespoons oil
2	tablespoons molasses
1	oz. unsweetened chocolate, melted
1½	cups all purpose flour
1	cup medium rye flour
1	teaspoon caraway seed

In large bowl, dissolve yeast in warm water (105 to 115°F.). Add sugar, salt, onion powder, instant coffee, oil, molasses and chocolate; blend well. Add 1 cup all purpose flour to yeast mixture. Blend at low speed until moistened; beat 3 minutes at medium speed. By hand, stir in remaining ½ cup all purpose flour, rye flour and caraway seed to form a stiff batter. Cover loosely with plastic wrap and cloth towel. Let rise in warm place (80 to 85°F.) until light and doubled in size, about 45 minutes.

Generously grease 8x4 or 9x5-inch loaf pan. Stir down dough to remove all air bubbles. Turn into greased pan. Cover with greased plastic wrap; let rise in warm place until light and doubled in size, 30 to 45 minutes.

Heat oven to 375°F. Uncover dough. Bake 28 to 35 minutes or until loaf is deep golden brown and sounds hollow when lightly tapped. Immediately remove from pan; cool on wire rack.

1 (16-slice) loaf.

HIGH ALTITUDE – Above 3500 Feet: Increase all purpose flour to 1¾ cups. Bake as directed above.

NUTRITION INFORMATION PER SERVING:

1 SLICE		PERCENT U.S. RDA	
Calories	100	Protein	2%
Protein	2 g	Vitamin A	*
Carbohydrate	17 g	Vitamin C	*
Dietary Fiber	2 g	Thiamine	8%
Fat	3 g	Riboflavin	4%
Polyunsaturated	1 g	Niacin	4%
Saturated	1 g	Calcium	*
Cholesterol	0 mg	Iron	6%
Sodium	135 mg	*Less than 2% U.S. RDA	
Potassium	100 mg		

DIETARY EXCHANGES: 1 Starch, 1/2 Fat

MEXICAN CILANTRO BATTER BREAD

1 tablespoon poppy seed
4½ cups all purpose flour
2 tablespoons sugar
1 teaspoon salt
1 teaspoon garlic powder
1 pkg. active dry yeast
1 cup water
1 cup 2% milk
2 tablespoons margarine or butter
½ cup chopped fresh cilantro
3 teaspoons freeze-dried chives
1 (4-oz.) can chopped green chiles, drained

Because batter breads are not kneaded, the texture of the finished loaf won't be as refined as that of a traditional kneaded bread. Cilantro and green chiles accent the flavor of this easy, unique batter bread.

Generously grease 12-cup Bundt® pan or 10-inch tube pan. Sprinkle bottom and sides of pan with poppy seed. In large bowl, combine 2 cups flour, sugar, salt, garlic powder and yeast; blend well. In small saucepan, heat water, milk and margarine until very warm (120 to 130°F.). Add warm liquid to flour mixture. Beat 2 minutes at medium speed. By hand, stir in remaining 2½ cups flour, cilantro, chives and green chiles to form a stiff batter. Cover; let rise in warm place (80 to 85°F.) until light and doubled in size, 45 to 60 minutes.

Stir down dough. Carefully spoon into greased pan. Cover loosely with greased plastic wrap and cloth towel. Let rise in warm place until light and doubled in size, 30 to 45 minutes.

Heat oven to 375°F. Uncover dough. Bake 35 to 40 minutes or until deep golden brown. Cool 5 minutes; remove from pan.
1 (16-slice) loaf.

HIGH ALTITUDE – Above 3500 Feet: No change.

NUTRITION INFORMATION PER SERVING:

1 SLICE		PERCENT U.S. RDA	
Calories	160	Protein	6%
Protein	5 g	Vitamin A	4%
Carbohydrate	30 g	Vitamin C	*
Dietary Fiber	1 g	Thiamine	20%
Fat	2 g	Riboflavin	10%
Polyunsaturated	1 g	Niacin	10%
Saturated	1 g	Calcium	2%
Cholesterol	1 mg	Iron	10%
Sodium	200 mg	*Less than 2% U.S. RDA	
Potassium	90 mg		

DIETARY EXCHANGES: 2 Starch

Bundt® is a registered trademark of Northland Aluminum Products, Inc., Minneapolis, MN.

DILL ZUCCHINI BATTER BREAD

*B*atter breads do not require kneading but do need to be beaten with a mixer so the bread will rise correctly. Ricotta cheese and zucchini add moisture, flavor and texture to this savory round loaf.

2½	**cups all purpose flour**
1	**tablespoon sugar**
2	**teaspoons dried dill weed**
¼	**teaspoon salt**
1	**pkg. active dry yeast**
¾	**cup 2% milk**
¼	**cup margarine or butter**
½	**cup grated zucchini, well drained**
½	**cup ricotta cheese**
1	**egg**

NUTRITION INFORMATION PER SERVING:

1 SLICE		PERCENT U.S. RDA	
Calories	120	Protein	6%
Protein	4 g	Vitamin A	4%
Carbohydrate	17 g	Vitamin C	*
Dietary Fiber	1 g	Thiamine	10%
Fat	4 g	Riboflavin	10%
Polyunsaturated	1 g	Niacin	6%
Saturated	1 g	Calcium	4%
Cholesterol	17 mg	Iron	6%
Sodium	90 mg	*Less than 2% U.S. RDA	
Potassium	75 mg		

DIETARY EXCHANGES: 1 Starch, 1 Fat

CONVENTIONAL DIRECTIONS: Grease 1½-quart casserole. In large bowl, combine 1 cup flour, sugar, dill, salt and yeast; blend well. In small saucepan, heat milk and margarine until very warm (120 to 130°F.). Add warm liquid, zucchini, cheese and egg to flour mixture. Blend at low speed until moistened; beat 2 minutes at medium speed. By hand, stir in remaining 1½ cups flour to form a stiff batter. Spoon into greased casserole. Cover loosely with greased plastic wrap and cloth towel. Let rise in warm place (80 to 85°F.) until light, about 30 minutes.

Heat oven to 350°F. Uncover dough. Bake 30 to 40 minutes or until deep golden brown. Immediately remove from casserole; cool on wire rack.
1 (16-slice) loaf.

MICROWAVE DIRECTIONS: Grease 8-cup microwave-safe ring mold; coat with *cornflake crumbs*. Prepare batter as directed above. Spoon into greased mold; let rise as directed above. Microwave on MEDIUM for 9½ to 11 minutes or until no fingerprint remains when lightly touched. Let stand 3 minutes. Remove from ring mold; cool on wire rack.

HIGH ALTITUDE – Above 3500 Feet: No change.

Dill Zucchini Batter Bread (Microvave version)

RUSTIC OATS AND WHEAT BREAD

*T*hese large braided loaves have a hearty texture and old-fashioned flavor. An electric knife works well for slicing them.

1	cup cracked wheat	2	pkg. active dry yeast
¼	cup firmly packed brown sugar	⅔	cup warm water
2	teaspoons salt	4¾	to 5¾ cups all purpose flour
2	cups boiling water	1	cup rolled oats
¼	cup molasses	1	egg, beaten
3	tablespoons oil	1	tablespoon rolled oats

In large bowl, combine cracked wheat, brown sugar, salt, 2 cups boiling water, molasses and oil; blend well. Cool mixture to 105 to 115°F. In small bowl, dissolve yeast in ⅔ cup warm water (105 to 115°F.). Add to cooled cracked wheat mixture. Add 2 cups flour to cracked wheat mixture. Blend at low speed until moistened; beat 2 minutes at medium speed. By hand, stir in 1 cup oats and an additional 2¼ to 2¾ cups flour until dough pulls away from sides of bowl.

On floured surface, knead in remaining ½ to 1 cup flour until dough is smooth and elastic, about 10 minutes. Place dough in greased bowl; cover loosely with plastic wrap and cloth towel. Let rise in warm place (80 to 85°F.) until light and doubled in size, 45 to 60 minutes.

Grease 2 cookie sheets. Punch dough down several times to remove all air bubbles. Divide dough in half; divide each half into 3 equal parts. Roll each part into 16-inch rope; place 3 ropes side by side on each greased cookie sheet. Braid 3 ropes loosely from center to each end. Pinch ends together; tuck under to seal. Repeat with other 3 ropes of dough. Cover; let rise in warm place until light and doubled in size, 45 to 60 minutes.

Heat oven to 350°F. Uncover dough. Brush loaves with beaten egg; sprinkle with 1 tablespoon oats. Bake at 350°F. for 35 to 45 minutes or until loaves are deep golden brown and sound hollow when lightly tapped. Remove from cookie sheets; cool on wire racks.

2 (16-slice) loaves.

TIP:

To make round loaves, divide dough in half and shape into balls. Place on greased cookie sheets. With sharp knife, slash a ¼-inch deep lattice design in top of each loaf. Continue as directed above.

HIGH ALTITUDE – Above 3500 Feet: Bake at 375°F. for 30 to 40 minutes.

NUTRITION INFORMATION PER SERVING:

1 SLICE		PERCENT U.S. RDA	
Calories	140	Protein	6%
Protein	4 g	Vitamin A	*
Carbohydrate	26 g	Vitamin C	*
Dietary Fiber	2 g	Thiamine	15%
Fat	2 g	Riboflavin	8%
Polyunsaturated	1 g	Niacin	8%
Saturated	0 g	Calcium	*
Cholesterol	7 mg	Iron	8%
Sodium	140 mg	*Less than 2% U.S. RDA	
Potassium	105 mg		

DIETARY EXCHANGES: 1-1/2 Starch, 1/2 Fat

RYE BUNS

2 cups all purpose flour

⅓ cup firmly packed brown sugar

3 teaspoons salt

½ teaspoon baking soda

2 pkg. active dry yeast

1 cup water

1 cup buttermilk

¼ cup oil

¼ cup molasses

4 to 4½ cups medium rye flour

In large bowl, combine all purpose flour, brown sugar, salt, baking soda and yeast; blend well. In small saucepan, heat water, buttermilk, oil and molasses until very warm (120 to 130°F.). Add warm liquid to flour mixture. Blend at low speed until moistened; beat 3 minutes at medium speed. By hand, stir in 3 to 3½ cups rye flour to make a stiff dough.

On floured surface, knead in remaining ½ to 1 cup rye flour until dough is smooth and elastic, about 5 minutes. Place in greased bowl; cover loosely with plastic wrap and cloth towel. Let rise in warm place (80 to 85°F.) until light and doubled in size, 45 to 60 minutes.

Generously grease 2 cookie sheets. Punch down dough. Divide into 36 pieces; shape each into a ball. Place on greased cookie sheets. Cover; let rise in warm place until doubled in size, 45 to 60 minutes.

Heat oven to 350°F. Uncover dough. Bake 12 to 14 minutes or until golden brown. If desired, brush tops with melted margarine. Immediately remove from cookie sheets; cool on wire racks.

36 buns.

HIGH ALTITUDE – Above 3500 Feet: No change.

Rolls such as these tender rye buns freeze well. Bake as usual, cool completely and wrap for the freezer. They'll keep up to 12 months. To serve them, unwrap slightly and thaw at room temperature 2 to 3 hours.

NUTRITION INFORMATION PER SERVING:			
1 BUN		**PERCENT U.S. RDA**	
Calories	100	Protein	2%
Protein	2 g	Vitamin A	*
Carbohydrate	19 g	Vitamin C	*
Dietary Fiber	2 g	Thiamine	6%
Fat	2 g	Riboflavin	4%
Polyunsaturated	1 g	Niacin	4%
Saturated	0 g	Calcium	*
Cholesterol	0 mg	Iron	4%
Sodium	200 mg	*Less than 2% U.S. RDA	
Potassium	110 mg		

DIETARY EXCHANGES: 1 Starch, 1/2 Fat

SWEDISH WHOLE WHEAT DINNER ROLLS

Fast-acting dry yeast allows bread to rise in about one-third less time than with regular yeast. In this recipe, because of the fast-acting yeast, there is only one rise time.

NUTRITION INFORMATION PER SERVING:

1 ROLL		PERCENT U.S. RDA	
Calories	180	Protein	6%
Protein	5 g	Vitamin A	2%
Carbohydrate	31 g	Vitamin C	*
Dietary Fiber	2 g	Thiamine	20%
Fat	4 g	Riboflavin	10%
Polyunsaturated	1 g	Niacin	10%
Saturated	1 g	Calcium	*
Cholesterol	13 mg	Iron	10%
Sodium	320 mg	*Less than 2% U.S. RDA	
Potassium	140 mg		

DIETARY EXCHANGES: 1-1/2 Starch, 1 Fat

1   **cup whole wheat flour**
½   **cup mashed potato flakes**
2   **tablespoons brown sugar**
2   **teaspoons salt**
1   **teaspoon anise seed, crushed**
1   **teaspoon fennel seed, crushed**
1½   **teaspoons grated orange peel**
1   **pkg. fast-acting dry yeast**
1⅓   **cups water**
¼   **cup margarine or butter**
1   **tablespoon instant coffee granules or crystals**
2   **tablespoons molasses**
1   **teaspoon orange extract, if desired**
1   **egg**
2½   **to 3½ cups all purpose flour**
1   **tablespoon margarine or butter, softened**
½   **teaspoon grated orange peel, if desired**

Grease two 8 or 9-inch round cake pans. In large bowl, combine whole wheat flour, potato flakes, brown sugar, salt, anise seed, fennel seed, 1½ teaspoons orange peel and yeast; blend well. In small saucepan, heat water, ¼ cup margarine, instant coffee, molasses and orange extract until very warm (120 to 130°F.). Add warm liquid and egg to flour mixture. Blend at low speed until moistened; beat 3 minutes at medium speed. Stir in an additional 2 to 2½ cups all purpose flour until dough pulls cleanly away from sides of bowl.

On floured surface, knead in remaining ½ to 1 cup all purpose flour until dough is smooth and elastic, about 5 minutes. Divide dough in half. Divide each half into 8 equal pieces; shape into balls. Place 8 balls in each greased pan. Cover loosely with plastic wrap and cloth towel. Let rise in warm place (80 to 85°F.) until light and doubled in size, about 1 hour.

Heat oven to 375°F. Uncover dough. Bake 20 to 25 minutes or until rolls are golden brown and sound hollow when lightly tapped. Immediately remove from pans; place on wire racks. Brush warm rolls with 1 tablespoon margarine; sprinkle with ½ teaspoon orange peel.
16 rolls.

HIGH ALTITUDE – Above 3500 Feet: No change.

Swedish Whole Wheat Dinner Rolls

WHOLE WHEAT MUSTARD BUNS

*T*he subtle mustard flavor is delicious with shaved ham, corned beef, roast beef or burgers.

NUTRITION INFORMATION PER SERVING:

1 BUN		PERCENT U.S. RDA	
Calories	210	Protein	10%
Protein	7 g	Vitamin A	*
Carbohydrate	39 g	Vitamin C	*
Dietary Fiber	3 g	Thiamine	25%
Fat	3 g	Riboflavin	20%
Polyunsaturated	1 g	Niacin	15%
Saturated	1 g	Calcium	2%
Cholesterol	36 mg	Iron	15%
Sodium	300 mg	*Less than 2% U.S. RDA	
Potassium	140 mg		

DIETARY EXCHANGES: 2-1/2 Starch, 1/2 Fat

1¾ to 2½ cups all purpose flour

1 tablespoon sugar

1 teaspoon salt

1 pkg. active dry yeast

½ cup 2% milk

½ cup water

1 tablespoon oil

1 to 2 tablespoons prepared mustard

1 egg

1 cup whole wheat flour

Beaten egg

In large bowl, combine 1 cup all purpose flour, sugar, salt and yeast; mix well. In small saucepan, heat milk, water and oil until very warm (120 to 130°F.). Add warm liquid, mustard and egg to flour mixture. Blend at low speed until moistened; beat 3 minutes at medium speed. By hand, stir in whole wheat flour and an additional ½ to 1 cup all purpose flour until a soft dough forms.

On floured surface, knead in remaining ¼ to ½ cup all purpose flour until dough is smooth and elastic, about 5 minutes. Place dough in greased bowl; cover loosely with plastic wrap and cloth towel. Let rise in warm place (80 to 85°F.) until light and doubled in size, 50 to 60 minutes.

Grease cookie sheet. Punch down dough several times to remove all air bubbles. Divide dough into 3 parts; divide each part into 3 pieces. Shape each piece into a smooth ball. Place on greased cookie sheet; if desired, flatten slightly. Cover; let rise in warm place until doubled in size, about 30 minutes.

Heat oven to 375°F. Uncover dough; carefully brush buns with beaten egg. Bake 15 to 20 minutes or until golden brown. Immediately remove from cookie sheet; cool on wire racks.

9 buns.

TIP:

To make a smaller cocktail-size bun, divide dough into 15 pieces.

HIGH ALTITUDE – Above 3500 Feet: No change.

OAT BRAN POTATO BUNS

3½ to 4½ cups all purpose flour
1 cup mashed potato flakes
1 cup instant nonfat dry milk
1 cup oat bran
2 teaspoons salt
2 pkg. active dry yeast
2½ cups water
¼ cup shortening
3 tablespoons honey
Margarine or butter, melted

These nutty, moist buns are made with oat bran and potato flakes. Enjoy them as dinner rolls or as sandwich buns.

In large bowl, combine 1 cup flour, potato flakes, dry milk, oat bran, salt and yeast; blend well. In small saucepan, heat water, shortening and honey until very warm (120 to 130°F.). Add warm liquid to flour mixture. Blend at low speed until moistened; beat 3 minutes at medium speed. By hand, stir in an additional 1½ to 2 cups flour until dough pulls cleanly away from sides of bowl.

On floured surface, knead in remaining 1 to 1½ cups flour until dough is smooth and elastic, about 5 minutes. Place dough in greased bowl; cover loosely with plastic wrap and cloth towel. Let rise in warm place (80 to 85°F.) until light and doubled in size, 45 to 60 minutes.

Grease cookie sheets. Punch down dough several times to remove all air bubbles. On floured surface, roll out dough to ¾-inch thickness; cut with floured 2 to 2½-inch round cutter.* Place 2 inches apart on greased cookie sheets. Cover; let rise in warm place until light and doubled in size, about 30 minutes.

Heat oven to 375°F. Uncover dough. Bake 12 to 16 minutes or until golden brown. Immediately remove from cookie sheets; place on wire racks. Brush tops of warm rolls with melted margarine. Serve warm or cool.
24 to 30 rolls.

TIP:
 * For sandwich-sized rolls, cut dough with floured 3-inch round cutter. Makes about twelve 3-inch rolls.

HIGH ALTITUDE – Above 3500 Feet: No change.

NUTRITION INFORMATION PER SERVING:

1 ROLL		PERCENT U.S. RDA	
Calories	120	Protein	6%
Protein	4 g	Vitamin A	*
Carbohydrate	21 g	Vitamin C	*
Dietary Fiber	1 g	Thiamine	15%
Fat	3 g	Riboflavin	10%
Polyunsaturated	1 g	Niacin	6%
Saturated	1 g	Calcium	2%
Cholesterol	0 mg	Iron	6%
Sodium	160 mg	*Less than 2% U.S. RDA	
Potassium	105 mg		

DIETARY EXCHANGES: 1 Starch, 1/2 Fat

CORNMEAL BREADSTICKS

1¾ to 2¼ cups all purpose flour
1 cup cornmeal
¼ cup sugar
1 teaspoon salt
1 pkg. fast-acting dry yeast
1 cup water

¼ cup margarine or butter
1 to 2 tablespoons cornmeal
Margarine or butter, melted
Cornmeal

The use of fast-acting dry yeast and the food processor will save you time in the preparation of these breadsticks. Fast-acting yeast reduces rising time and the food processor eliminates kneading. The breadsticks are easy to prepare while a pot of soup is simmering.

In large bowl, combine 1 cup flour, 1 cup cornmeal, sugar, salt and yeast; blend well. In small saucepan, heat water and ¼ cup margarine until very warm (120 to 130°F.). Add warm liquid to flour mixture. Blend at low speed until moistened; beat 2 minutes at medium speed. By hand, stir in an additional ½ to 1 cup flour until dough pulls away from sides of bowl.

On floured surface, knead in remaining ¼ cup flour until dough is smooth and elastic, about 2 minutes. Place in greased bowl; cover loosely with plastic wrap and cloth towel. Let rise in warm place (80 to 85°F.) until light and doubled in size, about 10 minutes.

Grease 2 large cookie sheets; sprinkle with 1 to 2 tablespoons cornmeal. Punch down dough several times to remove all air bubbles. Divide dough into 24 parts; roll each into 10-inch rope. Place on greased cookie sheets. Cover; let rise in warm place until light and doubled in size, about 10 minutes.

Heat oven to 375°F. Uncover dough. Carefully brush sticks with melted margarine; sprinkle with cornmeal. Bake at 375°F. for 12 to 16 minutes or until bottoms are golden brown. Immediately remove from cookie sheets; cool on wire racks.

24 breadsticks.

FOOD PROCESSOR DIRECTIONS: In food processor bowl with metal blade, combine 1¼ cups flour, 1 cup cornmeal, sugar, salt, yeast and ¼ cup margarine. Cover; process 5 seconds. With machine running, pour 1 cup water heated to 120 to 130°F. through feed tube; continue processing until blended, about 20 seconds. Add ½ to 1 cup flour; process an additional 10 to 20 seconds or until a stiff dough forms. With rubber scraper, carefully pull dough from blade and bowl; place in lightly greased bowl. Continue as directed above.

HIGH ALTITUDE – Above 3500 Feet: No change.

NUTRITION INFORMATION PER SERVING:

1 BREADSTICK		PERCENT U.S. RDA	
Calories	90	Protein	2%
Protein	2 g	Vitamin A	2%
Carbohydrate	16 g	Vitamin C	*
Dietary Fiber	1 g	Thiamine	8%
Fat	3 g	Riboflavin	4%
Polyunsaturated	1 g	Niacin	4%
Saturated	1 g	Calcium	*
Cholesterol	0 mg	Iron	4%
Sodium	120 mg	*Less than 2% U.S. RDA	
Potassium	35 mg		

DIETARY EXCHANGES: 1 Starch, 1/2 Fat

Cornmeal Breadsticks

THICK CRUST PIZZA DOUGH

*C*rown this Chicago-style pizza crust with your favorite toppings. Using reduced-fat mozzarella and vegetable toppings will help keep the fat to a minimum.

NUTRITION INFORMATION PER SERVING:

1/8 OF CRUST		PERCENT U.S. RDA	
Calories	130	Protein	4%
Protein	4 g	Vitamin A	*
Carbohydrate	24 g	Vitamin C	*
Dietary Fiber	1 g	Thiamine	20%
Fat	2 g	Riboflavin	10%
Polyunsaturated	1 g	Niacin	10%
Saturated	0 g	Calcium	*
Cholesterol	0 mg	Iron	8%
Sodium	270 mg	*Less than 2% U.S. RDA	
Potassium	50 mg		

DIETARY EXCHANGES: 1-1/2 Starch, 1/2 Fat

1½ to 2 cups all purpose flour

1 teaspoon salt

½ teaspoon sugar

1 pkg. active dry yeast

¾ cup water

1 tablespoon oil

In large bowl, combine ¾ cup flour, salt, sugar and yeast; blend well. In small saucepan, heat water and oil until very warm (120 to 130°F.). Add to flour mixture. Blend at low speed until moistened; beat 2 minutes at medium speed. Stir in an additional ½ to ¾ cup flour to form a stiff dough.

On floured surface, knead in remaining ¼ to ½ cup flour until dough is smooth and elastic, 3 to 5 minutes. Place dough in greased bowl; cover loosely with plastic wrap and cloth towel. Let rise in warm place (80 to 85°F.) until light and doubled in size, 30 to 40 minutes.

Grease 12-inch pizza pan. Punch down dough several times to remove all air bubbles. With greased fingers, press dough in greased pan, forming ½-inch rim. Cover; let rise in warm place (80 to 85°F.) until light and doubled in size, 15 to 30 minutes.

Heat oven to 400°F. Uncover dough. Bake crust 8 to 10 minutes or until set and very light golden brown. Top as desired with favorite pizza toppings. Bake an additional 15 to 20 minutes or until crust is golden brown and toppings are thoroughly heated.
8 servings.

HIGH ALTITUDE – Above 3500 Feet: No change.

VARIATIONS:

THIN CRUST PIZZA DOUGH: Prepare dough as directed above; divide in half. Press each half in greased 12-inch pizza pan. Top as desired with favorite pizza toppings. Bake at 400°F. for 18 to 25 minutes or until crust is golden brown and toppings are thoroughly heated.
2 thin crust pizzas.

WHOLE WHEAT PIZZA DOUGH: Substitute ½ cup whole wheat flour for part of the all purpose flour. Prepare as directed above.

ITALIAN WHOLE WHEAT FOCACCIA

1½ cups whole wheat flour
1 to 1½ cups all purpose flour
1 teaspoon sugar
½ teaspoon salt
1 pkg. fast-acting dry yeast
1 cup very warm water
2 tablespoons olive oil or oil
1 egg
½ cup thinly sliced fresh mushrooms
3 tablespoons olive oil or oil
2 tablespoons shelled sunflower seeds
1 tablespoon grated Parmesan cheese
1 teaspoon dried thyme leaves

This whole wheat version of the classic flat bread, focaccia (foh-CAH-chee-ah), includes sunflower seeds and fresh mushrooms. It is best when served warm from the oven.

In large bowl, combine 1 cup whole wheat flour, ½ cup all purpose flour, sugar, salt and yeast; mix well. Add very warm water (120 to 130°F.), 2 tablespoons olive oil and egg to flour mixture. Blend at low speed until moistened; beat 2 minutes at medium speed. By hand, stir in remaining ½ cup whole wheat flour and an additional ¼ to ½ cup all purpose flour until dough pulls away from sides of bowl.

On floured surface, knead in remaining ¼ to ½ cup all purpose flour until dough is smooth and elastic, about 5 minutes. Cover with large bowl; let rest 5 minutes.

Meanwhile, grease cookie sheet. Place dough on greased cookie sheet. Roll or press into 12-inch circle. Cover loosely with greased plastic wrap and cloth towel. Let rise in warm place (80 to 85°F.) until light and doubled in size, about 30 minutes.

Heat oven to 400°F. Uncover dough. With handle of wooden spoon, poke holes in dough at 1-inch intervals. Arrange mushrooms over dough; drizzle with 3 tablespoons olive oil, coating mushroom slices. Sprinkle remaining ingredients evenly over top, pressing in lightly.

Bake at 400°F. for 17 to 27 minutes or until golden brown. Immediately remove from cookie sheet; cool slightly on wire rack. Serve warm, cut into wedges.

1 (24-wedge) loaf.

HIGH ALTITUDE – Above 3500 Feet: No change.

NUTRITION INFORMATION PER SERVING:

1 WEDGE		PERCENT U.S. RDA	
Calories	90	Protein	4%
Protein	3 g	Vitamin A	*
Carbohydrate	12 g	Vitamin C	*
Dietary Fiber	1 g	Thiamine	6%
Fat	4 g	Riboflavin	6%
Polyunsaturated	1 g	Niacin	6%
Saturated	1 g	Calcium	*
Cholesterol	9 mg	Iron	4%
Sodium	55 mg	*Less than 2% U.S. RDA	
Potassium	65 mg		

DIETARY EXCHANGES: 1 Starch, 1/2 Fat

NO-KNEAD REFRIGERATOR DOUGH

*T*his versatile basic dough keeps up to four days in the refrigerator—ready to shape and bake into your choice of delicious recipes. One recipe will make two coffee cakes, two braided loaves or two dozen rolls. Read the recipe for the desired variation before preparing the basic dough.

4 **to 4½ cups all purpose flour**
½ **cup sugar**
1 **teaspoon salt**
2 **pkg. active dry yeast**
1 **cup water**
½ **cup margarine or butter**
3 **eggs**

In large bowl, combine 2 cups flour, sugar, salt and yeast; blend well. In small saucepan, heat water and margarine until very warm (120 to 130°F.). Add warm liquid and eggs to flour mixture. Blend at low speed until moistened; beat 2 minutes at medium speed. By hand, stir in remaining 2 to 2½ cups flour to form a stiff dough. Cover tightly with plastic wrap; refrigerate at least 2 hours or up to 4 days.

Shape and bake dough as directed in the following recipes: *Almond-Filled Swedish Tea Rings, Braided Cardamom Bread, Herbed Dinner Rolls or Spiced Cranberry Rolls.* Or, dough can be shaped and baked into 24 plain dinner rolls, following directions for *Herbed Dinner Rolls.*

HIGH ALTITUDE – Above 3500 Feet: No change.

NUTRITION INFORMATION PER SERVING:
1 PLAIN DINNER ROLL PERCENT U.S. RDA

Calories	150	Protein	4%
Protein	3 g	Vitamin A	4%
Carbohydrate	22 g	Vitamin C	*
Dietary Fiber	1 g	Thiamine	10%
Fat	5 g	Riboflavin	10%
Polyunsaturated	1 g	Niacin	8%
Saturated	1 g	Calcium	*
Cholesterol	27 mg	Iron	6%
Sodium	140 mg	*Less than 2% U.S. RDA	
Potassium	45 mg		

DIETARY EXCHANGES: 1-1/2 Starch, 1 Fat

HERBED DINNER ROLLS

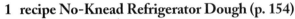

1 **recipe No-Knead Refrigerator Dough (p. 154)**

2 **teaspoons dried basil leaves**

1 **teaspoon dried thyme leaves**

1 **teaspoon fennel seed**

1 **tablespoon margarine or butter, melted**

Prepare dough as directed in recipe, adding basil, thyme and fennel seed with liquid ingredients. Refrigerate as directed.

Lightly grease two 8 or 9-inch round cake pans. On lightly floured surface, divide chilled dough into 4 equal parts. Cut each part into 6 equal pieces; shape into balls. Place 12 balls in each greased pan. Brush with melted margarine. Cover loosely with plastic wrap and cloth towel; let rise in warm place (80 to 85°F.) until doubled in size, 45 to 60 minutes.

Heat oven to 375°F. Uncover dough. Bake for 18 to 28 minutes or until golden brown. Immediately remove from pans.
24 rolls.

HIGH ALTITUDE – Above 3500 Feet: No change.

Shape and bake just part of these flavorful rolls at a time and have fresh dinner rolls four days in a row.

NUTRITION INFORMATION PER SERVING:

1 ROLL		PERCENT U.S. RDA	
Calories	150	Protein	4%
Protein	3 g	Vitamin A	4%
Carbohydrate	22 g	Vitamin C	*
Dietary Fiber	1 g	Thiamine	15%
Fat	5 g	Riboflavin	10%
Polyunsaturated	2 g	Niacin	8%
Saturated	1 g	Calcium	*
Cholesterol	27 mg	Iron	6%
Sodium	150 mg	*Less than 2% U.S. RDA	
Potassium	50 mg		

DIETARY EXCHANGES: 1-1/2 Starch, 1 Fat

HEALTH NOTES

GOOD NEWS ABOUT BREAD

Bread lovers, take heart. Man does not gain weight by bread alone. Along with grains, the staff of life is revered as the basis of a wholesome diet for a number of reasons. Bread is chock-full of complex carbohydrates, B vitamins and minerals. And it is typically low in fat and calories, and nearly or totally free of cholesterol. Additionally, whole grain breads are fiber-rich.

SPICED CRANBERRY ROLLS

*P*erfectly festive for a holiday dinner, these pretty and easy-to-shape rolls are made with our easy No-Knead Refrigerator Dough. Serve one panful and freeze the other.

1 recipe No-Knead Refrigerator Dough (p. 154)
1 teaspoon cinnamon
½ teaspoon ginger
½ teaspoon nutmeg
1 cup chopped fresh or frozen cranberries
1 tablespoon margarine or butter, if desired

Prepare dough as directed in recipe, adding cinnamon, ginger and nutmeg with first addition of flour. Stir in cranberries with last addition of flour. Refrigerate as directed.

Grease two 9-inch round cake pans. On lightly floured surface, divide chilled dough into 4 parts. Cut each part into 12 equal pieces; shape into balls. Place 24 balls in each greased pan. Cover loosely with plastic wrap and cloth towel. Let rise in warm place (80 to 85°F.) until almost doubled in size, 1 hour to 1 hour 15 minutes.

Heat oven to 375°F. Uncover dough. Bake 20 to 30 minutes or until golden brown. Immediately remove from pans; place on wire racks. Brush margarine over warm rolls.
48 rolls.

HIGH ALTITUDE – Above 3500 Feet: No change.

NUTRITION INFORMATION PER SERVING:			
1 ROLL		**PERCENT U.S. RDA**	
Calories	80	Protein	2%
Protein	2 g	Vitamin A	2%
Carbohydrate	12 g	Vitamin C	*
Dietary Fiber	1 g	Thiamine	6%
Fat	3 g	Riboflavin	4%
Polyunsaturated	1 g	Niacin	4%
Saturated	1 g	Calcium	*
Cholesterol	13 mg	Iron	2%
Sodium	75 mg	*Less than 2% U.S. RDA	
Potassium	25 mg		

DIETARY EXCHANGES: 1/2 Starch, 1/2 Fat

Spiced Cranberry Rolls

Braided Cardamom Bread

BRAIDED CARDAMOM BREAD

1 recipe No-Knead Refrigerator Dough (p. 154)

1 teaspoon cardamom or nutmeg

TOPPING

1 egg

1 tablespoon 2% milk

¼ cup sliced almonds

Prepare dough as directed in recipe, adding cardamom with liquid ingredients. Refrigerate as directed.

Grease 2 cookie sheets. On lightly floured surface, divide chilled dough in half; divide each half into 3 pieces. On lightly floured surface, roll each piece into a 16-inch rope. Place 3 ropes lengthwise on each greased cookie sheet. Braid ropes loosely from center to each end. Pinch ends together; tuck under to seal. Cover loosely with plastic wrap and cloth towel; let rise in warm place (80 to 85°F.) until doubled in size, 45 to 60 minutes.

Heat oven to 375°F. Uncover dough. In small bowl, beat egg and milk; brush over loaves. Sprinkle with almonds. Bake at 375°F. for 18 to 28 minutes or until loaves sound hollow when lightly tapped. Immediately remove from cookie sheets; cool on wire racks.

2 (16-slice) loaves.

HIGH ALTITUDE – Above 3500 Feet: No change.

You'll find cardamom to have a pungent aroma and a warm, spicy-sweet flavor. It's delicious in this Scandinavian coffee bread that's made with our easy No-Knead Refrigerator Dough.

NUTRITION INFORMATION PER SERVING:

1 SLICE		PERCENT U.S. RDA	
Calories	120	Protein	4%
Protein	3 g	Vitamin A	2%
Carbohydrate	17 g	Vitamin C	*
Dietary Fiber	1 g	Thiamine	10%
Fat	4 g	Riboflavin	8%
Polyunsaturated	1 g	Niacin	6%
Saturated	1 g	Calcium	*
Cholesterol	27 mg	Iron	6%
Sodium	110 mg	*Less than 2% U.S. RDA	
Potassium	45 mg		

DIETARY EXCHANGES: 1 Starch, 1 Fat

ALMOND-FILLED
SWEDISH TEA RINGS

*F*rom one recipe of our No-Knead Refrigerator Dough you can make two of these delicious tea rings. Serve one and freeze one, or shape and bake one today, another tomorrow.

1 recipe No-Knead Refrigerator Dough (p. 154)

FILLING
½ **cup finely chopped blanched almonds, toasted**
½ **cup firmly packed brown sugar**
1½ **teaspoons cinnamon**
2 **tablespoons margarine or butter, melted**

GLAZE
1 **cup powdered sugar**
1 **to 3 tablespoons orange juice**

Prepare and refrigerate dough as directed in recipe.

Grease 2 large cookie sheets. On lightly floured surface, divide chilled dough in half. Return half to bowl; cover and refrigerate. Roll half of dough to 15x12-inch rectangle. In small bowl, combine almonds, brown sugar and cinnamon; mix well. Spread dough evenly with 1 tablespoon of the margarine; sprinkle with half of almond mixture. Starting with 15-inch side, roll up tightly, pinching seam firmly to seal. Place seam side down on greased cookie sheet, joining ends to form ring; pinch to seal. With scissors, make cuts at 1-inch intervals to within ½ inch of inside of ring. Turn each slice on its side, cut side up. Repeat with remaining half of dough, margarine and almond mixture. Cover loosely with plastic wrap and cloth towel; let rise in warm place (80 to 85°F.) until doubled in size, 45 to 60 minutes.

Heat oven to 350°F. Uncover dough. Bake 25 to 35 minutes or until deep golden brown. Immediately remove from cookie sheets; cool 10 minutes on wire racks.

In small bowl, combine powdered sugar and enough orange juice for desired drizzling consistency; blend until smooth. Drizzle over warm tea rings.

2 (16-slice) tea rings.

HIGH ALTITUDE – Above 3500 Feet: No change.

NUTRITION INFORMATION PER SERVING:

1 SLICE		PERCENT U.S. RDA	
Calories	160	Protein	4%
Protein	3 g	Vitamin A	2%
Carbohydrate	24 g	Vitamin C	*
Dietary Fiber	1 g	Thiamine	10%
Fat	5 g	Riboflavin	8%
Polyunsaturated	1 g	Niacin	6%
Saturated	1 g	Calcium	*
Cholesterol	20 mg	Iron	6%
Sodium	115 mg	*Less than 2% U.S. RDA	
Potassium	65 mg		

DIETARY EXCHANGES: 1 Starch, 1/2 Fruit, 1 Fat

APPLE ROUND-O-ROLLS

ROLLS

1 pkg. active dry yeast

1½ cups warm 2% milk

3 to 3½ cups all purpose flour

½ cup sugar

½ teaspoon salt

⅓ cup margarine or butter, melted

2 eggs

2 cups whole wheat flour

FILLING

4 cups finely chopped peeled apples

¼ cup dried currants

¼ cup firmly packed brown sugar

2 teaspoons cinnamon

⅛ teaspoon salt

1 tablespoon lemon juice

¼ cup margarine or butter, softened

GLAZE

2 cups powdered sugar

3 tablespoons apple juice

1 tablespoon lemon juice

These lightly glazed rolls are flavored with whole wheat flour, apple pieces, currants and cinnamon. Prepare one pan for a sweet morning start and freeze the other for another time.

NUTRITION INFORMATION PER SERVING:

1 ROLL		PERCENT U.S. RDA	
Calories	160	Protein	4%
Protein	3 g	Vitamin A	2%
Carbohydrate	29 g	Vitamin C	*
Dietary Fiber	2 g	Thiamine	8%
Fat	4 g	Riboflavin	6%
Polyunsaturated	1 g	Niacin	6%
Saturated	1 g	Calcium	2%
Cholesterol	12 mg	Iron	6%
Sodium	80 mg	*Less than 2% U.S. RDA	
Potassium	100 mg		

DIETARY EXCHANGES: 1 Starch, 1/2 Fruit, 1 Fat

In small bowl, dissolve yeast in warm milk (105 to 115°F.). In large bowl, combine 1½ cups all purpose flour, sugar and ½ teaspoon salt; blend well. Add dissolved yeast, ⅓ cup margarine and eggs to flour mixture. Blend at low speed until moistened; beat 3 minutes at medium speed. Stir in whole wheat flour and an additional 1 cup all purpose flour until dough pulls cleanly away from sides of bowl.

On floured surface, knead in remaining ½ to 1 cup all purpose flour until dough is smooth and elastic, about 5 minutes. Place dough in greased bowl; cover loosely with plastic wrap and cloth towel. Let rise in warm place (80 to 85°F.) until light and doubled in size, about 1 hour.

Grease three 9-inch round cake pans or one 15x10x1-inch baking pan. Punch down dough several times to remove all air bubbles. Divide dough in half; shape into balls. In medium bowl, combine all filling ingredients except ¼ cup margarine; blend well. Roll each ball into 18x8-inch rectangle. Spread each with 2 tablespoons of the margarine and half of filling. Starting with longest side, roll up; pinch edges firmly to seal. Cut each into eighteen 1-inch slices. Place 12 slices cut side down in each greased round pan or 36 slices in greased baking pan. Cover loosely with plastic wrap and cloth towel; let rise in warm place until light and doubled in size, about 1 hour. Heat oven to 350°F. Uncover dough. Bake 30 to 35 minutes or until golden brown. Immediately remove from pans; cool on wire racks. In small bowl, combine all glaze ingredients; blend until smooth. Drizzle over warm rolls.
36 rolls.

HIGH ALTITUDE – Above 3500 Feet: No change.

Honey Almond Twist

HONEY ALMOND TWIST

BREAD

6 to 7 cups all purpose flour

½ cup sugar

2 teaspoons salt

2 pkg. active dry yeast

1 cup water

1 cup 2% milk

½ cup margarine or butter

1 egg

FILLING

⅓ cup sugar

1 teaspoon cinnamon

3 tablespoons margarine or butter, softened

GLAZE

¼ cup sugar

¼ cup honey

2 tablespoons margarine or butter

½ cup slivered almonds

These stunning pretzel-shaped loaves have a cinnamon filling and are topped with an almond-honey glaze. They are perfect for breakfast or brunch.

NUTRITION INFORMATION PER SERVING:

1 SLICE		PERCENT U.S. RDA	
Calories	130	Protein	4%
Protein	3 g	Vitamin A	2%
Carbohydrate	21 g	Vitamin C	*
Dietary Fiber	1 g	Thiamine	10%
Fat	4 g	Riboflavin	8%
Polyunsaturated	1 g	Niacin	6%
Saturated	1 g	Calcium	*
Cholesterol	5 mg	Iron	6%
Sodium	130 mg	*Less than 2% U.S. RDA	
Potassium	50 mg		

DIETARY EXCHANGES: 1 Starch, 1 Fat

In large bowl, combine 2 cups flour, ½ cup sugar, salt and yeast; blend well. In small saucepan, heat water, milk and ½ cup margarine until very warm (120 to 130°F.). Add warm liquid and egg to flour mixture. Blend at low speed until moistened; beat 3 minutes at medium speed. By hand, stir in an additional 3 cups flour until dough pulls away from sides of bowl.

On floured surface, knead in remaining 1 to 2 cups flour until dough is smooth and elastic, about 5 minutes. Place dough in greased bowl; cover loosely with plastic wrap and cloth towel. Let rise in warm place (80 to 85°F.) until light and doubled in size, about 45 minutes.

Grease 2 cookie sheets. Punch down dough several times to remove all air bubbles. In small bowl, combine ⅓ cup sugar and cinnamon; set aside. Divide dough into 3 equal parts. On lightly floured surface, roll each part into 25x6-inch rectangle. Spread each with 1 tablespoon margarine. Sprinkle with sugar-cinnamon mixture. Starting with longer side, roll up tightly; pinch edges to seal. Twist each roll, stretching slightly. Form into pretzel shape; tuck ends under to seal. Place on greased cookie sheets. Cover; let rise in warm place until doubled in size, about 30 minutes.

Heat oven to 350°F. Uncover dough. Bake 20 to 30 minutes or until deep golden brown. Immediately remove from cookie sheets; cool on wire racks. In small saucepan, combine all glaze ingredients. Bring to a boil, stirring constantly. Spoon hot glaze over warm breads, completely covering tops and sides.

3 (16-slice) loaves.

HIGH ALTITUDE – Above 3500 Feet: Decrease each rise time by 15 minutes. Bake as directed above.

LIGHT GRAIN BREAD

Because bread machines have become an integral appliance in many kitchens, we've included six healthful recipes for you to try. Each gives the option for making either a small or large loaf. In addition to being truly delicious, these breads are chock full of a variety of wholesome ingredients!

	SMALL LOAF (8 slices)	LARGE LOAF (12 slices)
Water	¾ cup	1¼ cups
Bread flour	2 cups	3 cups
Instant nonfat dry milk	1 tablespoon	1½ tablespoons
Molasses	1 tablespoon	1½ tablespoons
Honey	1 tablespoon	1½ tablespoons
Salt	¾ teaspoon	1¼ teaspoons
Margarine or butter	1 tablespoon	2 tablespoons
Wheat germ	3 tablespoons	¼ cup
Shelled sunflower seeds	2 tablespoons	3 tablespoons
Active dry yeast	1½ teaspoons	2½ teaspoons

1. If bread machine typically uses 2 cups flour, use small loaf recipe. If machine uses 3 cups flour, use large loaf recipe.
2. Follow manufacturer's directions for loading ingredients into machine. Measure ingredients carefully.
3. Select regular, rapid or delayed-time bake cycle and follow manufacturer's directions for starting machine.

HIGH ALTITUDE – Above 3500 Feet: For small loaf, increase water by 1 to 2 tablespoons and decrease yeast by ¼ to ½ teaspoon. For large loaf, increase water by 1½ to 3 tablespoons and decrease yeast by ¼ to ¾ teaspoon. Continue as directed above.

NUTRITION INFORMATION PER SERVING:

1 SLICE		PERCENT U.S. RDA	
Calories	180	Protein	8%
Protein	6 g	Vitamin A	*
Carbohydrate	31 g	Vitamin C	*
Dietary Fiber	2 g	Thiamine	25%
Fat	4 g	Riboflavin	15%
Polyunsaturated	2 g	Niacin	15%
Saturated	1 g	Calcium	2%
Cholesterol	0 mg	Iron	10%
Sodium	250 mg	*Less than 2% U.S. RDA	
Potassium	135 mg		

DIETARY EXCHANGES: 2 Starch, 1/2 Fat

HEARTY HONEY GRANOLA BREAD

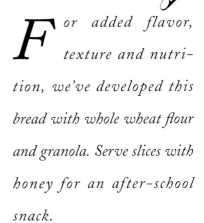

	SMALL LOAF (8 slices)	LARGE LOAF (12 slices)
Water	¾ cup plus 2 tablespoons	1¼ cups
Margarine or butter	1 tablespoon	2 tablespoons
Honey	1 tablespoon	1½ tablespoons
Bread flour	1½ cups	2¼ cups
Whole wheat flour	½ cup	¾ cup
Lowfat granola cereal	¼ cup	⅓ cup
Instant nonfat dry milk	1 tablespoon	2 tablespoons
Salt	¾ teaspoon	1¼ teaspoons
Active dry yeast	1 teaspoon	2 teaspoons

*F*or added flavor, texture and nutrition, we've developed this bread with whole wheat flour and granola. Serve slices with honey for an after-school snack.

NUTRITION INFORMATION PER SERVING:

1 SLICE		PERCENT U.S. RDA	
Calories	170	Protein	8%
Protein	5 g	Vitamin A	4%
Carbohydrate	31 g	Vitamin C	*
Dietary Fiber	2 g	Thiamine	20%
Fat	3 g	Riboflavin	15%
Polyunsaturated	1 g	Niacin	15%
Saturated	1 g	Calcium	*
Cholesterol	0 mg	Iron	10%
Sodium	300 mg	*Less than 2% U.S. RDA	
Potassium	100 mg		

DIETARY EXCHANGES: 2 Starch, 1/2 Fat

1. If bread machine typically uses 2 cups flour, use small loaf recipe. If machine uses 3 cups flour, use large loaf recipe.

2. Follow manufacturer's directions for loading ingredients into machine. Measure ingredients carefully.

3. Select regular, rapid or delayed-time bake cycle and follow manufacturer's directions for starting machine.

HIGH ALTITUDE – Above 3500 Feet: For small loaf, increase water by 1 to 2 tablespoons and decrease yeast by ¼ to ½ teaspoon. For large loaf, increase water by 1½ to 3 tablespoons and decrease yeast by ¼ to ¾ teaspoon. Continue as directed above.

BUTTERMILK WALNUT BREAD

To make breads in the bread machine, we recommend using bread flour. It is specially formulated to help provide the desired elasticity and structure needed to properly raise and bake the bread.

	SMALL LOAF (8 slices)	LARGE LOAF (12 slices)
Water	½ cup	¾ cup
Buttermilk	¼ cup	½ cup
Bread flour	2 cups	3 cups
Sugar	4 teaspoons	3 tablespoons
Salt	½ teaspoon	¾ teaspoon
Chopped walnuts	⅓ cup	½ cup
Active dry yeast	1½ teaspoons	2½ teaspoons

1. If bread machine typically uses 2 cups flour, use small loaf recipe. If machine uses 3 cups flour, use large loaf recipe.

2. Follow manufacturer's directions for loading ingredients into machine. Measure ingredients carefully.

3. Select regular, rapid or delayed-time bake cycle and follow manufacturer's directions for starting machine.

HIGH ALTITUDE – Above 3500 Feet: For small loaf, increase water by 1 to 2 tablespoons and decrease yeast by ¼ to ½ teaspoon. For large loaf, increase water by 1½ to 3 tablespoons and decrease yeast by ¼ to ¾ teaspoon. Continue as directed above.

NUTRITION INFORMATION PER SERVING:

1 SLICE		PERCENT U.S. RDA	
Calories	170	Protein	8%
Protein	5 g	Vitamin A	*
Carbohydrate	30 g	Vitamin C	*
Dietary Fiber	1 g	Thiamine	20%
Fat	4 g	Riboflavin	15%
Polyunsaturated	2 g	Niacin	15%
Saturated	0 g	Calcium	*
Cholesterol	0 mg	Iron	10%
Sodium	150 mg	*Less than 2% U.S. RDA	
Potassium	90 mg		

DIETARY EXCHANGES: 1-1/2 Starch, 1 Fat

Carrot Onion Dill Bread, p. 167

CARROT-ONION-DILL BREAD

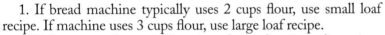

	SMALL LOAF (8 slices)	LARGE LOAF (12 slices)
Water	¾ cup	1¼ cups
Shredded carrots	⅓ cup	½ cup
Bread flour	2 cups	3 cups
Instant nonfat dry milk	1 tablespoon	2 tablespoons
Sugar	1 teaspoon	2 teaspoons
Salt	1 teaspoon	1¼ teaspoons
Margarine or butter	1 tablespoon	2 tablespoons
Dried dill weed	⅛ teaspoon	¼ teaspoon
Dried minced onion	1 tablespoon	1½ tablespoons
Active dry yeast	1¼ teaspoons	2 teaspoons

*Y*ou'll like the fresh-from-the-garden flavors in this healthful bread. It's great for sandwiches, breakfast or just as a snack.

NUTRITION INFORMATION PER SERVING:

1 SLICE		PERCENT U.S. RDA	
Calories	150	Protein	6%
Protein	5 g	Vitamin A	25%
Carbohydrate	27 g	Vitamin C	*
Dietary Fiber	1 g	Thiamine	20%
Fat	3 g	Riboflavin	10%
Polyunsaturated	1 g	Niacin	15%
Saturated	1 g	Calcium	*
Cholesterol	0 mg	Iron	8%
Sodium	290 mg	*Less than 2% U.S. RDA	
Potassium	85 mg		

DIETARY EXCHANGES: 1-1/2 Starch, 1/2 Fat

1. If bread machine typically uses 2 cups flour, use small loaf recipe. If machine uses 3 cups flour, use large loaf recipe.

2. Follow manufacturer's directions for loading ingredients into machine. Measure ingredients carefully.

3. Select regular, rapid or delayed-time bake cycle and follow manufacturer's directions for starting machine.

HIGH ALTITUDE – Above 3500 Feet: For small loaf, increase water by 1 to 2 tablespoons and decrease yeast by ¼ to ½ teaspoon. For large loaf, increase water by 1½ to 3 tablespoons and decrease yeast by ¼ to ¾ teaspoon. Continue as directed above.

POTATO CHIVE BREAD

This moist bread is low-fat and deliciously nutritious. Serve it often!

NUTRITION INFORMATION PER SERVING:

1 SLICE		PERCENT U.S. RDA	
Calories	170	Protein	8%
Protein	5 g	Vitamin A	2%
Carbohydrate	30 g	Vitamin C	*
Dietary Fiber	1 g	Thiamine	20%
Fat	3 g	Riboflavin	15%
Polyunsaturated	1 g	Niacin	15%
Saturated	1 g	Calcium	2%
Cholesterol	0 mg	Iron	10%
Sodium	300 mg	*Less than 2% U.S. RDA	
Potassium	100 mg		

DIETARY EXCHANGES: 2 Starch, 1/2 Fat

	SMALL LOAF (8 slices)	LARGE LOAF (12 slices)
Water	½ cup	¾ cup
Buttermilk	⅓ cup	½ cup
Bread flour	2 cups	3 cups
Instant mashed potato flakes	⅓ cup	½ cup
Sugar	1½ tablespoons	2½ tablespoons
Salt	1 teaspoon	1½ teaspoons
Chopped dried chives	1 tablespoon	2 tablespoons
Margarine or butter	2 tablespoons	3 tablespoons
Active dry yeast	1½ teaspoons	2½ teaspoons

1. If bread machine typically uses 2 cups flour, use small loaf recipe. If machine uses 3 cups flour, use large loaf recipe.

2. Follow manufacturer's directions for loading ingredients into machine. Measure ingredients carefully.

3. Select regular, rapid or delayed-time bake cycle and follow manufacturer's directions for starting machine.

HIGH ALTITUDE – Above 3500 Feet: For small loaf, increase water by 1 to 2 tablespoons and decrease yeast by ¼ to ½ teaspoon. For large loaf, increase water by 1½ to 3 tablespoons and decrease yeast by ¼ to ¾ teaspoon. Continue as directed above.

SAGE BREAD

	SMALL LOAF (8 slices)	LARGE LOAF (12 slices)
Water	¾ cup	1¼ cups
Bread flour	2 cups	3 cups
Instant nonfat dry milk	1 tablespoon	1½ tablespoons
Sugar	1 teaspoon	2 teaspoons
Salt	1 teaspoon	1¼ teaspoons
Margarine or butter	1 teaspoon	2 teaspoons
Instant minced onion	1 tablespoon	1½ tablespoons
Dried rosemary leaves	⅛ teaspoon	¼ teaspoon
Ground sage	⅛ teaspoon	¼ teaspoon
Dried thyme leaves	Dash	⅛ teaspoon
White pepper	Dash	⅛ teaspoon
Active dry yeast	1¼ teaspoons	2 teaspoons

*T*his aromatic bread is flavored with sage, rosemary and thyme. All three of these herbs are native to the Mediterranean area and at one time or another were used for medicinal purposes!

NUTRITION INFORMATION PER SERVING:

1 SLICE		PERCENT U.S. RDA	
Calories	140	Protein	6%
Protein	5 g	Vitamin A	*
Carbohydrate	26 g	Vitamin C	*
Dietary Fiber	1 g	Thiamine	20%
Fat	1 g	Riboflavin	10%
Polyunsaturated	0 g	Niacin	15%
Saturated	0 g	Calcium	*
Cholesterol	0 mg	Iron	8%
Sodium	280 mg	*Less than 2% U.S. RDA	
Potassium	65 mg		

DIETARY EXCHANGES: 1-1/2 Starch

1. If bread machine typically uses 2 cups flour, use small loaf recipe. If machine uses 3 cups flour, use large loaf recipe.

2. Follow manufacturer's directions for loading ingredients into machine. Measure ingredients carefully.

3. Select regular, rapid or delayed-time bake cycle and follow manufacturer's directions for starting machine.

HIGH ALTITUDE – Above 3500 Feet: For small loaf, increase water by 1 to 2 tablespoons and decrease yeast by ¼ to ½ teaspoon. For large loaf, increase water by 1½ to 3 tablespoons and decrease yeast by ¼ to ¾ teaspoon. Continue as directed above.

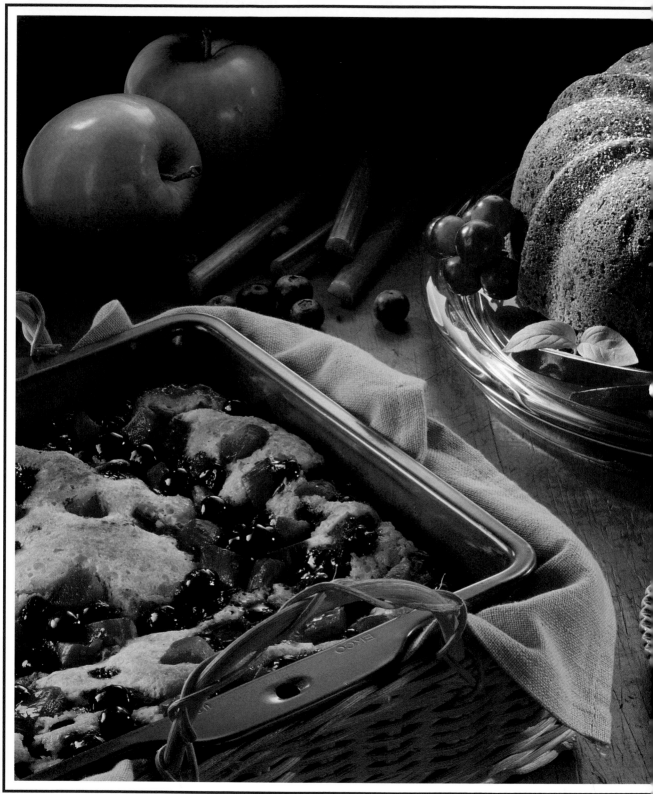

Apple Wheat Ring Cake, p. 180; Saucy Rhu–Berry Cake, p. 177

CAKES, PIES & TARTS

*A*t 10 grams of fat or fewer per serving, our luscious cakes and pies will win raves for their great taste. They're so scrumptious, it's hard to believe these delicacies contain almost half the fat of traditional fare.

TRIPLE TREAT BLUEBERRY SQUARES

This tender, delicious cake has a crisp and chewy macaroon topping with blueberries hidden beneath. It's a wonderful sweet touch at the end of any family meal.

NUTRITION INFORMATION PER SERVING:

1/12 OF RECIPE		PERCENT U.S. RDA	
Calories	230	Protein	4%
Protein	3 g	Vitamin A	*
Carbohydrate	46 g	Vitamin C	2%
Dietary Fiber	2 g	Thiamine	8%
Fat	4 g	Riboflavin	8%
Polyunsaturated	1 g	Niacin	4%
Saturated	3 g	Calcium	*
Cholesterol	35 mg	Iron	6%
Sodium	160 mg	*Less than 2% U.S. RDA	
Potassium	55 mg		

DIETARY EXCHANGES: 1 Starch, 2 Fruit, 1 Fat

CAKE

1¼ **cups all purpose flour**

¾ **cup sugar**

½ **teaspoon salt**

½ **teaspoon baking soda**

½ **cup water**

2 **egg yolks (reserve egg whites for topping)**

FILLING

1 **(21-oz.) can blueberry fruit pie filling**

1 **tablespoon all purpose flour**

1 **teaspoon grated lemon peel**

1 **tablespoon lemon juice**

TOPPING

4 **egg whites (includes 2 reserved whites)**

1 **tablespoon water**

Dash salt

⅓ **cup sugar**

1 **cup coconut**

2 **tablespoons all purpose flour**

2 **tablespoons coconut**

Heat oven to 350°F. Grease 13x9-inch pan. In large bowl, combine all cake ingredients; mix well. Spread batter in greased pan.

In small bowl, combine all filling ingredients; mix well. Drop by tablespoonfuls over batter.

In large bowl, combine egg whites, 1 tablespoon water and dash salt; beat at high speed until soft peaks form. Add ⅓ cup sugar 1 tablespoon at a time, beating at high speed until stiff peaks form. Fold in 1 cup coconut and 2 tablespoons flour. Spread carefully over filling. Sprinkle evenly with 2 tablespoons coconut.

Bake at 350°F. for 25 to 35 minutes or until meringue is golden brown. Serve warm or at room temperature; top with light whipped topping or ice milk, if desired.

12 servings.

HIGH ALTITUDE – Above 3500 Feet: Increase flour in cake to 1⅓ cups; decrease sugar in cake to ⅔ cup. Bake at 375°F. for 25 to 30 minutes.

APPLESAUCE DATE CAKE

2 cups all purpose flour

½ cup quick-cooking rolled oats

2 teaspoons baking soda

1 teaspoon cinnamon

½ teaspoon salt

½ teaspoon cloves

1 cup sugar

6 tablespoons margarine or butter, softened

1 teaspoon vanilla

1 egg

1¾ cups applesauce

1 cup chopped dates

1 to 2 tablespoons powdered sugar

This good-for-you cake is filled with wholesome ingredients such as oats, applesauce and dates. The spicy aroma and flavor will tempt the whole family!

Heat oven to 350°F. Spray 13x9-inch baking pan with nonstick cooking spray. In small bowl, combine flour, oats, baking soda, cinnamon, salt and cloves; set aside. In large bowl, combine sugar and margarine; beat until light and fluffy. Add vanilla and egg; beat well. Add flour mixture alternately with applesauce, beating well after each addition. Stir in dates. Spread batter in spray-coated pan.

Bake at 350°F. for 30 to 40 minutes or until toothpick inserted in center comes out clean. Cool completely. Sprinkle with powdered sugar just before serving.

18 servings.

HIGH ALTITUDE – Above 3500 Feet: Decrease sugar to ⅔ cup. Bake as directed above.

NUTRITION INFORMATION PER SERVING:

1/18 OF RECIPE		PERCENT U.S. RDA	
Calories	190	Protein	4%
Protein	2 g	Vitamin A	2%
Carbohydrate	35 g	Vitamin C	*
Dietary Fiber	2 g	Thiamine	8%
Fat	4 g	Riboflavin	6%
Polyunsaturated	1 g	Niacin	6%
Saturated	1 g	Calcium	2%
Cholesterol	12 mg	Iron	6%
Sodium	140 mg	*Less than 2% U.S. RDA	
Potassium	110 mg		

DIETARY EXCHANGES: 1 Starch, 1 Fruit, 1 Fat

APPLESAUCE SPICE CAKE

This down-home cake is a treat you won't have to say "no thanks" to. Even with a buttery frosting, the recipe weighs in at only 7 grams of fat per serving.

NUTRITION INFORMATION PER SERVING:

1/16 OF RECIPE		PERCENT U.S. RDA	
Calories	310	Protein	4%
Protein	3 g	Vitamin A	2%
Carbohydrate	60 g	Vitamin C	*
Dietary Fiber	1 g	Thiamine	10%
Fat	7 g	Riboflavin	8%
Polyunsaturated	3 g	Niacin	6%
Saturated	2 g	Calcium	2%
Cholesterol	32 mg	Iron	6%
Sodium	260 mg	*Less than 2% U.S. RDA	
Potassium	95 mg		

DIETARY EXCHANGES: 1 Starch, 3 Fruit, 1-1/2 Fat

CAKE

2¼   cups all purpose flour

1½   cups sugar

1   teaspoon baking powder

1   teaspoon baking soda

1   teaspoon salt

2   teaspoons cinnamon

1⅓   cups applesauce

⅓   cup oil

2   eggs

¾   cup (1 medium) chopped peeled apple

½   cup raisins, if desired

BROWNED BUTTER FROSTING

2   tablespoons butter (do not substitute margarine)

2   cups powdered sugar

¼   teaspoon cinnamon

½   teaspoon vanilla

3   to 4 tablespoons apple juice or 2% milk

Heat oven to 350°F. Grease and flour 13x9-inch pan. In large bowl, combine flour, sugar, baking powder, baking soda, salt and 2 teaspoons cinnamon; blend well. Add applesauce, oil and eggs; blend at low speed until moistened. Beat 2 minutes at high speed. Stir in apple and raisins. Pour batter into greased and floured pan.

Bake at 350°F. for 28 to 38 minutes or until toothpick inserted in center comes out clean. Cool completely.

Brown butter in medium saucepan over medium heat until light golden brown, stirring frequently. Remove from heat; cool slightly. Add powdered sugar, ¼ teaspoon cinnamon, vanilla and enough apple juice for desired spreading consistency; mix well. Immediately spread over top of cooled cake. (Frosting sets up quickly.)

16 servings.

HIGH ALTITUDE – Above 3500 Feet: Decrease sugar to 1¼ cups. Bake as directed above.

Applesauce Spice Cake

CRANBERRY UPSIDE-DOWN CAKE

*C*rimson cranberries almost glow when this dessert is turned out of the pan. Although it's perfect for the holiday season, you can enjoy it any time frozen cranberries are available.

NUTRITION INFORMATION PER SERVING:

1/9 OF RECIPE		PERCENT U.S. RDA	
Calories	280	Protein	4%
Protein	3 g	Vitamin A	*
Carbohydrate	54 g	Vitamin C	4%
Dietary Fiber	1 g	Thiamine	10%
Fat	7 g	Riboflavin	8%
Polyunsaturated	2 g	Niacin	4%
Saturated	2 g	Calcium	6%
Cholesterol	25 mg	Iron	6%
Sodium	220 mg	*Less than 2% U.S. RDA	
Potassium	70 mg		

DIETARY EXCHANGES: 1 Starch, 2-1/2 Fruit, 1-1/2 Fat

⅔ cup sugar

2 cups fresh or frozen cranberries

CAKE

1¼ cups all purpose flour

1 cup sugar

1½ teaspoons baking powder

½ teaspoon salt

1 teaspoon grated lemon peel

⅔ cup 2% milk

¼ cup shortening

¼ teaspoon vanilla

1 egg

Heat oven to 350°F. Grease 8-inch square pan. Sprinkle ⅓ cup sugar in pan. Arrange cranberries over sugar; sprinkle with ⅓ cup sugar. Cover with foil. Bake at 350°F. for 30 minutes. Remove foil; cool.

In large bowl, combine all cake ingredients; blend at low speed until moistened. Beat 2 minutes at medium speed. Pour batter evenly over cranberries.

Bake at 350°F. for 40 to 50 minutes or until toothpick inserted in center comes out clean. For easy removal, run knife around edge of pan. Invert onto serving plate, leaving pan over cake for 2 minutes; remove pan. Serve warm or at room temperature.

9 servings.

HIGH ALTITUDE – Above 3500 Feet: Decrease sugar in cake to ¾ cup. Bake as directed above.

SAUCY RHU-BERRY CAKE

¼ cup margarine or butter, melted
1 cup all purpose flour
½ cup sugar
2 teaspoons baking powder
½ cup 2% milk
2 cups fresh or frozen chopped rhubarb
1 cup fresh or frozen blueberries
¾ cup hot apple cider or water
½ cup sugar
   Cinnamon

Heat oven to 350°F. Pour margarine evenly into 9-inch square pan. In medium bowl, combine flour, ½ cup sugar and baking powder; mix well. Stir in milk. Spoon batter into prepared pan. DO NOT MIX. Top with rhubarb and blueberries.

In small bowl or glass measuring cup, combine hot cider and ½ cup sugar; stir until sugar is dissolved. Pour syrup over fruit; sprinkle with cinnamon. Bake at 350°F. for 45 to 55 minutes or until golden brown. Serve warm or at room temperature.
9 servings.

HIGH ALTITUDE – Above 3500 Feet: Decrease baking powder to 1 teaspoon. Bake as directed above.

Although most cooks consider rhubarb a fruit, did you know that it is botanically a vegetable? We've combined rhubarb with blueberries in this delicious dessert. Serve it warm with vanilla ice milk.

NUTRITION INFORMATION PER SERVING:

1/9 OF RECIPE		PERCENT U.S. RDA	
Calories	210	Protein	2%
Protein	2 g	Vitamin A	6%
Carbohydrate	40 g	Vitamin C	4%
Dietary Fiber	1 g	Thiamine	8%
Fat	6 g	Riboflavin	6%
Polyunsaturated	2 g	Niacin	4%
Saturated	1 g	Calcium	10%
Cholesterol	1 mg	Iron	4%
Sodium	180 mg		
Potassium	160 mg		

DIETARY EXCHANGES: 1 Starch, 1-1/2 Fruit, 1 Fat

Saucy Rhu-Berry Cake

LIGHT CHOCOLATE LAYER CAKE

*S*atisfy your chocolate craving and maintain your goal of reduced fat and calories with this rich, chocolaty layer cake. It has about half the fat of a typical chocolate cake.

CAKE
1¾ cups all purpose flour
½ cup unsweetened cocoa
1¼ teaspoons baking soda
½ teaspoon salt
1¼ cups sugar
½ cup margarine or butter, softened
1 teaspoon vanilla
4 egg whites
1 cup buttermilk

FROSTING
2 cups frozen light whipped topping, thawed

Heat oven to 350°F. Grease and flour two 8 or 9-inch round cake pans.* In medium bowl, combine flour, cocoa, baking soda and salt. In large bowl, beat sugar and margarine until light and fluffy. Beat in vanilla and egg whites. Alternately add dry ingredients and buttermilk, beating well after each addition. Spread batter evenly in greased and floured pans.

Bake at 350°F. for 27 to 35 minutes or until toothpick inserted in center comes out clean. Cool 10 minutes; remove from pans. Cool completely. Fill and frost with whipped topping.
12 servings.

TIP:
> * Cake can be baked in greased and floured 13x9-inch pan. Prepare as directed above. Bake at 350°F. for 33 to 40 minutes. Cool completely.

HIGH ALTITUDE – Above 3500 Feet: Decrease sugar to 1 cup. Bake as directed above.

NUTRITION INFORMATION PER SERVING:

1/12 OF RECIPE		PERCENT U.S. RDA	
Calories	260	Protein	6%
Protein	5 g	Vitamin A	6%
Carbohydrate	40 g	Vitamin C	*
Dietary Fiber	2 g	Thiamine	10%
Fat	10 g	Riboflavin	10%
Polyunsaturated	2 g	Niacin	6%
Saturated	3 g	Calcium	4%
Cholesterol	1 mg	Iron	6%
Sodium	370 mg	*Less than 2% U.S. RDA	
Potassium	105 mg		

DIETARY EXCHANGES: 1-1/2 Starch, 1 Fruit, 2 Fat

WHOLE WHEAT WALNUT CRUMB CAKE

STREUSEL

1 cup chopped walnuts
or pecans

⅓ cup firmly packed brown
sugar

1 teaspoon cinnamon

CAKE

2 cups whole wheat flour

1 cup sugar

3 teaspoons baking powder

½ teaspoon salt

1 cup 2% milk

⅓ cup margarine or butter,
softened

1 egg

GLAZE

¾ cup powdered sugar

1 to 2 tablespoons water

This lightly spiced whole wheat cake can be baked in cake layer pans or in a 13x9-inch pan. It's great for picnics.

NUTRITION INFORMATION PER SERVING:		
1/16 OF RECIPE		PERCENT U.S. RDA
Calories	230	Protein	6%
Protein	4 g	Vitamin A	4%
Carbohydrate	36 g	Vitamin C	*
Dietary Fiber	2 g	Thiamine	6%
Fat	9 g	Riboflavin	4%
Polyunsaturated	4 g	Niacin	4%
Saturated	1 g	Calcium	8%
Cholesterol	14 mg	Iron	6%
Sodium	220 mg	*Less than 2% U.S. RDA
Potassium	140 mg	

DIETARY EXCHANGES: 2 Starch, 1-1/2 Fat

Heat oven to 350°F. Grease and flour two 8 or 9-inch round cake pans.* In small bowl, mix all streusel ingredients until well blended; set aside.

In large bowl, combine all cake ingredients. Beat at low speed until moistened; beat 2 minutes at medium speed. Spread about ¾ cup of batter in each greased and floured pan; sprinkle ¼ of streusel mixture evenly over batter in each pan. Carefully spread remaining batter over streusel in each pan; sprinkle with remaining streusel mixture.

Bake at 350°F. for 20 to 30 minutes or until toothpick inserted in center comes out clean. Cool slightly. In small bowl, combine powdered sugar and enough water for desired drizzling consistency; blend until smooth. Drizzle over warm cakes.

2 cakes; 6 to 8 servings each.

TIP:

* Cake can be baked in 13x9-inch pan. Spread half of batter in greased and floured pan; sprinkle half of streusel mixture evenly over batter. Carefully spread remaining batter over streusel; sprinkle with remaining streusel mixture. Bake at 350°F. for 25 to 35 minutes or until toothpick inserted in center comes out clean.

HIGH ALTITUDE – Above 3500 Feet: Increase flour to 2¼ cups. Bake at 375°F. for 20 to 30 minutes.

APPLE WHEAT RING CAKE

*O*ne hundred percent whole wheat goodness and generous amounts of fresh apple make this cake a flavorful way to eat healthier. Take along slices of this moist cake when traveling, hiking or cross-country skiing.

2	**cups whole wheat flour**
¼	**cup wheat germ**
2	**teaspoons baking soda**
1	**teaspoon cinnamon**
½	**teaspoon nutmeg**
½	**teaspoon salt**
3½	**cups diced peeled apples**
1	**cup firmly packed brown sugar**
½	**cup oil**
1	**teaspoon vanilla**
2	**eggs or ½ cup frozen fat-free egg product, thawed**

Heat oven to 350°F. Generously grease and flour 12-cup Bundt® pan. In large bowl, combine flour, wheat germ, baking soda, cinnamon, nutmeg and salt; blend well. In medium bowl, combine apples, brown sugar, oil, vanilla and eggs; mix well. Pour over flour mixture. Stir just until dry ingredients are moistened. Spoon batter into greased and floured pan.

Bake at 350°F. for 30 to 40 minutes or until toothpick inserted in center comes out clean. (Cake will not rise to top of pan.) Cool 15 minutes; invert onto serving plate. Dust with powdered sugar, if desired.

16 servings.

HIGH ALTITUDE – Above 3500 Feet: No change.

NUTRITION INFORMATION PER SERVING:

1/16 OF RECIPE		PERCENT U.S. RDA	
Calories	200	Protein	4%
Protein	3 g	Vitamin A	*
Carbohydrate	29 g	Vitamin C	*
Dietary Fiber	3 g	Thiamine	6%
Fat	8 g	Riboflavin	4%
Polyunsaturated	4 g	Niacin	4%
Saturated	1 g	Calcium	2%
Cholesterol	27 mg	Iron	6%
Sodium	240 mg	*Less than 2% U.S. RDA	
Potassium	160 mg		

DIETARY EXCHANGES: 1 Starch, 1 Fruit, 1-1/2 Fat

Bundt® is a registered trademark of Northland Aluminum Products, Inc., Minneapolis, MN.

WARM CHOCOLATE CINNAMON CAKE

CAKE

- 1 cup all purpose flour
- 1 cup firmly packed brown sugar
- 3 tablespoons unsweetened cocoa
- 1 teaspoon baking soda
- ¾ teaspoon cinnamon
- ¾ cup skim or 2% milk
- ⅓ cup margarine or butter, softened
- 2 teaspoons white vinegar
- 1 teaspoon vanilla
- 2 egg whites

TOPPING

- ½ cup frozen light whipped topping, thawed
- ½ teaspoon cinnamon

Heat oven to 350°F. Spray 9-inch round cake pan with nonstick cooking spray. In large bowl, combine all cake ingredients. Beat at low speed until moistened; beat 2 minutes at medium speed. Pour into spray-coated pan.

Bake at 350°F. for 25 to 30 minutes or until toothpick inserted in center comes out clean.

Meanwhile, combine whipped topping and ½ teaspoon cinnamon. To serve, cut warm cake into wedges; garnish with topping.

10 servings.

HIGH ALTITUDE – Above 3500 Feet: Decrease brown sugar to ¾ cup. Bake as directed above.

How could anyone resist warm, chocolaty cake fresh from the oven? This definitely decadent dessert will have everyone asking for seconds!

NUTRITION INFORMATION PER SERVING:

1/10 OF RECIPE		PERCENT U.S. RDA	
Calories	200	Protein	4%
Protein	3 g	Vitamin A	6%
Carbohydrate	33 g	Vitamin C	*
Dietary Fiber	1 g	Thiamine	6%
Fat	7 g	Riboflavin	8%
Polyunsaturated	2 g	Niacin	4%
Saturated	2 g	Calcium	4%
Cholesterol	0 mg	Iron	8%
Sodium	220 mg	*Less than 2% U.S. RDA	
Potassium	150 mg		

DIETARY EXCHANGES: 1 Starch, 1 Fruit, 1-1/2 Fat

ANGEL FOOD CAKE

*A*ngel food cakes are light, airy cakes made with stiffly beaten egg whites. Because they are prepared with egg whites and no shortening or oil, they contain no fat or cholesterol. The cake is delicious plain or it can be topped with fresh fruit.

NUTRITION INFORMATION PER SERVING:

1/12 OF RECIPE		PERCENT U.S. RDA	
Calories	140	Protein	6%
Protein	4 g	Vitamin A	*
Carbohydrate	32 g	Vitamin C	*
Dietary Fiber	0 g	Thiamine	4%
Fat	0 g	Riboflavin	10%
Polyunsaturated	0 g	Niacin	2%
Saturated	0 g	Calcium	*
Cholesterol	0 mg	Iron	2%
Sodium	100 mg	*Less than 2% U.S. RDA	
Potassium	120 mg		

DIETARY EXCHANGES: 2 Starch

¾   cup all purpose flour

¾   cup sugar

1½   cups (about 12) egg whites, room temperature

1½   teaspoons cream of tartar

¼   teaspoon salt

1½   teaspoons vanilla

½   teaspoon almond extract

¾   cup sugar

Place oven rack at lowest position. Heat oven to 375°F. In small bowl, combine flour and ¾ cup sugar. In large bowl, beat egg whites, cream of tartar, salt, vanilla and almond extract until mixture forms soft peaks. Gradually add ¾ cup sugar, beating at high speed until stiff peaks form. Spoon flour-sugar mixture ¼ cup at a time over beaten egg whites; fold in gently just until blended. Pour batter into ungreased 10-inch tube pan. With knife, cut gently through batter to remove large air bubbles.

Bake at 375°F. on lowest oven rack for 30 to 40 minutes or until crust is golden brown and cracks are very dry. Immediately invert cake onto funnel or soft drink bottle; let hang until completely cool. Remove cooled cake from pan.

12 servings.

TIP:

To make loaves, bake in 2 ungreased 9x5-inch loaf pans for 25 to 30 minutes.

HIGH ALTITUDE − Above 3500 Feet: Increase flour to 1 cup; increase egg whites to 1¾ cups (about 13). Bake at 400°F. for 30 to 35 minutes.

VARIATION:

CHOCOLATE-CHERRY ANGEL FOOD CAKE: Fold ⅓ cup well-drained, chopped maraschino cherries and 1 oz. grated semi-sweet chocolate into batter. Bake as directed above. In small saucepan over low heat, melt 2 tablespoons margarine or butter and 1 oz. semi-sweet chocolate with 1 tablespoon corn syrup. Stir in 1 cup powdered sugar and 2 to 3 tablespoons maraschino cherry liquid until smooth and of desired drizzling consistency. Immediately drizzle over cooled cake.

PASTRY FOR ONE-CRUST PIE OR TART

1 **cup all purpose flour**

½ **teaspoon salt**

⅓ **cup shortening**

2 **to 4 tablespoons ice water**

*O*ur basic pastry recipe with whole wheat, extra flaky and food processor variations shows the way to numerous combinations of pie crusts to mix and match with your favorite fillings.

In medium bowl, combine flour and salt. Using pastry blender or fork, cut in shortening until mixture resembles coarse crumbs. Sprinkle flour mixture with water, 1 tablespoon at a time, while tossing and mixing lightly with fork. Add water until dough is just moist enough to form a ball when lightly pressed together. (Too much water causes dough to become sticky and tough; too little water causes edges to crack and pastry to tear easily while rolling.)

Shape dough into ball. Flatten ball to ½-inch thickness, rounding and smoothing edges. On lightly floured surface, roll from center to edge into 11-inch circle. Fold pastry in half; place in 9-inch pie pan or 9 or 10-inch tart pan. Unfold; gently press in bottom and up sides of pan. Do not stretch.

If using pie pan, fold edge under to form a standing rim; flute edges. If using tart pan, trim pastry edges if necessary.

For Filled One-Crust Pie: Fill and bake as directed in recipe.

For Baked Pie Shell (Unfilled): Prick bottom and sides of pastry generously with fork. Bake at 450°F. for 9 to 12 minutes or until light golden brown; cool. Continue as directed in recipe. **One-crust pastry.**

🍲 FOOD PROCESSOR DIRECTIONS: Place flour, salt and shortening in processor bowl fitted with steel blade. Process 20 to 30 seconds until mixture resembles coarse crumbs. With machine running, add *minimum* amount of ice water all at once through feed tube. Process 20 to 30 seconds or just until ball forms. (If ball does not form in 30 seconds, shape into ball with hands.) Wrap dough in plastic wrap; refrigerate 30 minutes or freeze 10 minutes before continuing as directed above.

VARIATIONS:

EXTRA FLAKY PASTRY: Add 1 teaspoon sugar with flour and 1 teaspoon vinegar with water.

WHOLE WHEAT PASTRY: Substitute up to ½ cup whole wheat flour for all purpose flour. Additional water may be necessary.

NUTRITION INFORMATION PER SERVING:			
1/8 OF RECIPE		PERCENT U.S. RDA	
Calories	130	Protein	2%
Protein	2 g	Vitamin A	*
Carbohydrate	12 g	Vitamin C	*
Dietary Fiber	0 g	Thiamine	8%
Fat	8 g	Riboflavin	4%
Polyunsaturated	2 g	Niacin	4%
Saturated	2 g	Calcium	*
Cholesterol	0 mg	Iron	4%
Sodium	135 mg	*Less than 2% U.S. RDA	
Potassium	15 mg		

DIETARY EXCHANGES: 1 Starch, 1-1/2 Fat

Sunshine Paradise Meringue Pie

SUNSHINE PARADISE MERINGUE PIE

MERINGUE

- 3 egg whites
- ¼ teaspoon cream of tartar
- ¼ to ½ teaspoon cinnamon
- ¾ cup sugar

FILLING

- ⅔ cup sugar
- 2 tablespoons cornstarch
- 1 (8-oz.) can crushed pineapple, drained, reserving liquid
- ⅔ cup orange juice
- 2 egg yolks, slightly beaten
- 1 (11-oz.) can mandarin orange segments, drained
- 1 medium banana, sliced
- ½ cup macadamia nuts
- 2 tablespoons coconut

Even before the rotary egg beater was invented in 1870, meringue tarts and crusts were popular. For a successful meringue crust, it is important to gradually beat in the sugar and allow the standing time in the oven after baking.

Heat oven to 275°F. Line cookie sheet with brown or parchment paper. Draw 10-inch circle on paper. In small bowl, beat egg whites, cream of tartar and cinnamon until foamy. Gradually add ¾ cup sugar 2 tablespoons at a time, beating continuously until sugar is dissolved and stiff peaks form. DO NOT UNDERBEAT. Spread ⅔ of meringue onto 10-inch circle on paper-lined cookie sheet. Using remaining ⅓ of meringue, spoon or pipe dollops around edge of circle.

Bake at 275°F. for 30 minutes. Turn oven off; let meringue set in oven with door closed for 1 hour. Remove from oven; cool completely. Carefully remove paper from meringue shell; place shell on serving plate.

In medium saucepan, combine ⅔ cup sugar and cornstarch. Stir in reserved pineapple liquid, orange juice and egg yolks. Cook over medium heat until mixture boils and thickens, stirring constantly. Boil 1 minute; remove from heat. Fold in pineapple, orange segments and banana slices. Spoon into meringue shell. Cool. Cover with plastic wrap; refrigerate 1 to 2 hours. To serve, sprinkle with nuts and coconut; cut into wedges.
10 to 12 servings.

TIP:
The meringue shell can be made a day ahead. Cover loosely; store at room temperature.

HIGH ALTITUDE – Above 3500 Feet: No change.

NUTRITION INFORMATION PER SERVING:

1/12 OF RECIPE		PERCENT U.S. RDA	
Calories	190	Protein	2%
Protein	2 g	Vitamin A	4%
Carbohydrate	35 g	Vitamin C	15%
Dietary Fiber	1 g	Thiamine	4%
Fat	5 g	Riboflavin	4%
Polyunsaturated	0 g	Niacin	*
Saturated	1 g	Calcium	*
Cholesterol	36 mg	Iron	2%
Sodium	15 mg	*Less than 2% U.S. RDA	
Potassium	170 mg		

DIETARY EXCHANGES: 1/2 Starch, 2 Fruit, 1 Fat

NEW-FASHIONED PUMPKIN PIE

*Y*ou'll never guess this all-time favorite pie is made with evaporated skimmed milk and fat-free egg product. It's every bit as delicious as the traditional version—with much less fat!

CRUST

Pastry for One-Crust Pie (p. 183)

FILLING

¾ **cup sugar**

1½ **teaspoons pumpkin pie spice**

½ **teaspoon salt**

1 **(16-oz.) can (2 cups) pumpkin**

1 **(12-oz.) can (1½ cups) evaporated skimmed milk**

½ **cup frozen fat-free egg product, thawed, or 3 egg whites, slightly beaten**

TOPPING

1 **cup frozen light whipped topping, thawed, or 1 pint frozen nonfat vanilla yogurt, if desired***

Prepare pastry for *Filled One-Crust Pie* using 9-inch pie pan.

Heat oven to 425°F. In large bowl, combine all filling ingredients; blend well. Pour into pastry-lined pan. Carefully transfer to oven rack. Bake at 425°F. for 15 minutes. Reduce oven temperature to 350°F.; bake an additional 40 to 50 minutes or until knife inserted near center comes out clean. Cool; refrigerate until serving time. Serve with whipped topping. Store in refrigerator.

8 to 10 servings.

TIP:

* For a fluffy topping made with frozen yogurt, let yogurt stand at room temperature for 10 to 15 minutes or until softened. Place in small bowl; beat at high speed for 1 to 2 minutes or just until fluffy.

NUTRITION INFORMATION PER SERVING:			
1/10 OF RECIPE		**PERCENT U.S. RDA**	
Calories	230	Protein	8%
Protein	6 g	Vitamin A	210%
Carbohydrate	34 g	Vitamin C	2%
Dietary Fiber	2 g	Thiamine	10%
Fat	8 g	Riboflavin	15%
Polyunsaturated	2 g	Niacin	4%
Saturated	3 g	Calcium	15%
Cholesterol	1 mg	Iron	8%
Sodium	280 mg		
Potassium	260 mg		

DIETARY EXCHANGES: 2 Starch, 1-1/2 Fat

New-Fashioned Pumpkin Pie

SLIM CHOCOLATE CHEESECAKE PIE

*S*atisfy your chocolate craving and maintain your goal of reduced fat with this rich, creamy cheesecake. A dusting of powdered sugar through a stencil design makes a nice garnish if you choose not to use the fruit topping.

NUTRITION INFORMATION PER SERVING:

1/16 OF RECIPE		PERCENT U.S. RDA	
Calories	170	Protein	8%
Protein	6 g	Vitamin A	8%
Carbohydrate	29 g	Vitamin C	35%
Dietary Fiber	2 g	Thiamine	4%
Fat	5 g	Riboflavin	6%
Polyunsaturated	0 g	Niacin	2%
Saturated	2 g	Calcium	8%
Cholesterol	15 mg	Iron	4%
Sodium	150 mg		
Potassium	220 mg		

DIETARY EXCHANGES: 1 Starch, 1/2 Fruit, 1 Fat

CRUST

1 cup graham cracker crumbs

1 tablespoon sugar

CHEESECAKE

1 (15-oz.) container light ricotta cheese

1 cup sugar

½ cup unsweetened cocoa

1 (8-oz.) pkg. light cream cheese (Neufchatel), softened

½ cup frozen fat-free egg product, thawed, or 2 egg whites

⅓ cup skim or 2% milk

2 teaspoons vanilla

TRIPLE FRUIT TOPPING

1 cup orange juice

4 teaspoons cornstarch

2 (11-oz.) cans mandarin orange segments, drained

2 kiwifruit, peeled, sliced

1 cup sliced strawberries

FOOD PROCESSOR DIRECTIONS: Heat oven to 325°F. Spray 9-inch pie pan thoroughly (6 to 8 seconds) with nonstick cooking spray. In small bowl, combine crust ingredients; mix well. Add cookie crumbs; tilt pan to coat evenly. (Avoid tapping pan, which will loosen crumbs from sides.) Gently press crumbs against sides and bottom of pan. (Crumbs will stick loosely together but will be held firmly in place when filling is added.) Set aside.

In food processor bowl with metal blade, process ricotta cheese until smooth.* Add 1 cup sugar, cocoa and cream cheese; process until smooth. Add egg product, milk and vanilla; process until blended. Carefully pour mixture into crust.

Bake at 325°F. for 45 to 55 minutes or until edges are firm. (Center will be soft.) Turn oven off; let cheesecake stand in oven 30 minutes with door open at least 4 inches. Remove from oven; cool to room temperature on wire rack. Cover; refrigerate at least 2 hours.

To prepare topping, in small saucepan cook orange juice and cornstarch over medium heat until mixture thickens and comes to a full boil. Remove from heat; cool to room temperature. Fold in orange segments, kiwifruit and strawberries. Serve over cheesecake. Store in refrigerator.

16 servings.

TIP:

* Ricotta cheese can be pureed in blender container in 2 batches, using half of the milk for each batch. Transfer pureed ricotta mixture to large bowl. Continue as directed using an electric mixer.

Slim Chocolate Cheesecake Pie

STRAWBERRY LEMON TART

*I*mpressive and easy to make ahead, this luscious spring dessert is a sure winner for any menu. Strawberries are a great source of vitamin C. Be sure to use the freshest, prettiest strawberries available for a luscious presentation.

NUTRITION INFORMATION PER SERVING:

1/10 OF RECIPE		PERCENT U.S. RDA	
Calories	200	Protein	6%
Protein	4 g	Vitamin A	6%
Carbohydrate	32 g	Vitamin C	25%
Dietary Fiber	1 g	Thiamine	8%
Fat	6 g	Riboflavin	10%
Polyunsaturated	2 g	Niacin	4%
Saturated	1 g	Calcium	2%
Cholesterol	64 mg	Iron	6%
Sodium	125 mg		
Potassium	95 mg		

DIETARY EXCHANGES: 1 Starch, 1 Fruit, 1 Fat

CRUST

- 1 **cup all purpose flour**
- 1 **tablespoon sugar**
- 1 **teaspoon grated lemon peel**
- ⅛ **teaspoon salt**
- ¼ **cup margarine or butter**
- 1 **egg, slightly beaten**
- 2 **to 6 teaspoons water**

FILLING

- 2 **eggs, slightly beaten**
- ¾ **cup sugar**
- 2 **tablespoons all purpose flour**
- 2 **teaspoons grated lemon peel**
- ½ **teaspoon baking powder**
- 2 **tablespoons lemon juice**

TOPPING

- 2 **cups strawberries, halved**
- 2 **tablespoons apple jelly, melted**

Heat oven to 375°F. In medium bowl, combine 1 cup flour, 1 tablespoon sugar, 1 teaspoon lemon peel and salt; mix well. Using pastry blender or fork, cut in margarine until mixture resembles coarse crumbs. With fork, stir in 1 egg and enough water until mixture forms a ball. Press in bottom and up sides of 9½ or 10-inch tart pan with removable bottom. Bake at 375°F. for 15 minutes.

Reduce oven temperature to 350°F. In medium bowl, combine all filling ingredients except lemon juice; blend well. Stir in lemon juice. Pour mixture over warm crust. Bake at 350°F. for 20 to 25 minutes or until top is light golden brown. Cool to room temperature. Arrange strawberries over top; brush with melted jelly. Store in refrigerator.

10 servings.

HIGH ALTITUDE – Above 3500 Feet: No change.

Strawberry Lemon Tart

APRICOT MERINGUE TART

This meringue tart is an ideal low-fat, low-calorie dessert because it contains no fat and has a low calorie count. You'll enjoy the melt-in-your-mouth cinnamon-flavored meringue and tart apricot filling.

MERINGUE

- **3 egg whites**
- **¼ teaspoon cream of tartar**
- **½ teaspoon cinnamon**
- **¾ cup sugar**

FILLING

- **½ cup apricot preserves**
- **6 to 9 apricots, halved, pitted, or 16-oz. can apricot halves, drained**

Heat oven to 275°F. Line cookie sheet with brown paper. Draw 10-inch circle on paper. In small bowl, beat egg whites, cream of tartar and cinnamon until foamy. Gradually add sugar, beating until stiff peaks form. Spread ⅔ of meringue into 10-inch circle on paper-lined cookie sheet. Using remaining ⅓ of meringue, spoon or pipe dollops around top edge of circle to form rim.

Bake at 275°F. for 30 minutes. Turn oven off; leave meringue in oven with door closed for an additional 1 hour. Remove from oven; cool completely.

Carefully remove paper from meringue; place on serving plate. If desired, reserve 2 tablespoons of the preserves for glaze; spread remaining preserves in bottom of meringue shell. Arrange apricot halves cut side down over preserves. Melt reserved preserves; brush over apricot halves. Serve immediately or refrigerate up to 3 hours.

12 servings.

NUTRITION INFORMATION PER SERVING:

1/12 OF RECIPE		PERCENT U.S. RDA	
Calories	100	Protein	2%
Protein	1 g	Vitamin A	15%
Carbohydrate	24 g	Vitamin C	4%
Dietary Fiber	1 g	Thiamine	*
Fat	0 g	Riboflavin	2%
Polyunsaturated	0 g	Niacin	*
Saturated	0 g	Calcium	*
Cholesterol	0 mg	Iron	*
Sodium	20 mg	*Less than 2% U.S. RDA	
Potassium	110 mg		

DIETARY EXCHANGES: 1-1/2 Fruit

HEALTH NOTES
CHOLESTEROL CRUNCHING

Health experts suggest that limiting daily dietary cholesterol consumption to 300 milligrams is one way to keep blood cholesterol levels in check. But counting cholesterol is tedious and may not be as effective as focusing on a low-fat diet. Why? Because low-fat diets are typically low in cholesterol as well as saturated fat. Too much saturated fat in the diet is the primary cause of high blood cholesterol levels. To keep blood cholesterol levels under control, eat more low-fat foods, such as bread, which typically contains little or no cholesterol. And remember to work in at least five servings of fruits and vegetables daily: Eating more of these foods leaves little room for fatty meals and snacks.

MINCE APPLE TARTS

CRUST

 2 **cups all purpose flour**
 1 **teaspoon salt**
 ⅔ **cup shortening**
 5 **to 7 tablespoons ice water**

FILLING

 ¾ **cup prepared mincemeat**
 ½ **cup chopped peeled apple**
 ¼ **cup finely chopped walnuts**
 1 **tablespoon brandy or ½ teaspoon brandy extract**

*T*iny pastry cutouts top these delectable fruit tarts. Use various shapes of canape cutters (such as hearts, stars, diamonds and triangles) that are about one inch in diameter.

Heat oven to 400°F. In medium bowl, combine flour and salt. Using pastry blender or fork, cut in shortening until mixture resembles coarse crumbs. Sprinkle flour mixture with water, 1 tablespoon at a time, while tossing and mixing lightly with fork. Add water until dough is just moist enough to form a ball when lightly pressed together. (Too much water causes dough to become sticky and tough; too little water causes edges to crack and pastry to tear easily while rolling.)

Shape dough into 2 balls. Flatten 1 ball to ½-inch thickness, rounding and smoothing edges. On lightly floured surface, roll from center to edge into 11-inch circle. Repeat with remaining dough. Using 2½-inch round cookie cutter, cut 12 rounds from each pastry circle. Press into bottom and up sides of 24 ungreased miniature muffin cups; set aside.

Using canape cutters of desired shapes, cut 24 shapes from remaining pastry. Place on ungreased cookie sheet. Sprinkle with sugar. Bake cutouts at 400°F. for 7 to 9 minutes or until light golden brown. Remove from cookie sheet; cool.

In small bowl, combine all filling ingredients. Spoon into pastry-lined cups, filling each ⅔ full. Bake at 400°F. for 15 to 25 minutes or until filling is bubbly and crust is light golden brown. Cool 2 minutes. Remove from pans. Top each tart with pastry cutout.

24 tarts.

NUTRITION INFORMATION PER SERVING:			
1 TART		**PERCENT U.S. RDA**	
Calories	120	Protein	2%
Protein	1 g	Vitamin A	*
Carbohydrate	14 g	Vitamin C	*
Dietary Fiber	0 g	Thiamine	6%
Fat	7 g	Riboflavin	2%
Polyunsaturated	2 g	Niacin	2%
Saturated	1 g	Calcium	*
Cholesterol	0 mg	Iron	4%
Sodium	115 mg	*Less than 2% U.S. RDA	
Potassium	40 mg		

DIETARY EXCHANGES: 1 Starch, 1 Fat

CREAMY LEMON LIME TARTS

*S*oft meringues are used to top pies, puddings or tarts such as these. Always spoon the meringue over the hot filling and spread until it touches the crust. This produces a tight seal and helps prevent shrinkage during baking. For that extra flair, use a medium-sized star tip to pipe the meringue onto your filling.

NUTRITION INFORMATION PER SERVING:

1 TART		PERCENT U.S. RDA	
Calories	270	Protein	4%
Protein	3 g	Vitamin A	6%
Carbohydrate	46 g	Vitamin C	4%
Dietary Fiber	0 g	Thiamine	2%
Fat	8 g	Riboflavin	8%
Polyunsaturated	2 g	Niacin	2%
Saturated	2 g	Calcium	2%
Cholesterol	73 mg	Iron	2%
Sodium	240 mg		
Potassium	80 mg		

DIETARY EXCHANGES: 1 Starch, 2 Fruit, 1-1/2 Fat

FILLING

¾ cup sugar
3 tablespoons cornstarch
¼ teaspoon salt
½ cup cold water
¼ cup 2% milk
2 egg yolks
1 tablespoon margarine or butter
2 tablespoons fresh lemon juice
2 tablespoons fresh lime juice
1 teaspoon grated lime peel

CRUSTS

1 (4-oz.) pkg. (6) individual graham cracker pie shells

MERINGUE

2 egg whites, room temperature
⅛ teaspoon cream of tartar
2 tablespoons sugar

In small saucepan, combine ¾ cup sugar, cornstarch and salt; mix well. Gradually stir in water and milk until smooth. Cook over medium heat until mixture boils, stirring constantly; boil 1 minute, stirring constantly. Remove from heat. In small bowl, beat egg yolks; stir about ¼ cup of hot mixture into egg yolks. Gradually stir yolk mixture into hot mixture. Cook over medium-low heat until mixture boils, stirring constantly. Boil 1 minute, stirring constantly. Remove from heat; stir in margarine, lemon juice, lime juice and lime peel. Cool slightly, about 15 minutes. Pour into pie shells.

Heat oven to 350°F. In small deep bowl, beat egg whites and cream of tartar at medium speed until soft peaks form, about 1 minute. Add 2 tablespoons sugar, 1 tablespoon at a time, beating at high speed until stiff glossy peaks form and sugar is dissolved. Spoon or pipe meringue onto hot filling, spreading or piping to edge of crust to seal well and prevent shrinkage. If meringue was spread, use narrow spatula or knife to swirl.

Bake at 350°F. for 12 to 15 minutes or until peaks of meringue are light golden brown. Cool completely. Refrigerate 2 hours or until filling is set. Store in refrigerator.
6 tarts.

ORANGE PEAR TART

CRUST

Pastry for One-Crust Pie (p. 183)

FILLING

1 envelope unflavored gelatin

2 tablespoons sugar

¾ cup orange juice

1 (16-oz.) container vanilla yogurt

1 (16-oz.) can pear halves, well drained, thinly sliced

2 orange slices, peeled, cut into sixths

GLAZE

1 tablespoon apricot preserves

2 teaspoons orange juice

This light dessert is pretty enough for company but easy enough to prepare for a busy-day family dinner.

NUTRITION INFORMATION PER SERVING:			
1/10 OF RECIPE		**PERCENT U.S. RDA**	
Calories	180	Protein	6%
Protein	4 g	Vitamin A	*
Carbohydrate	26 g	Vitamin C	10%
Dietary Fiber	1 g	Thiamine	8%
Fat	7 g	Riboflavin	10%
Polyunsaturated	2 g	Niacin	4%
Saturated	2 g	Calcium	8%
Cholesterol	2 mg	Iron	4%
Sodium	140 mg	*Less than 2% U.S. RDA	
Potassium	180 mg		

DIETARY EXCHANGES: 1 Starch, 1/2 Fruit, 1-1/2 Fat

Prepare and bake pastry as directed for *Baked Pie Shell* using 10-inch tart pan with removable bottom; cool.

In small saucepan, combine gelatin, sugar and ¼ cup of the orange juice; let stand 1 minute. Stir over medium heat until gelatin is dissolved. Cool slightly. Stir in remaining ½ cup orange juice and yogurt. Pour into cooled baked shell. Refrigerate until filling is firm.

Shortly before serving, arrange pear slices in concentric circles over tart. Insert orange pieces between pear slices. In small saucepan, heat preserves with 2 teaspoons orange juice until melted. Cool slightly. Strain mixture, if desired. Brush over fruit. Refrigerate until serving time.

10 servings.

Bavarian Apple Tart

BAVARIAN APPLE TART

CRUST

1½ cups all purpose flour

½ cup sugar

½ cup margarine or butter, softened

1 egg

¼ teaspoon almond extract

FILLING

½ cup golden or dark raisins

⅓ cup sliced almonds

2 large apples, peeled, cored and cut into ¼-inch slices

2 teaspoons cornstarch

¼ cup 2% milk

1 tablespoon lemon juice

¼ teaspoon almond extract

¼ teaspoon vanilla

1 (8-oz.) container vanilla yogurt

1 egg, beaten

¼ cup apricot preserves, melted

Granny Smith or Rome Beauty apples are a good choice for this yogurt custard tart. These varieties of apples are wonderfully tart, will keep their firm texture when baked, and are widely available throughout the country.

NUTRITION INFORMATION PER SERVING:

1/12 OF RECIPE		PERCENT U.S. RDA	
Calories	250	Protein	6%
Protein	5 g	Vitamin A	8%
Carbohydrate	37 g	Vitamin C	2%
Dietary Fiber	2 g	Thiamine	10%
Fat	10 g	Riboflavin	10%
Polyunsaturated	3 g	Niacin	6%
Saturated	2 g	Calcium	6%
Cholesterol	37 mg	Iron	6%
Sodium	120 mg		
Potassium	190 mg		

DIETARY EXCHANGES: 1-1/2 Starch, 1/2 Fruit, 2 Fat

Heat oven to 375°F. In large bowl, combine flour, sugar and margarine; beat at low speed until well blended. Beat in 1 egg and ¼ teaspoon almond extract until crumbly. Press crumb mixture in bottom and 1½ inches up sides of ungreased 9-inch springform pan. Sprinkle raisins and almonds onto pastry. Arrange apple slices over raisins and almonds in desired pattern.

In medium bowl, dissolve cornstarch in milk. Add lemon juice, ¼ teaspoon almond extract, vanilla, yogurt and 1 egg; blend well. Pour over apples.

Bake at 375°F. for 55 to 65 minutes or until apples are tender. Cool 30 minutes; remove sides of pan. Brush preserves over apples. Garnish with whipped topping, if desired. Store in refrigerator. **10 to 12 servings.**

APPLE CIDER TARTLETS

*B*ake these flaky tartlets ahead and freeze them for your holiday cookie tray or dessert buffet. For a pretty presentation, pipe whipped topping on each one.

NUTRITION INFORMATION PER SERVING:

1 TARTLET		PERCENT U.S. RDA	
Calories	130	Protein	2%
Protein	1 g	Vitamin A	*
Carbohydrate	15 g	Vitamin C	*
Dietary Fiber	0 g	Thiamine	6%
Fat	7 g	Riboflavin	4%
Polyunsaturated	2 g	Niacin	2%
Saturated	2 g	Calcium	*
Cholesterol	9 mg	Iron	2%
Sodium	105 mg	*Less than 2% U.S. RDA	
Potassium	65 mg		

DIETARY EXCHANGES: 1 Starch, 1-1/2 Fat

CRUST
2 cups all purpose flour

1 teaspoon salt

⅔ cup shortening

5 to 7 tablespoons ice water

FILLING
¾ cup frozen apple juice concentrate, thawed

⅓ cup firmly packed brown sugar

¼ teaspoon cinnamon

1 tablespoon margarine or butter, melted

½ teaspoon vanilla

1 egg

1 cup frozen light whipped topping, thawed, if desired

Heat oven to 400°F. In medium bowl, combine flour and salt. Using pastry blender or fork, cut in shortening until mixture resembles coarse crumbs. Sprinkle flour mixture with water, 1 tablespoon at a time, while tossing and mixing lightly with fork. Add water until dough is just moist enough to form a ball when lightly pressed together. (Too much water causes dough to become sticky and tough; too little water causes edges to crack and pastry to tear easily while rolling.)

Shape dough into 2 balls. Flatten 1 ball to ½-inch thickness, rounding and smoothing edges. On lightly floured surface, roll from center to edge into 11-inch circle. Repeat with remaining dough. Using 2½-inch round cookie cutter, cut 12 rounds from each pastry circle. Press into bottom and up sides of 24 ungreased miniature muffin cups until pastry extends ¼ inch above each cup; set aside.

In small bowl, combine all filling ingredients except whipped topping. Spoon scant 1 tablespoon filling into each pastry-lined cup, filling each ¾ full.

Bake at 400°F. for 17 to 24 minutes or until filling is set and crust is light golden brown. Cool 2 minutes; remove from pans. When ready to serve, pipe or spoon whipped topping onto each tart. Store in refrigerator.

24 tartlets.

SENSATIONAL BLACKBERRY TART

CRUST

Pastry for One-Crust Pie (p. 183)

FILLING

4 cups (2 pints) fresh blackberries or raspberries, or 3 cups blueberries*

¼ cup sugar

2 tablespoons cornstarch

¾ cup water

½ cup blackberry wine

Prepare and bake pastry as directed for *Baked Pie Shell* using 9-inch tart pan with removable bottom; cool.

Arrange blackberries in bottom of cooled baked shell. In small saucepan, combine sugar and cornstarch; mix well. Stir in water and wine. Bring to a boil over medium-high heat; cook, stirring constantly, until thickened. Pour over berries. Refrigerate until set. **10 servings.**

TIP:

* When substituting blueberries for blackberries, fold blueberries into thickened wine glaze and spoon into cooled baked shell.

Also called bramble because of the thorny bushes it grows on, the black-berry is the largest of the wild berries. The combination of these sweet and tangy berries and blackberry wine is indescribable!

NUTRITION INFORMATION PER SERVING:

1/10 OF RECIPE		PERCENT U.S. RDA	
Calories	180	Protein	2%
Protein	2 g	Vitamin A	*
Carbohydrate	25 g	Vitamin C	15%
Dietary Fiber	3 g	Thiamine	8%
Fat	7 g	Riboflavin	4%
Polyunsaturated	2 g	Niacin	4%
Saturated	2 g	Calcium	2%
Cholesterol	0 mg	Iron	4%
Sodium	110 mg	*Less than 2% U.S. RDA	
Potassium	140 mg		

DIETARY EXCHANGES: 1 Starch, 1/2 Fruit, 1-1/2 Fat

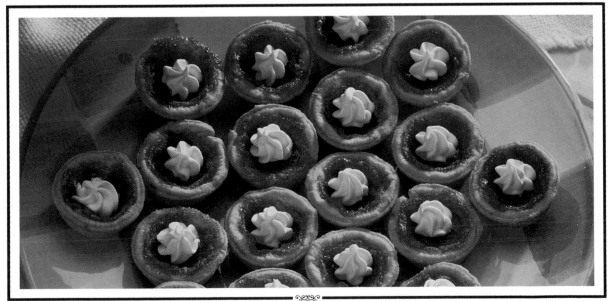

Apple Cider Tartlets, p. 198

California Orange Ricotta Cheesecake with Strawberry Sauce, p. 230; Individual Hot Fudge Sundae Cakes, p. 238

DESSERTS

*F*or a guilt-free grand finale to any meal, serve a delectable dessert with no more than 10 grams of fat per serving. You'll be happy to know these recipes contain considerably less fat than typical desserts, which have as much as 30 grams per serving!

GRAPEFRUIT BAKED ALASKAS

*T*raditionally, baked Alaska is an intriguing dessert of sponge cake and ice cream all baked in an airy meringue. This unusual version of baked Alaska combines grapefruit halves with healthful frozen yogurt and a golden meringue. It's a great choice for a sit-down brunch menu.

2 **cups frozen raspberry, mixed berry, orange or lime yogurt**
2 **medium grapefruit**
2 **egg whites**
¼ **teaspoon cream of tartar**
  Dash salt
¼ **cup sugar**

Scoop yogurt into 4 paper baking cups; wrap each in foil. Freeze until very firm, about 2 to 3 hours.

Cut each grapefruit in half crosswise; remove seeds and cut around sections to loosen completely. Cover; refrigerate until ready to bake.

In small bowl, beat egg whites until soft peaks form. Add cream of tartar and salt. Gradually add sugar 1 tablespoon at a time, beating continuously until stiff peaks form and mixture is glossy.

Heat oven to 400°F. Place grapefruit halves in 9-inch square pan. Remove yogurt balls from freezer; remove foil and gently peel off paper baking cups. Place 1 yogurt ball on top of each grapefruit half. Working quickly, spoon ¼ of meringue over each yogurt ball; spread to cover ball completely, sealing meringue to edges of grapefruit. Decoratively swirl tops of meringue with back of spoon. Bake at 400°F. for 6 to 8 minutes or until well browned. Serve immediately.

4 servings.

NUTRITION INFORMATION PER SERVING:

1/4 OF RECIPE		PERCENT U.S. RDA	
Calories	190	Protein	8%
Protein	5 g	Vitamin A	2%
Carbohydrate	43 g	Vitamin C	50%
Dietary Fiber	1 g	Thiamine	6%
Fat	0 g	Riboflavin	20%
Polyunsaturated	0 g	Niacin	*
Saturated	0 g	Calcium	10%
Cholesterol	0 mg	Iron	*
Sodium	120 mg	*Less than 2% U.S. RDA	
Potassium	220 mg		

DIETARY EXCHANGES: 1-1/2 Starch, 1 Fruit

FRUIT-FILLED CHOCOLATE MERINGUES

MERINGUES

2 egg whites

¼ teaspoon salt

¼ teaspoon vinegar

½ cup sugar

½ teaspoon vanilla

1 tablespoon unsweetened cocoa

FILLING

1 to 1½ cups assorted fresh fruits (peach or kiwifruit slices, strawberries, blueberries, grapes and/or raspberries)

½ cup purchased fudge sauce, if desired

Heat oven to 275°F. Line cookie sheet with parchment paper. In small bowl, beat egg whites, salt and vinegar until foamy. Gradually add sugar and vanilla, beating until stiff peaks form. Sift cocoa over beaten egg whites; fold into mixture. Drop 6 heaping tablespoonfuls meringue onto parchment-lined cookie sheet. Make deep well in center of each, spreading meringue to form 3-inch circles.*

Bake at 275°F. for 45 minutes or until crisp. Turn oven off; leave meringues in oven with door closed for 1½ hours. Remove meringues from oven; cool completely. Remove from parchment paper. To serve, fill meringues with fresh fruit; serve with fudge sauce.

6 servings.

TIP:

* Meringue can be spooned into decorating bag with large star tip. Pipe six 3-inch circles; pipe meringue to fill in bottoms.

When making meringues, be sure to add the sugar about 1 tablespoon at a time so that it dissolves completely. Serve these lovely chocolate-flavored meringues with any fresh fruit that is in season. If you're watching fat and calories, omit the fudge sauce.

NUTRITION INFORMATION PER SERVING:			
1/6 OF RECIPE		PERCENT U.S. RDA	
Calories	180	Protein	4%
Protein	3 g	Vitamin A	*
Carbohydrate	37 g	Vitamin C	25%
Dietary Fiber	2 g	Thiamine	*
Fat	4 g	Riboflavin	8%
Polyunsaturated	1 g	Niacin	*
Saturated	1 g	Calcium	2%
Cholesterol	3 mg	Iron	2%
Sodium	140 mg	*Less than 2% U.S. RDA	
Potassium	160 mg		

DIETARY EXCHANGES: 2-1/2 Fruit, 1 Fat

Strawberry Meringue Torte

STRAWBERRY MERINGUE TORTE

MERINGUE

   6 egg whites
   ½ teaspoon cream of tartar
      Dash salt
1½ cups sugar
   ½ teaspoon vanilla

FILLING

   3 cups half-and-half
   1 (5¼-oz.) pkg. instant vanilla pudding and pie filling mix
   1 teaspoon almond extract

TOPPING

   3 cups strawberries, halved
   2 tablespoons currant jelly, if desired

Heat oven to 275°F. Line 2 cookie sheets with brown or parchment paper. In large bowl, beat egg whites, cream of tartar and salt until frothy. Gradually add sugar, beating continuously until stiff peaks form, about 10 minutes. Beat in vanilla. Spoon half of meringue mixture onto each paper-lined sheet. Shape into two 9-inch circles, building up sides slightly with back of spoon.

Bake at 275°F. for 1¼ hours. Turn oven off; leave meringues in oven with door closed for 2 hours. Remove from oven; cool completely. Remove meringues from paper.

To prepare filling, in medium bowl combine half-and-half and pudding mix; beat at low speed 1 minute. Stir in almond extract.

To assemble, place 1 meringue on large serving plate. Spread filling to edges of meringue; top with remaining meringue. Arrange strawberries over top. In small saucepan, melt jelly over low heat; brush over berries. Refrigerate at least 2 hours before serving to soften meringues.

12 servings.

TIP:

   Meringues can be made 1 or 2 days ahead. Cover loosely;store at room temperature. Fill and top with berries; refrigerate at least 2 hours before serving to soften meringues.

*F*or a perfect meringue, be sure egg whites are at room temperature and the bowl and beaters are completely free of fat. Store baked dessert meringues at room temperature for up to two days or freeze them for up to one month.

NUTRITION INFORMATION PER SERVING:			
1/12 OF RECIPE		PERCENT U.S. RDA	
Calories	250	Protein	6%
Protein	4 g	Vitamin A	6%
Carbohydrate	45 g	Vitamin C	50%
Dietary Fiber	1 g	Thiamine	2%
Fat	7 g	Riboflavin	10%
Polyunsaturated	0 g	Niacin	*
Saturated	4 g	Calcium	6%
Cholesterol	22 mg	Iron	*
Sodium	240 mg	*Less than 2% U.S. RDA	
Potassium	210 mg		

DIETARY EXCHANGES: 1 Starch, 2 Fruit, 1-1/2 Fat

FRUIT-TOPPED MERINGUES

*M*eringues, virtually free of fat and cholesterol, are a great choice for a light dessert. Top the heavenly filling in this meringue with your favorite fresh fruits. Choose a variety of colors for a pretty presentation.

MERINGUES

4 **egg whites**

¼ **teaspoon cream of tartar**

⅔ **cup sugar**

FILLING

1 **cup low-fat large curd cottage cheese**

2 **tablespoons powdered sugar**

1 **teaspoon vanilla**

3 **cups assorted fresh fruits (peach or kiwifruit slices, strawberries, blueberries, grapes, raspberries and/or orange segments)**

Heat oven to 275°F. Line cookie sheet with parchment or brown paper. In large bowl, beat egg whites and cream of tartar until soft peaks form. Add ⅔ cup sugar 1 tablespoon at a time, beating continuously until stiff peaks form and mixture is glossy, about 14 minutes. Spoon or pipe meringue onto paper-lined cookie sheet in six 4-inch circles, forming a 1-inch rim around sides. Bake at 275°F. for 45 minutes or until light golden brown and dry. Cool completely.

In food processor bowl with metal blade or blender container, combine cottage cheese, powdered sugar and vanilla; process until smooth. Spoon into meringue shells; top with fruit. Refrigerate until serving time.

6 servings.

NUTRITION INFORMATION PER SERVING:

1/6 OF RECIPE		PERCENT U.S. RDA	
Calories	180	Protein	10%
Protein	8 g	Vitamin A	6%
Carbohydrate	36 g	Vitamin C	60%
Dietary Fiber	2 g	Thiamine	4%
Fat	1 g	Riboflavin	10%
Polyunsaturated	0 g	Niacin	*
Saturated	1 g	Calcium	4%
Cholesterol	3 mg	Iron	*
Sodium	190 mg	*Less than 2% U.S. RDA	
Potassium	250 mg		

DIETARY EXCHANGES: 1 Lean Meat, 2 Fruit

Fruit–Topped Meringues

APPLE OAT CRISP

*U*npeeled apples, rolled oats, wheat germ and whole wheat flour add fiber to this homey dessert. It can be cooked in the microwave or you can bake it in the conventional oven.

NUTRITION INFORMATION PER SERVING:

1/6 OF RECIPE		PERCENT U.S. RDA	
Calories	190	Protein	2%
Protein	2 g	Vitamin A	*
Carbohydrate	36 g	Vitamin C	10%
Dietary Fiber	5 g	Thiamine	6%
Fat	6 g	Riboflavin	2%
Polyunsaturated	3 g	Niacin	2%
Saturated	1 g	Calcium	2%
Cholesterol	0 mg	Iron	6%
Sodium	25 mg	*Less than 2% U.S. RDA	
Potassium	240 mg		

DIETARY EXCHANGES: 1/2 Starch, 1-1/2 Fruit, 1 Fat

6 **medium baking apples, unpeeled, sliced**
1 **teaspoon cinnamon**
1 **tablespoon lemon juice**
1 **tablespoon water**
¼ **cup rolled oats**
¼ **cup firmly packed brown sugar**
2 **tablespoons whole wheat flour**
2 **tablespoons wheat germ**
  Dash salt
2 **tablespoons oil**

Heat oven to 375°F. Prepare apples and crumb mixture as directed above. Arrange apples in ungreased 8-inch square (1½-quart) baking dish. Sprinkle crumb mixture over apples. Bake at 375°F. for 40 to 45 minutes or until apples are tender.

MICROWAVE DIRECTIONS: In large bowl, combine apple slices and cinnamon. Sprinkle lemon juice and water over apples; mix well. Arrange in ungreased 8-inch square (1½-quart) microwave-safe dish. In small bowl, combine all remaining ingredients; stir until crumbly. Sprinkle crumb mixture over apples. Microwave on HIGH for 12 to 14 minutes or until apples are tender, rotating dish ¼ turn once halfway through cooking.
6 servings.

BLUEBERRY PEACH CRISP

FRUIT MIXTURE

- **4 cups fresh or frozen sliced peeled peaches, thawed**
- **2 teaspoons lemon juice**
- **3 cups fresh or frozen blueberries, thawed**
- **3 tablespoons all purpose flour**
- **3 to 4 tablespoons sugar**

TOPPING

- **¼ cup firmly packed brown sugar**
- **¼ cup quick-cooking rolled oats**
- **2 tablespoons all purpose flour**
- **2 tablespoons chopped almonds**
- **½ teaspoon cinnamon**
- **⅛ teaspoon nutmeg**
- **2 tablespoons margarine or butter**

Heat oven to 350°F. In ungreased 8-inch square (1½-quart) baking dish, combine peaches and lemon juice; toss gently. Add blueberries, 3 tablespoons flour and sugar; toss with peaches.

In small bowl, combine all topping ingredients except margarine. With fork or pastry blender, cut in margarine until crumbly. Sprinkle topping over fruit mixture.

Bake at 350°F. for 30 minutes or until golden brown and bubbly. If desired, serve with light whipped topping or frozen yogurt. **9 servings.**

⬛ MICROWAVE DIRECTIONS: Using 8-inch square (1½-quart) microwave-safe dish, prepare recipe as directed above. Microwave on HIGH for 11 to 15 minutes or until fruit is tender, rotating dish ¼ turn once during cooking. If desired, serve with light whipped topping or frozen yogurt.

*I*f you make this easy fruit crisp in the summer when days are warm, bake it in the microwave and keep your kitchen cool!

NUTRITION INFORMATION PER SERVING:

1/9 OF RECIPE		PERCENT U.S. RDA	
Calories	170	Protein	2%
Protein	2 g	Vitamin A	2%
Carbohydrate	29 g	Vitamin C	10%
Dietary Fiber	3 g	Thiamine	6%
Fat	4 g	Riboflavin	4%
Polyunsaturated	1 g	Niacin	2%
Saturated	1 g	Calcium	2%
Cholesterol	0 mg	Iron	4%
Sodium	35 mg		
Potassium	160 mg		

DIETARY EXCHANGES: 1 Starch, 1 Fruit, 1 Fat

GINGER APPLE CRISP

*C*rystallized ginger is gingerroot that has been cooked in a sugar syrup and coated with coarse sugar. Its hot, spicy, sweet flavor is delicious in this easy crisp.

NUTRITION INFORMATION PER SERVING:

1/6 OF RECIPE		PERCENT U.S. RDA	
Calories	260	Protein	2%
Protein	2 g	Vitamin A	8%
Carbohydrate	56 g	Vitamin C	15%
Dietary Fiber	3 g	Thiamine	10%
Fat	4 g	Riboflavin	15%
Polyunsaturated	1 g	Niacin	8%
Saturated	1 g	Calcium	8%
Cholesterol	0 mg	Iron	10%
Sodium	130 mg		
Potassium	330 mg		

DIETARY EXCHANGES: 1 Starch, 2-1/2 Fruit, 1 Fat

⅓ **cup purchased cornflake crumbs**

¼ **cup firmly packed brown sugar**

3 **tablespoons all purpose flour**

2 **tablespoons crystallized ginger, chopped, or 1 teaspoon ginger**

2 **tablespoons margarine or butter, melted**

6 **Rome Beauty or Macintosh apples, peeled, cored, thinly sliced and slices cut in half (6 cups)**

2 **tablespoons sugar**

2 **teaspoons lemon juice**

1½ **cups frozen nonfat vanilla yogurt or ice milk**

Heat oven to 400°F. Spray 8-inch square (1½-quart) baking dish with nonstick cooking spray. In small bowl, combine cornflake crumbs, brown sugar, flour and ginger; mix well. Stir in melted margarine until well mixed.

Place apples in spray-coated dish. Add sugar and lemon juice; toss to coat. Sprinkle apples with crumb mixture; press gently.

Bake at 400°F. for 25 to 30 minutes or until apples are tender and mixture is bubbly. Cool slightly; serve warm with frozen vanilla yogurt.

6 servings.

Ginger Apple Crisp

PASSOVER FRUIT CRISP

*M*atzo cake meal is available in Jewish markets and most super-markets. It's used instead of flour in this traditional Jewish holiday dessert.

2 **(8-oz.) pkg. dried mixed fruit**
⅔ **cup sugar**
2 **cinnamon sticks**
1½ **cups water**
¾ **cup red wine or water**

TOPPING

⅔ **cup matzo cake meal**
⅓ **cup sugar**
¼ **cup finely chopped almonds**
½ **teaspoon cinnamon**
½ **teaspoon ginger**
¼ **teaspoon nutmeg**
3 **tablespoons margarine or butter**

In medium saucepan, combine fruit, ⅔ cup sugar, cinnamon sticks, water and wine. Bring to a boil, stirring occasionally. Reduce heat; simmer 10 to 15 minutes or until fruit is tender, stirring occasionally. Remove cinnamon sticks.

Heat oven to 400°F. In medium bowl, combine cake meal, ⅓ cup sugar, almonds, cinnamon, ginger and nutmeg; mix well. With pastry blender or fork, cut in margarine until fine crumbs form. Pour hot fruit mixture into ungreased 1½-quart casserole. Sprinkle evenly with topping.

Bake at 400°F. for 15 to 20 minutes or until topping is light golden brown. Cool slightly; serve warm or cool. Fruit mixture will thicken as it cools.

8 servings.

NUTRITION INFORMATION PER SERVING:			
1/8 OF RECIPE		PERCENT U.S. RDA	
Calories	350	Protein	4%
Protein	3 g	Vitamin A	25%
Carbohydrate	71 g	Vitamin C	2%
Dietary Fiber	6 g	Thiamine	*
Fat	7 g	Riboflavin	8%
Polyunsaturated	2 g	Niacin	6%
Saturated	1 g	Calcium	4%
Cholesterol	0 mg	Iron	10%
Sodium	70 mg	*Less than 2% U.S. RDA	
Potassium	490 mg		

DIETARY EXCHANGES: 1 Starch, 3-1/2 Fruit, 1-1/2 Fat

BLUEBERRY CRUMBLE

FRUIT MIXTURE

- 4 **cups fresh or frozen blueberries**
- ¼ **cup raisins**
- 2 **tablespoons cornstarch**
- 1 **teaspoon grated lemon peel**
- 1 **tablespoon lemon juice**
- ⅓ **cup apricot preserves**

TOPPING

- ½ **cup all purpose flour**
- ½ **cup firmly packed brown sugar**
- 1 **teaspoon cinnamon**
- ¼ **cup margarine or butter, softened**

Heat oven to 400°F. Grease 10x6-inch (1½-quart) or 8-inch square baking dish. In large bowl, combine blueberries, raisins, cornstarch, lemon peel and lemon juice. Spoon mixture evenly into greased baking dish. Dot with apricot preserves.

In medium bowl, combine flour, brown sugar and cinnamon; mix well. With pastry blender or fork, cut in margarine until mixture is crumbly. Sprinkle topping evenly over fruit mixture.

Bake at 400°F. for 20 to 30 minutes or until topping is golden brown. Serve warm or at room temperature; top with light whipped topping or vanilla ice milk, if desired.

6 servings.

A crumble is an old-fashioned British dessert that consists of fruit topped with a crumbly pastry mixture before it is baked.

NUTRITION INFORMATION PER SERVING:

1/6 OF RECIPE		PERCENT U.S. RDA	
Calories	300	Protein	2%
Protein	2 g	Vitamin A	8%
Carbohydrate	59 g	Vitamin C	15%
Dietary Fiber	3 g	Thiamine	8%
Fat	8 g	Riboflavin	6%
Polyunsaturated	2 g	Niacin	4%
Saturated	1 g	Calcium	4%
Cholesterol	0 mg	Iron	10%
Sodium	105 mg		
Potassium	230 mg		

DIETARY EXCHANGES: 1 Starch, 2-1/2 Fruit, 1-1/2 Fat

PEACH BERRY CRUMBLE

This colorful triple-fruit dessert is the perfect ending for a meal or can be served for a coffee break anytime.

NUTRITION INFORMATION PER SERVING:

1/9 OF RECIPE		PERCENT U.S. RDA	
Calories	300	Protein	4%
Protein	3 g	Vitamin A	10%
Carbohydrate	61 g	Vitamin C	10%
Dietary Fiber	3 g	Thiamine	8%
Fat	6 g	Riboflavin	8%
Polyunsaturated	2 g	Niacin	6%
Saturated	1 g	Calcium	*
Cholesterol	24 mg	Iron	4%
Sodium	70 mg	*Less than 2% U.S. RDA	
Potassium	160 mg		

DIETARY EXCHANGES: 1 Starch, 3 Fruit, 1 Fat

TOPPING

1 cup all purpose flour

¾ cup sugar

¼ cup margarine or butter, softened

1 egg, slightly beaten

FRUIT MIXTURE

1 cup sugar

3 tablespoons cornstarch

1 cup water

¼ teaspoon almond extract

1 (16-oz.) pkg. frozen sliced peaches, thawed

1 cup fresh or frozen cranberries

1 cup fresh or frozen blackberries

Heat oven to 400°F. In medium bowl, combine flour and ¾ cup sugar. Using pastry blender or fork, cut in margarine until crumbly. Stir in egg; mix well. Set aside.

In small saucepan, combine 1 cup sugar and cornstarch; add water. Cook over medium heat until mixture boils and thickens, stirring constantly. Stir in almond extract. In ungreased 8-inch square (1½-quart) baking dish, combine peaches, cranberries and blackberries; stir in hot cornstarch mixture. Sprinkle topping over fruit mixture.

Bake at 400°F. for 40 to 45 minutes or until topping is golden brown. Serve warm. If desired, serve with sweetened light sour cream, whipped topping or ice milk.

9 servings.

TIP:

To prepare cornstarch mixture in microwave, combine 1 cup sugar and cornstarch in 4-cup microwave-safe measuring cup. Stir in water. Microwave on HIGH for 4 to 4½ minutes or until mixture boils and thickens, stirring twice during cooking. Stir in almond extract.

Peach Berry Crumble

APPLE RASPBERRY COBBLER

Cobblers, those classic and simple fruit desserts, can be topped with a sheet of pastry or with a cake-like topping, as we've done here.

NUTRITION INFORMATION PER SERVING:

1/6 OF RECIPE		PERCENT U.S. RDA	
Calories	280	Protein	4%
Protein	3 g	Vitamin A	4%
Carbohydrate	54 g	Vitamin C	8%
Dietary Fiber	4 g	Thiamine	8%
Fat	5 g	Riboflavin	8%
Polyunsaturated	1 g	Niacin	6%
Saturated	1 g	Calcium	4%
Cholesterol	36 mg	Iron	6%
Sodium	230 mg		
Potassium	90 mg		

DIETARY EXCHANGES: 1 Starch, 2-1/2 Fruit, 1 Fat

FRUIT MIXTURE

1 (21-oz.) can apple fruit pie filling

1½ cups fresh or frozen raspberries

TOPPING

¾ cup all purpose flour

¼ cup sugar

1 teaspoon baking powder

3 tablespoons skim or 2% milk

2 tablespoons margarine or butter, melted

1 egg

Heat oven to 400°F. In medium saucepan, combine pie filling and raspberries. Cook and stir over medium heat until hot and bubbly. Pour into ungreased 8-inch square (1½-quart) baking dish.

In small bowl, combine flour, sugar and baking powder; mix well. Add milk, margarine and egg; mix until batter is smooth. Drop 6 spoonfuls of batter onto hot fruit mixture.

Bake at 400°F. for 15 to 22 minutes or until topping is light golden brown. If desired, serve with warm milk or half-and-half. **6 servings.**

HIGH ALTITUDE – Above 3500 Feet: No change.

PEACH CRANBERRY CRUNCH CUPS

FRUIT MIXTURE

- **1 (29-oz.) can peach slices, well drained**
- **1 cup fresh or frozen cranberries**
- **2 tablespoons sugar**

TOPPING

- **⅓ cup all purpose flour**
- **⅓ cup rolled oats**
- **⅓ cup firmly packed brown sugar**
- **½ teaspoon cinnamon**
- **3 tablespoons margarine or butter, melted**

Heat oven to 375°F. Spray six 6-oz. custard cups with nonstick cooking spray; place on cookie sheet. In medium bowl, combine peaches, cranberries and sugar; toss lightly. Spoon about ½ cup fruit mixture into each spray-coated custard cup.

In medium bowl, combine all topping ingredients until crumbly; sprinkle over fruit mixture. Bake at 375°F. for 20 to 25 minutes or until golden brown.

6 servings.

These individual fruit desserts, capped with a crunchy topping, are at their best when served warm from the oven. The cranberries do not need to be thawed before baking.

NUTRITION INFORMATION PER SERVING:

1/6 OF RECIPE		PERCENT U.S. RDA	
Calories	200	Protein	2%
Protein	2 g	Vitamin A	20%
Carbohydrate	35 g	Vitamin C	6%
Dietary Fiber	3 g	Thiamine	6%
Fat	6 g	Riboflavin	4%
Polyunsaturated	2 g	Niacin	6%
Saturated	1 g	Calcium	2%
Cholesterol	0 mg	Iron	6%
Sodium	75 mg		
Potassium	220 mg		

DIETARY EXCHANGES: 1 Starch, 1 Fruit, 1 Fat

Peach Cranberry Crunch Cups

COUNTRY PEACH COBBLER

This old-fashioned dessert got its name from the phrase "cobble up," which means to put together in a hurry. Although cobblers are usually as seasonal as the fruits that fill them, this version, made with peach pie filling, can be made any time of the year.

FRUIT MIXTURE

1 (21-oz.) can peach fruit pie filling
½ cup apricot preserves
¼ teaspoon almond extract

TOPPING

1 cup all purpose flour
2 tablespoons sugar
2 teaspoons baking powder
¼ teaspoon salt
¼ cup margarine or butter
2 to 3 tablespoons 2% milk
1 egg
½ teaspoon sugar

Heat oven to 425°F. In medium saucepan, combine pie filling, preserves and almond extract. Cook over medium-high heat for 2 to 3 minutes or until mixture boils, stirring occasionally. Pour mixture into ungreased 8-inch square pan; spread evenly.

In large bowl, combine flour, 2 tablespoons sugar, baking powder and salt; mix well. With pastry blender or fork, cut in margarine until crumbly. In small bowl, beat 2 tablespoons milk and egg until blended. Stir into flour mixture until blended, adding additional milk if necessary to form a stiff dough. Drop dough by spoonfuls evenly over pie filling mixture. Sprinkle with ½ teaspoon sugar.

Bake at 425°F. for 12 to 17 minutes or until fruit bubbles around edges and topping is golden brown. Serve warm.
6 to 8 servings.

HIGH ALTITUDE – Above 3500 Feet: No change.

NUTRITION INFORMATION PER SERVING:

1/8 OF RECIPE		PERCENT U.S. RDA	
Calories	270	Protein	4%
Protein	3 g	Vitamin A	6%
Carbohydrate	49 g	Vitamin C	*
Dietary Fiber	1 g	Thiamine	8%
Fat	7 g	Riboflavin	6%
Polyunsaturated	2 g	Niacin	6%
Saturated	1 g	Calcium	6%
Cholesterol	27 mg	Iron	6%
Sodium	240 mg	*Less than 2% U.S. RDA	
Potassium	55 mg		

DIETARY EXCHANGES: 1 Starch, 2 Fruit, 1-1/2 Fat

PEAR CRANBERRY APRICOT COBBLER

TOPPING

1¼ cups all purpose flour

 ½ cup sugar

 1 teaspoon baking powder

 ¼ teaspoon salt

 ¼ cup 2% milk

 1 tablespoon margarine or butter, melted

 2 eggs

FRUIT MIXTURE

 4 cups (4 to 5 medium) sliced peeled pears

 1 cup fresh or frozen cranberries

 1 (16-oz.) can apricot halves, undrained

 ½ cup sugar

 ¾ teaspoon cinnamon

 2 to 3 teaspoons grated orange peel

A cobbler is similar to a deep dish pie but with a rich biscuit topping. It's a flavorful old-fashioned dessert that can be served with ice milk or light whipped topping. This mixed fruit cobbler boasts only 240 calories and 3 grams of fat per serving!

Heat oven to 350°F. Grease 2-quart casserole. In medium bowl, combine flour, ½ cup sugar, baking powder and salt; blend well. Add milk, margarine and eggs; mix until batter is smooth. Set aside.

In medium saucepan, combine all fruit mixture ingredients. Cook over medium heat 10 to 15 minutes or until mixture is hot, stirring occasionally. Pour hot fruit mixture into greased casserole; spoon batter over top.

Bake at 350°F. for 30 to 40 minutes or until topping is golden brown. Serve warm.

8 to 10 servings.

HIGH ALTITUDE – Above 3500 Feet: No change.

NUTRITION INFORMATION PER SERVING:			
1/10 OF RECIPE		PERCENT U.S. RDA	
Calories	240	Protein	6%
Protein	4 g	Vitamin A	15%
Carbohydrate	54 g	Vitamin C	6%
Dietary Fiber	3 g	Thiamine	10%
Fat	3 g	Riboflavin	10%
Polyunsaturated	1 g	Niacin	6%
Saturated	1 g	Calcium	4%
Cholesterol	43 mg	Iron	6%
Sodium	120 mg		
Potassium	190 mg		

DIETARY EXCHANGES: 1 Starch, 2-1/2 Fruit, 1/2 Fat

PEACH BERRY SHORTCAKE

A hint of honey and cinnamon highlights the fruit mixture in this wonderful fruit-and-yogurt-topped dessert.

NUTRITION INFORMATION PER SERVING:

1/8 OF RECIPE		PERCENT U.S. RDA	
Calories	250	Protein	10%
Protein	7 g	Vitamin A	10%
Carbohydrate	43 g	Vitamin C	10%
Dietary Fiber	2 g	Thiamine	15%
Fat	7 g	Riboflavin	20%
Polyunsaturated	2 g	Niacin	10%
Saturated	1 g	Calcium	20%
Cholesterol	28 mg	Iron	8%
Sodium	430 mg		
Potassium	250 mg		

DIETARY EXCHANGES: 1-1/2 Starch, 1 Fruit, 1-1/2 Fat

CAKE

1⅔ cups all purpose flour

⅓ cup sugar

3 teaspoons baking powder

½ teaspoon salt

½ cup evaporated skimmed milk

¼ cup margarine or butter, melted

2 teaspoons vanilla

1 egg, slightly beaten

TOPPING

1 (8-oz.) container nonfat vanilla yogurt

2 teaspoons honey

¼ teaspoon cinnamon

2 cups fresh or frozen sliced peaches, thawed

1 cup fresh or frozen blueberries, thawed

Heat oven to 350°F. Grease and flour 8 or 9-inch round cake pan. In large bowl, combine flour, sugar, baking powder and salt. Add milk, margarine, vanilla and egg; stir just until dry ingredients are moistened. Spoon into greased and floured pan.

Bake at 350°F. for 17 to 24 minutes or until toothpick inserted in center comes out clean. Cool 10 minutes; remove from pan. In small bowl, combine yogurt, honey and cinnamon; blend well. Top shortcake with yogurt mixture and fruit.

8 servings.

HIGH ALTITUDE – Above 3500 Feet: Increase flour to 1¾ cups; decrease baking powder to 2 teaspoons. Bake at 375°F. for 18 to 25 minutes.

LIGHT STRAWBERRY SHORTCAKE

❧

SHORTCAKE

1⅔ cups all purpose flour

⅓ cup sugar

3 teaspoons baking powder

½ teaspoon salt

½ cup evaporated skimmed milk

¼ cup margarine or butter, melted

2 teaspoons vanilla

1 egg, slightly beaten, or ¼ cup frozen fat-free egg product, thawed

FRUIT AND TOPPING

4 cups sliced strawberries

¼ cup sugar

⅔ cup evaporated skimmed milk

3 tablespoons powdered sugar

1 teaspoon vanilla

This lighter version of strawberry shortcake reflects healthier eating styles by reducing the fat, sugar and calories. A special whipped topping allows all the creamy satisfaction of whipped cream without the fat.

Heat oven to 350°F. Grease and flour 8 or 9-inch round cake pan. In large bowl, combine flour, ⅓ cup sugar, baking powder and salt. Add ½ cup milk, margarine, 2 teaspoons vanilla and egg, stirring just until dry ingredients are moistened. Spoon into greased and floured pan.

Bake at 350°F. for 17 to 24 minutes or until toothpick inserted in center comes out clean. Cool 10 minutes; invert onto serving platter. Split layer in half, if desired.

Meanwhile, in medium bowl combine strawberries and ¼ cup sugar; mix well. Refrigerate 30 minutes or until serving time. To prepare topping, place small bowl and beaters in refrigerator to chill. Pour ⅔ cup milk into freezer container. Freeze until slushy, about 50 minutes.

Just before serving, spoon slushy milk into small chilled bowl. Beat with chilled beaters until fluffy. Add powdered sugar and 1 teaspoon vanilla; beat until soft peaks form, scraping bowl occasionally. Serve immediately with shortcake and sweetened strawberries.* Store in refrigerator.

8 servings.

TIP:

* Topping can be held in freezer for up to 20 minutes or in refrigerator for up to 10 minutes.

HIGH ALTITUDE – Above 3500 Feet: Increase flour to 1¾ cups; decrease baking powder to 2 teaspoons. Bake at 375°F. for 18 to 25 minutes.

NUTRITION INFORMATION PER SERVING:

1/8 OF RECIPE		PERCENT U.S. RDA	
Calories	290	Protein	10%
Protein	7 g	Vitamin A	8%
Carbohydrate	51 g	Vitamin C	120%
Dietary Fiber	4 g	Thiamine	15%
Fat	7 g	Riboflavin	20%
Polyunsaturated	2 g	Niacin	10%
Saturated	1 g	Calcium	25%
Cholesterol	28 mg	Iron	10%
Sodium	440 mg		
Potassium	370 mg		

DIETARY EXCHANGES: 2 Starch, 1 Fruit, 1-1/2 Fat

PLUM KUCHEN

*O*riginating in Germany, a kuchen (pronounced koo-ken) is a fruit or cheese-filled cake. Kuchens are often served for dessert but also make exquisite coffee cakes for breakfast or brunch. This plum version is lower in fat and luscious!

NUTRITION INFORMATION PER SERVING:			
1/12 OF RECIPE		**PERCENT U.S. RDA**	
Calories	170	Protein	2%
Protein	2 g	Vitamin A	6%
Carbohydrate	30 g	Vitamin C	4%
Dietary Fiber	1 g	Thiamine	6%
Fat	5 g	Riboflavin	6%
Polyunsaturated	1 g	Niacin	4%
Saturated	1 g	Calcium	2%
Cholesterol	18 mg	Iron	2%
Sodium	115 mg		
Potassium	100 mg		

DIETARY EXCHANGES: 1 Starch, 1 Fruit, 1 Fat

KUCHEN

¼ cup margarine or butter, softened

¼ cup sugar

1 teaspoon vanilla

1 egg

1 cup all purpose flour

½ teaspoon baking powder

¼ teaspoon salt

6 to 8 ripe plums, pitted, sliced*

2 tablespoons sugar

½ teaspoon cinnamon

GLAZE

1 cup powdered sugar

½ teaspoon vanilla

1 to 2 tablespoons 2% milk

Heat oven to 400°F. Spray 9-inch springform pan with nonstick cooking spray. In large bowl, beat margarine and ¼ cup sugar until light and fluffy. Add vanilla and egg; beat well. In small bowl, combine flour, baking powder and salt. Gradually add to margarine mixture, mixing well. With floured fingers, press dough over bottom and 1 inch up sides of spray-coated pan. Arrange sliced plums over dough. Combine 2 tablespoons sugar and cinnamon; sprinkle over plums.

Bake at 400°F. for 15 to 20 minutes or until edges are golden brown. Cool 10 minutes; remove sides of pan. Meanwhile, in small bowl combine all glaze ingredients, adding enough milk for desired drizzling consistency; blend until smooth. Drizzle over warm kuchen.

8 to 12 servings.

TIPS:

* Two 16-oz. cans purple plums, well drained, pitted and cut in half, can be substituted for fresh plums.

A 13x9-inch pan can be substituted for the springform pan. Press dough in bottom of spray-coated pan. Continue as directed above.

HIGH ALTITUDE – Above 3500 Feet: No change.

Plum Kuchen

GINGERBREAD WITH LEMON SAUCE

Gingerbread dates back to the Middle Ages when ladies presented the spice bread to dashing knights going into battle. We know you'll be proud to serve this lemon-topped version to your favorite knight or anyone else who appreciates good home cooking!

NUTRITION INFORMATION PER SERVING:

1/9 OF RECIPE		PERCENT U.S. RDA	
Calories	210	Protein	4%
Protein	3 g	Vitamin A	*
Carbohydrate	35 g	Vitamin C	*
Dietary Fiber	1 g	Thiamine	10%
Fat	7 g	Riboflavin	6%
Polyunsaturated	4 g	Niacin	6%
Saturated	1 g	Calcium	6%
Cholesterol	0 mg	Iron	10%
Sodium	115 mg	*Less than 2% U.S. RDA	
Potassium	290 mg		

DIETARY EXCHANGES: 1 Starch, 1 Fruit, 1-1/2 Fat

GINGERBREAD

- 1 cup all purpose flour
- ⅓ cup wheat germ
- ¼ cup firmly packed brown sugar
- ¾ teaspoon ginger
- ¾ teaspoon cinnamon
- ½ teaspoon baking powder
- ½ teaspoon baking soda
- ½ teaspoon allspice
- ½ cup boiling unsweetened apple juice
- ⅓ cup molasses
- ¼ cup oil
- ¼ cup frozen fat-free egg product, thawed, or 1 egg

LEMON SAUCE

- ¼ cup sugar
- 2 teaspoons cornstarch
- ½ cup hot water
- 1 tablespoon lemon juice
- 1 teaspoon grated lemon peel

Heat oven to 350°F. Grease bottom only of 8-inch square pan. In large bowl, combine flour, wheat germ, brown sugar, ginger, cinnamon, baking powder, baking soda and allspice; mix well. Add remaining gingerbread ingredients; blend well. Pour into greased pan. Bake at 350°F. for 30 to 40 minutes or until toothpick inserted in center comes out clean.

Meanwhile, in medium saucepan combine sugar and cornstarch. Gradually stir in hot water. Cook over medium heat until mixture comes to a boil and is slightly thickened and clear, stirring constantly. Stir in lemon juice and lemon peel. Serve warm sauce over warm gingerbread.

9 servings.

▤ MICROWAVE DIRECTIONS: Grease 8-inch round microwave-safe dish; line with waxed paper. Prepare gingerbread batter as directed above. Pour into greased paper-lined dish. Microwave on MEDIUM for 7 minutes, rotating dish ¼ turn once halfway through cooking. Rotate another ¼ turn; microwave on HIGH for 2 to 2½ minutes or until gingerbread starts to pull away from sides of pan. Let stand 5 minutes. Remove from pan; remove waxed paper.

In small bowl, combine sugar and cornstarch. Gradually stir in hot water. Microwave on HIGH for 1½ to 2 minutes or until mixture comes to a boil and is slightly thickened and clear, stirring once halfway through cooking. Stir in lemon juice and lemon peel. Serve warm sauce over warm gingerbread.

HIGH ALTITUDE – Above 3500 Feet: Increase flour to 1 cup plus 2 tablespoons. Bake as directed above.

CRAZY CRUST
APPLE SQUARES

1 cup all purpose flour

½ cup sugar

1 teaspoon baking powder

½ teaspoon salt

¼ teaspoon nutmeg

⅔ cup 2% milk

1 egg

½ cup raisins

3 cups (3 medium) sliced peeled apples

½ cup chopped pecans

⅓ cup sugar

1 teaspoon cinnamon

This easy dessert has real down-home appeal. It's especially nice for picnics because it requires no refrigeration.

NUTRITION INFORMATION PER SERVING:			
1/12 OF RECIPE		**PERCENT U.S. RDA**	
Calories	170	Protein	4%
Protein	3 g	Vitamin A	*
Carbohydrate	33 g	Vitamin C	*
Dietary Fiber	1 g	Thiamine	8%
Fat	4 g	Riboflavin	6%
Polyunsaturated	1 g	Niacin	4%
Saturated	1 g	Calcium	4%
Cholesterol	19 mg	Iron	4%
Sodium	130 mg	*Less than 2% U.S. RDA	
Potassium	135 mg		

DIETARY EXCHANGES: 1 Starch, 1 Fruit, 1 Fat

Heat oven to 350°F. Grease 13x9-inch pan. In large bowl, combine flour, ½ cup sugar, baking powder, salt and nutmeg; mix well. Add milk and egg; blend well. Spread in greased pan. Sprinkle raisins, apples and pecans over batter. In small bowl, combine ⅓ cup sugar and cinnamon; mix well. Sprinkle sugar mixture over top.

Bake at 350°F. for 30 to 40 minutes or until edges are light golden brown and apples are tender.

12 servings.

HIGH ALTITUDE – Above 3500 Feet: No change.

CHERRY CRANBERRY DESSERT SQUARES

*C*ranberries are some-
times called bounce-
berries because ripe ones
bounce. This pretty dessert
layered with cranberries
makes a delicious and festive
finale for holiday meals.

NUTRITION INFORMATION PER SERVING:

1/12 OF RECIPE		PERCENT U.S. RDA	
Calories	310	Protein	4%
Protein	3 g	Vitamin A	4%
Carbohydrate	63 g	Vitamin C	4%
Dietary Fiber	1 g	Thiamine	2%
Fat	6 g	Riboflavin	4%
Polyunsaturated	1 g	Niacin	*
Saturated	3 g	Calcium	6%
Cholesterol	5 mg	Iron	2%
Sodium	350 mg	*Less than 2% U.S. RDA	
Potassium	150 mg		

DIETARY EXCHANGES: 1 Starch, 3 Fruit, 1 Fat

Pastry for one-crust pie (p. 183)
3 **cups fresh or frozen cranberries**
1 **cup sugar**
¼ **cup cornstarch**
½ **teaspoon cinnamon**
¼ **cup water**
1 **(21-oz.) can cherry fruit pie filling**
2 **(3.4-oz.) pkg. instant vanilla pudding and pie filling mix**
2 **cups skim or 2% milk**
½ **teaspoon rum extract**
1 **cup frozen light whipped topping, thawed**

Heat oven to 425°F. Prepare pastry as directed, rolling to a 13x9-inch rectangle. Press pastry in bottom only of ungreased 13x9-inch pan. Prick crust generously with fork. Bake at 425°F. for 9 to 11 minutes or until light golden brown. Cool.

In medium nonstick saucepan, combine cranberries, sugar, cornstarch and cinnamon; mix well. Stir in water; bring to a boil. Cook and stir over medium-high heat for about 5 minutes or until cranberries pop and sauce is very thick and translucent. Add cherry pie filling; mix well. Cover surface with plastic wrap. Refrigerate until cool.

In medium bowl, combine pudding mix, milk and rum extract. Blend with wire whisk until thickened. Spoon over baked crust. Top evenly with cranberry mixture. Refrigerate 30 to 60 minutes or until set.* Cut into squares to serve; top with whipped topping. **12 servings.**

TIP:
   * To speed preparation, place in freezer for up to 30 minutes or until set.

Cherry Cranberry Dessert Squares

MINTY CHOCOLATE DESSERT SQUARES

*M*ake these special squares any time you need a rich, chocolaty dessert. Chocolate-mint instant coffee beverage is the secret ingredient.

NUTRITION INFORMATION PER SERVING:

1/9 OF RECIPE		PERCENT U.S. RDA	
Calories	210	Protein	4%
Protein	2 g	Vitamin A	6%
Carbohydrate	34 g	Vitamin C	*
Dietary Fiber	1 g	Thiamine	4%
Fat	7 g	Riboflavin	6%
Polyunsaturated	2 g	Niacin	2%
Saturated	2 g	Calcium	2%
Cholesterol	24 mg	Iron	8%
Sodium	105 mg	*Less than 2% U.S. RDA	
Potassium	135 mg		

DIETARY EXCHANGES: 1 Starch, 1 Fruit, 1-1/2 Fat

CAKE

½   **cup firmly packed brown sugar**

¼   **margarine or butter, softened**

⅔   **cup chocolate-flavored syrup**

1   **teaspoon vanilla**

1   **egg**

⅔   **cup all purpose flour**

2   **teaspoons Dutch chocolate-mint instant coffee beverage powder**

TOPPING

1   **cup frozen lite whipped topping, thawed**

1   **teaspoon Dutch chocolate-mint instant coffee beverage powder**

2   **drops green food color**

Heat oven to 350°F. Spray 8-inch square pan with nonstick cooking spray. In medium bowl, beat brown sugar and margarine until light and fluffy. Add chocolate syrup, vanilla and egg; blend well. Add flour and 2 teaspoons coffee beverage powder; mix well. Spread evenly in spray-coated pan.

Bake at 350°F. for 20 to 25 minutes or until toothpick inserted in center comes out clean. Cool in refrigerator 20 to 25 minutes.

In small bowl, combine all topping ingredients until well blended. Spread over cooled cake. Store in refrigerator.

9 servings.

HIGH ALTITUDE–Above 3500 Feet: No change.

APRICOT
SOUFFLE

SOUFFLE

   2 **tablespoons cornstarch**

   2 **tablespoons sugar**

   ¾ **cup evaporated skimmed milk**

   ¼ **cup apricot preserves**

   3 **tablespoons apricot nectar**

   1 **teaspoon vanilla**

   6 **egg whites**

   ½ **teaspoon cream of tartar**

SAUCE

   ⅓ **cup apricot preserves**

   2 **tablespoons apricot nectar**

*I*n this delicate souffle, we've eliminated the egg yolks and created an elegant dessert with no fat. Have the sauce ready and serve the souffle immediately after baking it.

Spray 2½-quart souffle dish with nonstick cooking spray. In small saucepan, combine cornstarch and sugar. Add milk, ¼ cup apricot preserves and 3 tablespoons apricot nectar; mix well. Cook over medium heat until mixture boils and thickens, stirring constantly. Pour into large bowl; stir in vanilla. Cover surface with plastic wrap; set aside to cool to room temperature.

Heat oven to 425°F. In large bowl, beat egg whites and cream of tartar until stiff peaks form, about 2 to 3 minutes. Gently fold egg white mixture into cooled apricot mixture. Spoon into spray-coated souffle dish. Place souffle dish in 13x9-inch pan; pour boiling water into pan around souffle dish to a depth of 1 inch.

Place in 425°F. oven. Immediately reduce heat to 350°F.; bake 25 minutes or until puffy, set and golden brown. Meanwhile, in small saucepan combine sauce ingredients; cook over medium heat until thoroughly heated. Serve souffle immediately with sauce.

6 to 8 servings.

HIGH ALTITUDE – Above 3500 Feet: No change.

NUTRITION INFORMATION PER SERVING:			
1/8 OF RECIPE		**PERCENT U.S. RDA**	
Calories	110	Protein	6%
Protein	5 g	Vitamin A	4%
Carbohydrate	24 g	Vitamin C	2%
Dietary Fiber	0 g	Thiamine	*
Fat	0 g	Riboflavin	10%
Polyunsaturated	0 g	Niacin	*
Saturated	0 g	Calcium	8%
Cholesterol	1 mg	Iron	*
Sodium	80 mg	*Less than 2% U.S. RDA	
Potassium	170 mg		

DIETARY EXCHANGES: 1/2 Lean Meat, 1-1/2 Fruit

CALIFORNIA ORANGE RICOTTA CHEESECAKE WITH STRAWBERRY SAUCE

*M*ake this sumptuous cheesecake the day before your dinner and keep it refrigerated until you're ready to serve it. To help reduce the fat, we've used low-fat ricotta cheese and egg whites.

CRUST

2 tablespoons margarine or butter

⅔ cup graham cracker crumbs (about 10 to 12 squares)

FILLING

3 cups low-fat part-skim ricotta cheese

1 cup sugar

2 tablespoons all purpose flour

¼ cup orange juice

3 tablespoons grated orange peel

3 egg whites

STRAWBERRY SAUCE

1 (10-oz.) pkg. frozen sliced strawberries, thawed

2 teaspoons cornstarch

Heat oven to 350°F. Spray 9-inch springform pan with removable bottom with nonstick cooking spray. Melt margarine in small saucepan. Remove from heat; stir in graham cracker crumbs. Press crumb mixture evenly in bottom of spray-coated pan. Bake at 350°F. for 8 to 10 minutes or until light golden brown. Cool.

In food processor bowl with metal blade or large bowl with electric mixer, combine all filling ingredients; process or beat until smooth. Pour mixture into crust-lined pan. Bake at 350°F. for 50 to 60 minutes or until cheesecake is set. Cool in pan 5 minutes; remove sides of pan. Cool completely.

In small saucepan, combine strawberries and cornstarch. Cook and stir over medium heat for 2 to 5 minutes or until sauce is slightly thickened and translucent. Cool. Serve strawberry sauce over wedges of cheesecake. Store in refrigerator.

10 to 12 servings.

NUTRITION INFORMATION PER SERVING:

1/12 OF RECIPE		PERCENT U.S. RDA	
Calories	190	Protein	10%
Protein	6 g	Vitamin A	4%
Carbohydrate	32 g	Vitamin C	15%
Dietary Fiber	1 g	Thiamine	2%
Fat	5 g	Riboflavin	4%
Polyunsaturated	1 g	Niacin	*
Saturated	2 g	Calcium	10%
Cholesterol	15 mg	Iron	2%
Sodium	120 mg	*Less than 2% U.S. RDA	
Potassium	55 mg		

DIETARY EXCHANGES: 1 Starch, 1 Fruit, 1 Fat

ORANGE CHEESECAKE

CRUST

1 **cup finely crushed vanilla wafers (about 20 wafers)**

2 **tablespoons margarine or butter, melted**

FILLING

⅓ **cup sugar**

¾ **cup orange juice**

2 **envelopes unflavored gelatin**

1 **(15-oz.) container light ricotta cheese**

1 **(16-oz.) container nonfat vanilla yogurt**

2 **tablespoons orange-flavored liqueur or orange juice, if desired**

1 **(11-oz.) can mandarin orange segments, well drained**

Heat oven to 375°F. In small bowl, combine crust ingredients; press in bottom of ungreased 9 or 10-inch springform pan. Bake at 375°F. for 8 to 10 minutes or until light golden brown. Cool.

In small saucepan, combine sugar, orange juice and gelatin; mix well. Let stand 1 minute. Stir over medium heat until dissolved. In blender container or food processor bowl with metal blade, process ricotta cheese until smooth. Add yogurt, liqueur and gelatin mixture; blend well. Stir in orange segments.

Pour into cooled baked crust. Cover; refrigerate several hours or until firm. Before serving, carefully remove sides of pan. Store in refrigerator.

12 servings.

This featherweight cheesecake is a perfect make-ahead dessert for a special event.

NUTRITION INFORMATION PER SERVING:

1/12 OF RECIPE		PERCENT U.S. RDA	
Calories	160	Protein	10%
Protein	6 g	Vitamin A	6%
Carbohydrate	23 g	Vitamin C	15%
Dietary Fiber	0 g	Thiamine	6%
Fat	5 g	Riboflavin	8%
Polyunsaturated	1 g	Niacin	*
Saturated	2 g	Calcium	15%
Cholesterol	9 mg	Iron	*
Sodium	110 mg	*Less than 2% U.S. RDA	
Potassium	150 mg		

DIETARY EXCHANGES: 1-1/2 Starch, 1 Fat

MINI-CHEESECAKES WITH STRAWBERRY SAUCE

*V*elvety rich but low in calories...these dainty desserts will fulfill any cheesecake lover's fantasy.

NUTRITION INFORMATION PER SERVING:

1/8 OF RECIPE		PERCENT U.S. RDA	
Calories	160	Protein	6%
Protein	5 g	Vitamin A	8%
Carbohydrate	18 g	Vitamin C	20%
Dietary Fiber	1 g	Thiamine	*
Fat	8 g	Riboflavin	8%
Polyunsaturated	0 g	Niacin	*
Saturated	5 g	Calcium	2%
Cholesterol	75 mg	Iron	2%
Sodium	130 mg	*Less than 2% U.S. RDA	
Potassium	80 mg		

DIETARY EXCHANGES: 1 High-Fat Meat, 1 Fruit

CHEESECAKE

1 **(8-oz.) pkg. light cream cheese (Neufchatel), softened**

¼ **cup sugar**

Dash nutmeg

¼ **teaspoon vanilla**

2 **eggs**

SAUCE

1 **(10-oz.) pkg. frozen strawberries with syrup, thawed, drained, reserving liquid**

1 **tablespoon orange-flavored liqueur or orange juice**

2 **teaspoons cornstarch**

2 **to 3 drops red food color, if desired**

Heat oven to 325°F. Line 8 muffin cups or eight 5-oz. custard cups with paper baking cups. In small bowl, beat all cheesecake ingredients until smooth. Spoon ¼ cup cheesecake mixture into each paper-lined muffin cup.

Bake at 325°F. for 15 to 22 minutes or just until set and slightly puffed. DO NOT OVERBAKE. Remove from pan; cool 5 minutes. Refrigerate at least 1 hour or until serving time. (Center may dip slightly during cooling.)

In small saucepan, combine reserved strawberry liquid, liqueur and cornstarch. Cook over medium heat until mixture boils and thickens, stirring constantly. Remove from heat; stir in strawberries and food color. Cool.

To serve, remove paper baking cups; place inverted cheesecakes in individual dessert dishes. Spoon 2 tablespoons sauce over each. **8 servings.**

TIP:

To prepare sauce in microwave, combine reserved strawberry liquid, liqueur and cornstarch in medium microwave-safe bowl. Microwave on HIGH for 2 to 2½ minutes or until thickened, stirring once halfway through cooking. Stir in strawberries and food color. Cool.

LEMON SPONGE DESSERT

1 **cup sugar**

¼ **cup all purpose flour**

  Dash salt

2 **tablespoons margarine or butter, melted**

1 **tablespoon grated lemon peel**

1½ **cups milk**

⅓ **cup lemon juice**

3 **eggs, separated**

Heat oven to 325°F. In small bowl, combine sugar, flour, salt and margarine; mix well. Stir in lemon peel, milk, lemon juice and egg yolks. In medium bowl, beat egg whites until stiff peaks form. Fold lemon mixture into egg whites. Pour into eight 6-oz. custard cups. Place 4 custard cups in each of two 8-inch square pans; pour hot water into pans around cups to a depth of 1 inch.

Bake at 325°F. for 45 to 50 minutes or until tops are golden brown and spring back when touched lightly in center. Remove custard cups from pans. Cool on wire racks 1 hour. Serve immediately or refrigerate until ready to serve.

8 servings.

TIP:

If desired, dessert can be baked in 1½-quart casserole. Bake at 325°F. for 60 to 70 minutes or until top is golden brown and springs back when touched lightly in center.

HIGH ALTITUDE – Above 3500 Feet: No change.

These individual desserts can be served either warm or chilled. For the best flavor, we recommend using fresh lemon juice.

NUTRITION INFORMATION PER SERVING:

1/8 OF RECIPE		PERCENT U.S. RDA	
Calories	190	Protein	6%
Protein	4 g	Vitamin A	6%
Carbohydrate	31 g	Vitamin C	4%
Dietary Fiber	0 g	Thiamine	4%
Fat	6 g	Riboflavin	10%
Polyunsaturated	1 g	Niacin	*
Saturated	2 g	Calcium	6%
Cholesterol	83 mg	Iron	2%
Sodium	100 mg	*Less than 2% U.S. RDA	
Potassium	110 mg		

DIETARY EXCHANGES: 2 Starch, 1 Fat

SNAPPY BAKED FRUIT

*S*erve these individual fruit cups for dessert or as a brunch side dish— they're deliciously low in fat and calories.

1 **(16-oz.) can sliced peaches, drained**
1 **(16-oz.) can pear halves, drained, chopped**
½ **teaspoon grated lemon peel, if desired**
1 **cup finely crushed gingersnap cookies (about 14 cookies)**
1 **tablespoon margarine or butter, melted**

Heat oven to 375°F. In medium bowl, combine peaches, pears and lemon peel; mix well. Divide fruit mixture evenly among six 6-oz. custard cups. In small bowl, combine crushed cookies and margarine; mix well. Sprinkle evenly over fruit. Bake at 375°F. for 12 to 15 minutes or until hot and bubbly.
6 (½-cup) servings.

NUTRITION INFORMATION PER SERVING:

1/2 CUP		PERCENT U.S. RDA	
Calories	140	Protein	2%
Protein	2 g	Vitamin A	10%
Carbohydrate	26 g	Vitamin C	4%
Dietary Fiber	0 g	Thiamine	4%
Fat	4 g	Riboflavin	2%
Polyunsaturated	1 g	Niacin	4%
Saturated	1 g	Calcium	*
Cholesterol	7 mg	Iron	6%
Sodium	135 mg	*Less than 2% U.S. RDA	
Potassium	200 mg		

DIETARY EXCHANGES: 1-1/2 Fruit, 1 Fat

Snappy Baked Fruit

FRUITED PEARS WITH RUM SAUCE

PEARS

1 (16-oz.) can pear halves in heavy or light syrup, drained, reserving ½ cup liquid

¼ cup prepared mincemeat

RUM SAUCE

½ cup reserved pear liquid

2 teaspoons cornstarch

1 tablespoon rum or ¼ teaspoon rum extract

1 tablespoon margarine or butter

Heat oven to 375°F. Place pear halves, cut side up, in ungreased 8-inch square (1½-quart) baking dish. Spoon about 1 tablespoon mincemeat into each pear half. Bake at 375°F. for 15 minutes or until thoroughly heated.

Meanwhile, in small saucepan stir together reserved pear liquid and cornstarch. Heat over medium heat until mixture comes to a boil, stirring frequently. Remove from heat; stir in rum and margarine. Serve warm over pears.

3 to 6 servings.

*F*ruit desserts are perfect for those watching fat and calories closely. This quick and simple dessert features dressed-up pear halves. Pears in heavy or light syrup can be used. It's proof that you can enjoy delicious desserts and watch calories and fat, too!

NUTRITION INFORMATION PER SERVING:

1/6 OF RECIPE		PERCENT U.S. RDA	
Calories	110	Protein	*
Protein	0 g	Vitamin A	*
Carbohydrate	21 g	Vitamin C	*
Dietary Fiber	2 g	Thiamine	*
Fat	2 g	Riboflavin	*
Polyunsaturated	1 g	Niacin	*
Saturated	0 g	Calcium	*
Cholesterol	0 mg	Iron	2%
Sodium	60 mg	*Less than 2% U.S. RDA	
Potassium	75 mg		

DIETARY EXCHANGES: 1-1/2 Fruit, 1/2 Fat

Maple Baked Apples

MAPLE
BAKED APPLES

6 large baking apples

2 tablespoons lemon juice

½ cup raisins

½ teaspoon cinnamon

1 cup maple or maple-flavored syrup

¼ cup water

Heat oven to 350°F. Core apples and remove a 1-inch strip of peel around top to prevent splitting. Brush tops and insides with lemon juice. Place apples in ungreased 8-inch square (1½-quart) baking dish. In small bowl, combine raisins and cinnamon; fill center of each apple with mixture. Pour syrup over apples. Add ¼ cup water to baking dish.

Bake at 350°F. for 45 to 50 minutes or until apples are tender, occasionally spooning syrup mixture over apples.

6 servings.

MICROWAVE DIRECTIONS: Prepare and fill apples as directed above; place in 12x8-inch (2-quart) microwave-safe dish. Pour syrup over apples. Add ¼ cup water to dish; cover with microwave-safe waxed paper. Microwave on HIGH for 10 to 12 minutes or until apples are tender, spooning syrup mixture over apples twice during cooking.

Select tart baking apples such as Granny Smith or Rome Beauty to make these yummy baked apples. Bake them conventionally or cook them in the microwave in just 12 minutes!

NUTRITION INFORMATION PER SERVING:

1/6 OF RECIPE		PERCENT U.S. RDA	
Calories	270	Protein	*
Protein	1 g	Vitamin A	*
Carbohydrate	69 g	Vitamin C	10%
Dietary Fiber	4 g	Thiamine	8%
Fat	1 g	Riboflavin	4%
Polyunsaturated	0 g	Niacin	*
Saturated	0 g	Calcium	8%
Cholesterol	0 mg	Iron	6%
Sodium	10 mg	*Less than 2% U.S. RDA	
Potassium	380 mg		

DIETARY EXCHANGES: 4-1/2 Fruit

INDIVIDUAL HOT FUDGE SUNDAE CAKES

*A*lthough we've reduced the fat and sugar, this delectable dessert is 100% delicious! Stencil the tops of the warm sundae cakes with powdered sugar or add a dollop of nonfat frozen yogurt.

1 **cup all purpose flour**

½ **cup sugar**

2 **tablespoons unsweetened cocoa**

1½ **teaspoons baking powder**

⅔ **cup skim or 2% milk**

2 **tablespoons margarine or butter, melted**

1 **teaspoon vanilla**

¾ **cup firmly packed brown sugar**

¼ **cup unsweetened cocoa**

1½ **cups hot water**

Heat oven to 350°F. In small bowl, combine flour, sugar, 2 tablespoons cocoa and baking powder. Stir in milk, margarine and vanilla; mix until well blended. Spoon evenly into six 10-oz. custard cups. Place cups in 15x10x1-inch baking pan.

In small bowl, combine brown sugar and ¼ cup cocoa. Spoon 2 to 3 tablespoons mixture evenly over batter in each cup. Pour ¼ cup hot water evenly over sugar mixture in each cup.

Bake at 350°F. for 20 to 25 minutes or until center is set and firm to the touch. Serve warm. If desired, sprinkle with powdered sugar, or serve with frozen nonfat yogurt or light whipped topping.*

6 servings.

TIP:

* To decorate the top of each dessert with powdered sugar, cut a stencil of a favorite holiday shape from paper, or use a paper doily. Place paper stencil or doily on dessert; dust with powdered sugar. Remove stencil or doily.

HIGH ALTITUDE – Above 3500 Feet: No change.

NUTRITION INFORMATION PER SERVING:

1/6 OF RECIPE		PERCENT U.S. RDA	
Calories	300	Protein	6%
Protein	4 g	Vitamin A	4%
Carbohydrate	64 g	Vitamin C	*
Dietary Fiber	2 g	Thiamine	10%
Fat	5 g	Riboflavin	8%
Polyunsaturated	1 g	Niacin	6%
Saturated	1 g	Calcium	10%
Cholesterol	0 mg	Iron	10%
Sodium	150 mg	*Less than 2% U.S. RDA	
Potassium	250 mg		

DIETARY EXCHANGES: 1-1/2 Starch, 2-1/2 Fruit, 1 Fat

INDIVIDUAL PUMPKIN PUDDING CAKES

2 tablespoons sugar

⅛ teaspoon pumpkin pie spice

½ cup all purpose flour

½ cup sugar

½ teaspoon baking powder

½ teaspoon pumpkin pie spice
   Dash salt

½ cup canned pumpkin

1 tablespoon orange juice or water

1 tablespoon margarine or butter, melted

½ cup water, heated to 115 to 120°F.

Heat oven to 350°F. In small bowl, combine 2 tablespoons sugar and ⅛ teaspoon pumpkin pie spice; mix well. Set aside.

In medium bowl, combine flour, ½ cup sugar, baking powder, ½ teaspoon pumpkin pie spice and salt; mix well. Stir in pumpkin, orange juice and margarine until well mixed. Spoon evenly into six 6-oz. custard cups. Place cups in 15x10x1-inch baking pan. Sprinkle 1 teaspoon sugar-spice mixture over each. Spoon hot water evenly (4 teaspoons each) over sugar-spice mixture.

Bake at 350°F. for 16 to 20 minutes or until center is set and firm to the touch. Let stand 5 minutes before serving. Serve warm.

6 servings.

HIGH ALTITUDE – Above 3500 Feet: No change.

Some homespun desserts, like these spiced pudding cakes, smell so good while they are baking it's hard to wait for them to come out of the oven. Serve the desserts warm with frozen whipped topping or a cool scoop of non-fat frozen yogurt. With only 140 calories and 2 grams of fat per serving, you can afford to indulge!

NUTRITION INFORMATION PER SERVING:

1/6 OF RECIPE		PERCENT U.S. RDA	
Calories	140	Protein	2%
Protein	1 g	Vitamin A	90%
Carbohydrate	30 g	Vitamin C	2%
Dietary Fiber	1 g	Thiamine	6%
Fat	2 g	Riboflavin	2%
Polyunsaturated	1 g	Niacin	2%
Saturated	0 g	Calcium	2%
Cholesterol	0 mg	Iron	4%
Sodium	70 mg		
Potassium	60 mg		

DIETARY EXCHANGES: 1 Starch, 1/2 Fruit, 1/2 Fat

Lowfat Creme Caramel

LOWFAT CREME CARAMEL

1 cup sugar

1¾ cups skim milk

1 cup frozen fat-free egg product, thawed, or 4 eggs

¼ teaspoon salt

1 teaspoon vanilla

1 teaspoon grated orange peel

1 cup raspberries, blackberries, blueberries and/or
   sliced strawberries

Heat oven to 325°F. Heat ½ cup of the sugar in medium nonstick skillet over medium heat for 7 to 10 minutes or until sugar has melted and turned a light caramel color, stirring frequently. Immediately pour mixture into 8-inch round cake pan. MIXTURE WILL BE VERY HOT. Turn pan to coat bottom with sugar. Place on wire rack.

In large bowl, combine remaining ½ cup sugar, milk, egg product, salt, vanilla and orange peel; mix well. Pour custard mixture into sugar-coated pan. Place in 13x9-inch pan; pour very hot water around cake pan to within ½ inch of top of pan.

Bake at 325°F. for 50 to 60 minutes or until knife inserted in center comes out clean. Remove custard pan from pan of water. Cover; refrigerate 3 hours or overnight until thoroughly chilled. To unmold, run knife around edge of custard to loosen; invert onto serving platter. Top with fruit. Garnish as desired.

8 servings.

*I*ndulge in the rich, creamy elegance of baked custard and caramel glaze without worrying about cholesterol and fat. By substituting low-fat ingredients in this recipe, we have eliminated the guilt, but not the flavor.

NUTRITION INFORMATION PER SERVING:

1/8 OF RECIPE		PERCENT U.S. RDA	
Calories	140	Protein	6%
Protein	4 g	Vitamin A	6%
Carbohydrate	30 g	Vitamin C	4%
Dietary Fiber	1 g	Thiamine	4%
Fat	0 g	Riboflavin	10%
Polyunsaturated	0 g	Niacin	*
Saturated	0 g	Calcium	8%
Cholesterol	1 mg	Iron	4%
Sodium	135 mg	*Less than 2% U.S. RDA	
Potassium	160 mg		

DIETARY EXCHANGES: 1/2 Skim Milk, 1-1/2 Fruit

HEALTH NOTES

ALL DAIRY PRODUCTS ARE NOT CREATED EQUAL

Reduced-fat dairy foods are good news for cooks who want the great taste of milk, yogurt and cheese without the extra calories. Dairy foods are rich in protein, phosphorus, calcium and vitamins A and D. Happily, low- and non-fat products don't skimp on nutrition. They contain the same amount of protein, vitamins and minerals as their whole-milk counterparts. To decrease calories, fat and cholesterol in baked goods, you can substitute lower-fat milk in many recipes with little change in quality or flavor.

RAISIN BREAD PUDDING

*W*arm bread pudding is an all-time family favorite. Our microwave version quickly produces a moist bread pudding. Bake it in the conventional oven if you want a crisper topping.

⅓ **cup raisins**

2 **tablespoons dark rum***

3½ **cups oatmeal bread cubes (about 5 slices)**

¼ **cup sugar**

2 **eggs**

2 **cups skim or 2% milk**

1 **teaspoon vanilla**

Nutmeg

NUTRITION INFORMATION PER SERVING:

1/4 OF RECIPE		PERCENT U.S. RDA	
Calories	270	Protein	15%
Protein	11 g	Vitamin A	8%
Carbohydrate	44 g	Vitamin C	*
Dietary Fiber	3 g	Thiamine	10%
Fat	4 g	Riboflavin	25%
Polyunsaturated	1 g	Niacin	8%
Saturated	1 g	Calcium	20%
Cholesterol	108 mg	Iron	10%
Sodium	280 mg	*Less than 2% U.S. RDA	
Potassium	410 mg		

DIETARY EXCHANGES: 2-1/2 Starch, 1/2 Fruit, 1 Fat

▤ MICROWAVE DIRECTIONS: In large microwave-safe bowl, combine raisins and rum. Microwave on HIGH for 1 to 1½ minutes or until mixture boils. Add bread; mix well. Set aside.

Spray four 1-cup microwave-safe souffle dishes or four 10-oz. custard cups with nonstick cooking spray.** In small bowl, beat sugar and eggs until well blended. Slowly beat in milk and vanilla. Pour milk mixture over bread mixture; mix well. Spoon evenly into spray-coated dishes. Sprinkle with nutmeg. Arrange dishes in circle in microwave oven. Cover with microwave-safe waxed paper.

Microwave on MEDIUM for 10 to 14 minutes or until knife inserted near center comes out clean, rotating dishes once halfway through cooking. Let stand 5 minutes before serving. Serve warm.

4 servings.

CONVENTIONAL DIRECTIONS: Heat oven to 350°F. In large bowl, combine raisins and rum; set aside to marinate and plump. Spray four 1-cup ovenproof souffle dishes or four 10-oz. custard cups with nonstick cooking spray.** Prepare bread puddings as directed above, adding bread to marinated raisins just before adding milk mixture. Spoon evenly into spray-coated dishes. Place dishes on cookie sheet.

Bake at 350°F. for 30 to 40 minutes or until knife inserted in center comes out clean. Sprinkle with nutmeg. Serve warm.

TIPS:

* To substitute for rum, use ¼ teaspoon rum extract plus 2 tablespoons water.
** One 1-quart microwave-safe casserole can be substituted for the 4 dishes or cups. Microwave as directed above. Or, use 1-quart casserole and bake as directed above.

HIGH ALTITUDE – Above 3500 Feet: No change.

LEMON PUDDING CAKE

3 **eggs, separated**

½ **cup skim or 2% milk**

¼ **cup lemon juice**

1 **teaspoon grated lemon peel**

½ **cup sugar**

⅓ **cup all purpose flour**

⅛ **teaspoon salt**

Heat oven to 350°F. Grease 1-quart casserole. In small bowl, beat egg yolks; stir in milk, lemon juice and lemon peel. Add sugar, flour and salt; beat until smooth. In another small bowl, beat egg whites until stiff peaks form. Gently fold yolk mixture into beaten egg whites. DO NOT OVERBLEND. Pour into greased casserole. Place casserole in 13 x 9-inch pan; pour hot water into pan around casserole to a depth of 1 inch.

Bake at 350°F. for 25 to 35 minutes or until light golden brown. Serve warm or cool.

6 (½-cup) servings.

Magically, as this dessert bakes, a lemony cake rises to the top, leaving a delicious sauce on the bottom. This reduced-calorie dessert uses skim milk to keep fat below 5 grams per serving.

NUTRITION INFORMATION PER SERVING:

1/2 CUP		PERCENT U.S. RDA	
Calories	140	Protein	6%
Protein	5 g	Vitamin A	4%
Carbohydrate	24 g	Vitamin C	6%
Dietary Fiber	0 g	Thiamine	4%
Fat	3 g	Riboflavin	10%
Polyunsaturated	0 g	Niacin	2%
Saturated	1 g	Calcium	4%
Cholesterol	107 mg	Iron	4%
Sodium	90 mg	*Less than 2% U.S. RDA	
Potassium	85 mg		

DIETARY EXCHANGES: 1 Starch, 1/2 Fruit, 1/2 Fat

FRUIT AND RICE PUDDING

*T*his low-fat version of an old favorite is tastefully tailored for healthier eating. Fruit bits are added for a new flavor twist.

1½ cups skim or 2% milk
2 cups cooked brown rice
½ cup dried fruit bits
¼ cup firmly packed brown sugar
¼ teaspoon cinnamon
½ cup frozen fat-free egg product, thawed, or 2 eggs
1 teaspoon vanilla

Heat oven to 350°F. Heat milk in small saucepan until very warm. In ungreased 1½-quart casserole, combine warm milk and all remaining ingredients; mix well. Place casserole in 13x9-inch pan; pour boiling water into pan around casserole to a depth of 1 inch.

Bake at 350°F. for 40 minutes. Carefully stir pudding; bake an additional 15 to 25 minutes or until knife inserted in center comes out clean. Serve warm.

6 servings.

NUTRITION INFORMATION PER SERVING:

1/6 OF RECIPE		PERCENT U.S. RDA	
Calories	170	Protein	8%
Protein	6 g	Vitamin A	10%
Carbohydrate	34 g	Vitamin C	*
Dietary Fiber	2 g	Thiamine	8%
Fat	1 g	Riboflavin	10%
Polyunsaturated	0 g	Niacin	6%
Saturated	0 g	Calcium	10%
Cholesterol	1 mg	Iron	6%
Sodium	65 mg	*Less than 2% U.S. RDA	
Potassium	270 mg		

DIETARY EXCHANGES: 2 Starch

CUSTARD NOODLE PUDDING

*S*erve this old-fashioned noodle-filled pudding warm or cool. To prevent spoilage, always store custard desserts in the refrigerator.

4 cups uncooked fine egg noodles
3 eggs
1 cup sugar
¼ cup raisins
2 cups 2% milk
1½ teaspoons vanilla
1 teaspoon nutmeg

Heat oven to 350°F. Grease 13x9-inch pan. Cook egg noodles to desired doneness as directed on package. Drain; keep warm.

Beat eggs in large bowl; stir in sugar, raisins, milk, vanilla and cooked noodles. Spoon mixture into greased pan. Sprinkle nutmeg over top; cover with foil.

Bake at 350°F. for 55 to 60 minutes or until knife inserted near center comes out clean. If desired, serve with light whipped topping. Store in refrigerator.

12 servings.

NUTRITION INFORMATION PER SERVING:

1/12 OF RECIPE		PERCENT U.S. RDA	
Calories	160	Protein	6%
Protein	5 g	Vitamin A	2%
Carbohydrate	30 g	Vitamin C	*
Dietary Fiber	1 g	Thiamine	10%
Fat	3 g	Riboflavin	10%
Polyunsaturated	0 g	Niacin	4%
Saturated	1 g	Calcium	6%
Cholesterol	68 mg	Iron	4%
Sodium	40 mg	*Less than 2% U.S. RDA	
Potassium	130 mg		

DIETARY EXCHANGES: 1 Starch, 1 Fruit, 1/2 Fat

EGGNOG BREAD PUDDING WITH RUM SAUCE

BREAD PUDDING

   1 **cup sugar**

   1 **teaspoon nutmeg**

   2 **cups skim or 2% milk**

   1 **teaspoon vanilla**

   2 **eggs**

 10 **cups French bread cubes (1-inch)**

  ⅔ **cup raisins**

RUM SAUCE

   1 **cup firmly packed brown sugar**

  ½ **cup light corn syrup**

   2 **tablespoons rum***

   2 **tablespoons margarine or butter**

  ½ **teaspoon vanilla**

Heat oven to 350°F. Spray 13x9-inch (3-quart) baking dish with nonstick cooking spray. In large bowl, combine sugar, nutmeg, milk, 1 teaspoon vanilla and eggs; blend until smooth with wire whisk. Fold in bread cubes and raisins. Pour into spray-coated dish. Bake at 350°F. for 40 to 45 minutes or until knife inserted in center comes out clean.

Meanwhile, in small saucepan combine all rum sauce ingredients. Cook over medium heat until mixture comes to a boil, stirring constantly. Boil 1 minute. Remove from heat; cool slightly. Serve warm sauce over warm bread pudding.

12 to 16 servings.

TIP:

  * To substitute for rum, use ½ teaspoon rum extract plus water to make 2 tablespoons.

*B*read pudding has graduated from "the poor man's dessert" of years past. This low-fat version is anything but ordinary and is served with an exceptional rum sauce. The whole dessert is deliciously low in calories!

NUTRITION INFORMATION PER SERVING:			
1/16 OF RECIPE		PERCENT U.S. RDA	
Calories	250	Protein	6%
Protein	4 g	Vitamin A	2%
Carbohydrate	53 g	Vitamin C	*
Dietary Fiber	1 g	Thiamine	10%
Fat	3 g	Riboflavin	10%
Polyunsaturated	1 g	Niacin	6%
Saturated	1 g	Calcium	6%
Cholesterol	27 mg	Iron	6%
Sodium	210 mg	*Less than 2% U.S. RDA	
Potassium	180 mg		

DIETARY EXCHANGES: 2 Starch, 1 Fruit, 1/2 Fat

CUSTARD WITH RASPBERRY PUREE

Custard—classic yet classy! You'll enjoy the unique flavor combination of raspberry sauce over individually baked custards. And best of all, the dessert is fat free.

CUSTARD

2 **tablespoons brown sugar**
⅛ **teaspoon salt**
1 **cup evaporated skimmed milk**
½ **cup frozen fat-free egg product, thawed, or 2 eggs**
½ **teaspoon vanilla**
   Nutmeg

RASPBERRY PUREE

1 **(10-oz.) pkg. frozen raspberries with syrup, thawed**

GARNISH

   Fresh fruit, if desired
   Mint leaves, if desired

Heat oven to 325°F. In 2-cup measuring cup, combine brown sugar, salt, milk, egg product and vanilla; blend well. Place 4 ungreased 5-oz. custard cups in 9-inch square pan; place on oven rack. Pour custard mixture into custard cups; pour boiling water into pan around custard cups to a depth of 1 inch. Bake at 325°F. for 30 to 35 minutes or until knife inserted in center comes out clean.

To unmold, loosen edges with knife. Invert dessert plate on top of each custard cup. Quickly invert to release hot custard onto plate. Sprinkle with nutmeg.

Pour raspberries into food processor bowl with metal blade or blender container. Cover; process until smooth. Strain to remove seeds. Spoon 2 tablespoons sauce onto each plate around custard. Garnish with fresh fruit and mint leaves. Serve with additional sauce. Store in refrigerator.

4 servings.

NUTRITION INFORMATION PER SERVING:			
1/4 OF RECIPE		**PERCENT U.S. RDA**	
Calories	160	Protein	10%
Protein	8 g	Vitamin A	10%
Carbohydrate	34 g	Vitamin C	15%
Dietary Fiber	4 g	Thiamine	6%
Fat	0 g	Riboflavin	20%
Polyunsaturated	0 g	Niacin	*
Saturated	0 g	Calcium	20%
Cholesterol	2 mg	Iron	8%
Sodium	180 mg	*Less than 2% U.S. RDA	
Potassium	370 mg		

DIETARY EXCHANGES: 1-1/2 Fruit, 1 Skim Milk

APPLE STREUSEL BREAD PUDDING

BREAD PUDDING

- **4 cups French bread cubes (1-inch)**
- **1 cup chunky applesauce**
- **¼ cup raisins**
- **¼ teaspoon cinnamon**
- **⅛ teaspoon nutmeg**
- **2 eggs**
- **2 cups 2% milk**
- **⅓ cup sugar**
- **½ teaspoon cinnamon**
- **½ teaspoon vanilla**

STREUSEL TOPPING

- **¼ cup all purpose flour**
- **¼ cup firmly packed brown sugar**
- **2 tablespoons margarine or butter**

You'll never be disappointed when you serve this warm, old-fashioned dessert! Although the pudding is already low in fat and calories, you can substitute skim milk and fat-free egg product to reduce the fat content even further.

Heat oven to 350°F. Grease 8-inch square (1½-quart) baking dish or 2-quart casserole. Place 3 cups of the bread cubes in greased dish. In small bowl, combine applesauce, raisins, ¼ teaspoon cinnamon and nutmeg; blend well. Spoon by scant teaspoonfuls evenly over bread cubes. Top with remaining 1 cup bread cubes.

Beat eggs in medium bowl. Add milk, sugar, ½ teaspoon cinnamon and vanilla; blend well. Pour over bread cubes; let stand 10 minutes.

In small bowl, combine flour and brown sugar; mix well. With fork or pastry blender, cut in margarine until mixture is crumbly. Sprinkle over top of bread cube mixture.

Bake at 350°F. for 50 to 60 minutes or until knife inserted in center comes out clean. Let stand 10 minutes before serving. If desired, serve warm with half-and-half. Store in refrigerator.

8 servings.

NUTRITION INFORMATION PER SERVING:			
1/8 OF RECIPE		**PERCENT U.S. RDA**	
Calories	240	Protein	8%
Protein	6 g	Vitamin A	6%
Carbohydrate	42 g	Vitamin C	*
Dietary Fiber	1 g	Thiamine	10%
Fat	6 g	Riboflavin	15%
Polyunsaturated	1 g	Niacin	6%
Saturated	2 g	Calcium	10%
Cholesterol	58 mg	Iron	6%
Sodium	210 mg	*Less than 2% U.S. RDA	
Potassium	220 mg		

DIETARY EXCHANGES: 2 Starch, 1/2 Fruit, 1 Fat

CINNAMON BREAD PUDDING WITH WHISKEY SAUCE

*O*ne of the earliest colonial desserts, bread pudding was originally cooked in a covered iron pudding pot hung over an open hearth fire. We no longer need to cook this way but we still appreciate the aroma and flavor of an old-fashioned dessert. Egg whites, skim milk and nonfat yogurt help make this version low in fat.

BREAD PUDDING

5	cups cinnamon bread cubes (1-inch)
¼	cup raisins or dried currants
2	eggs
2	egg whites
¾	cup sugar
2½	cups hot skim or 2% milk

WHISKEY SAUCE

1	cup sugar
1	cup water
¼	cup whiskey*
¼	cup nonfat vanilla yogurt

Heat oven to 375°F. Butter 13x9-inch (3-quart) baking dish. Combine bread cubes and raisins in buttered dish. In medium bowl, combine eggs, egg whites and ¾ cup sugar; beat well. Add hot milk; mix well. Pour mixture over bread and raisins; let stand 5 minutes. Stir gently. Bake at 375°F. for 25 to 35 minutes or until liquid is absorbed but mixture is not dry.

Meanwhile, in small saucepan combine 1 cup sugar and water; mix well. Bring to a boil; boil 5 minutes. Remove from heat; stir in whiskey. Cool to lukewarm. Stir in yogurt. Serve warm sauce over warm bread pudding. Store any remaining bread pudding and sauce in refrigerator.

8 servings.

TIP:
* To substitute for whiskey, use ¼ cup water and 1 teaspoon brandy extract.

NUTRITION INFORMATION PER SERVING:

1/8 OF RECIPE		PERCENT U.S. RDA	
Calories	330	Protein	10%
Protein	8 g	Vitamin A	4%
Carbohydrate	66 g	Vitamin C	*
Dietary Fiber	0 g	Thiamine	8%
Fat	2 g	Riboflavin	20%
Polyunsaturated	0 g	Niacin	4%
Saturated	1 g	Calcium	15%
Cholesterol	55 mg	Iron	6%
Sodium	220 mg	*Less than 2% U.S. RDA	
Potassium	230 mg		

DIETARY EXCHANGES: 3 Starch, 1 Fruit, 1/2 Fat

APPLE CLAFOUTI

2 **tablespoons margarine or butter**

3 **medium apples, peeled, cut into ¼-inch wedges**

2 **slices raisin bread, cubed**

3 **eggs**

½ **cup all purpose flour**

¼ **cup sugar**

½ **teaspoon cinnamon**

⅛ **teaspoon salt**

2 **teaspoons vanilla**

½ **teaspoon grated lemon peel**

1⅓ **cups 2% milk**

Melt margarine in large skillet. Add apples; cook until crisp-tender.

Heat oven to 350°F. Grease 1½ or 2-quart casserole. Layer apples in greased casserole; top with bread cubes. In small bowl, beat eggs until well blended. Add flour, sugar, cinnamon, salt, vanilla and lemon peel; mix well. Beat in milk. Pour over bread cubes.

Bake at 350°F. for 45 to 55 minutes or until knife inserted in center comes out clean. Let stand 15 minutes. Serve warm. Store in refrigerator. 6 servings.

MICROWAVE DIRECTIONS: In 2-quart microwave-safe casserole, combine margarine and apples. Microwave on HIGH for 2 to 3 minutes or until apples are crisp-tender, stirring once halfway through cooking. Top with bread cubes; set aside.

In 4-cup microwave-safe measuring cup, microwave milk on HIGH until very warm, about 2 minutes. In medium bowl, beat eggs until well blended. Add flour, sugar, cinnamon, salt, vanilla and lemon peel; mix well. Beat in warm milk. Pour over bread cubes. Microwave on MEDIUM for 15 to 20 minutes or until set. Let stand 5 minutes. Serve warm. Store in refrigerator.

HIGH ALTITUDE – Above 3500 Feet: No change.

*C*lafouti is a French-country dessert made by topping fresh fruit with batter. Some clafoutis have a cake-like topping while others are more like a pudding. We've topped this apple version with cubes of raisin bread, then added a creamy custard for a clafouti that is out of this world!

NUTRITION INFORMATION PER SERVING:

1/6 OF RECIPE		PERCENT U.S. RDA	
Calories	240	Protein	10%
Protein	7 g	Vitamin A	8%
Carbohydrate	35 g	Vitamin C	6%
Dietary Fiber	2 g	Thiamine	10%
Fat	8 g	Riboflavin	20%
Polyunsaturated	2 g	Niacin	4%
Saturated	2 g	Calcium	10%
Cholesterol	111 mg	Iron	8%
Sodium	180 mg		
Potassium	230 mg		

DIETARY EXCHANGES: 1-1/2 Starch, 1 Fruit, 1-1/2 Fat

How To Use Nutrition Information

PLAN A HEALTHFUL DIET

We have provided nutrition information for every recipe in *Healthy Baking* to help you plan a healthful diet. For each recipe, you'll find calories per serving, plus grams of protein. carbohydrate, dietary fiber and fat, and milligrams of cholesterol, sodium and potassium. Vitamins and minerals are given in percentages of U.S. Recommended Daily Allowances (dietary standards developed by the Food and Drug Administration).

Each recipe also lists dietary exchanges, for those on special diets.

If you are following a medically prescribed diet, consult your physician or registered dietitian about using this nutrition information.

HOW WE CALCULATE

The recipe nutrition calculations are based on:

- A single serving; when a range of servings is given, the larger number.
- The first ingredient listed when an option is given.
- The larger amount of an ingredient when a range is given.

- "If desired" or garnishing ingredients when they are included in the ingredients listing.

WHAT YOU NEED

The amount of nutrients you need is determined by your age, sex, size and activity level. The following are general guidelines for a moderately active person. In general, sedentary women and some older adults have lower caloric needs, and teens, men and more active women can consume higher levels.

Calories	**Fat**
2,000	67 grams or less
Protein	**Saturated Fat**
50 to 75 grams	22 grams or less
Carbohydrates	**Cholesterol**
275 to 300 grams	300 milligrams or less
Fiber	**Sodium**
25 grams	2400 milligrams or less

INDEX

A

B

MW = Microwave Option